SCHOLASTIC

SYSTEM 44

NEXTGENERATION

TEACHING RESOURCES
For Modeled & Independent Reading

SECONDARY

Credits and acknowledgments appear on page 176, which constitutes an extension of this copyright page.

Portions previously published in *Teaching Resources for the System 44 Library: Secondary*, copyright © 2009.

Copyright © 2014, 2009 by Scholastic Inc.

All rights reserved.   Published by Scholastic Inc.   Printed in the U.S.A.

ISBN-13: 978-0-545-50116-3
ISBN-10: 0-545-50116-4

SCHOLASTIC, SYSTEM 44, 44BOOK, SRI SCHOLASTIC READING INVENTORY, SCHOLASTIC READING COUNTS!, SCHOLASTIC U, READ 180, and associated logos are trademarks and/or registered trademarks of Scholastic Inc. LEXILE and LEXILE FRAMEWORK are registered trademarks of MetaMetrics, Inc. IPAD is a registered trademark of Apple Inc. Other company names, brand names, and product names are the property and/or trademarks of their respective owners. Scholastic does not endorse any product or business entity mentioned herein.

Scholastic is constantly working to lessen the environmental impact of our manufacturing processes. To view our industry-leading paper procurement policy, visit www.scholastic.com/paperpolicy.

1 2 3 4 5 6 7 8 9 10   40   22 21 20 19 18 17 16 15 14 13

 Text pages printed on 10% PCW recycled paper.

Table of Contents

Using This Book 4

Introduction to the *System 44* Library 6

System 44 Library Features 8

Using the *System 44* Library in the Classroom 12

Managing Independent Reading 16

Supporting All Students 18

Building Critical Academic Vocabulary 22

Library Overview 24

Comprehension Routines 36

Decoding Routines 40

Vocabulary/Word Study Routines 46

Fluency Routines 50

Lesson Plans and Graphic Organizers

Series 1–6 (Lexile® measure 100L–250L)

Big! (Series 2 and 3) 54

Bugs That Kill (Series 1 and 2) 56

Did You Know? Odd Body Facts
(Series 1 and 2) 58

*Fast! The World's Fastest Couch and
Other Fast Things* (Series 4 and 5) 60

Messy Jobs (Series 1 and 2) 62

*Plugged In: Technology Dream
Jobs* (Series 4 and 5) 64

Poster Power (Series 1 and 2) 66

Shamila's Goal (Series 4 and 6) 68

These Are Not Poems (and Other Poems)
(Series 4 and 5) 70

They Did What? (Series 2 and 3) 72

Wacky Attractions (Series 1 and 2) 74

What's New? A History of Invention (Series 6)... 76

Wonders of the World (Series 4 and 6) 78

Yes! (Series 3) 80

Series 7–12 (Lexile® measure 100L–350L)

African Journey (Series 9) 82

Big Steals
(Series 8 and 9) 84

Button Your Lip and Other Idioms (Series 9)..... 86

Cool Jobs in Basketball (Series 11) 88

Crash! (Series 12 and 13) 90

DJ Mystery (Series 8) 92

Fashion Flashback (Series 8) 94

Home From War (Series 11) 96

Is This Art? (Series 7 and 8) 98

The Princess Brat (Series 10) 100

Ripped From the Headlines (Series 10) 102

Survival Guide: How to Keep Your Job
(Series 7 and 8) 104

*Unstoppable: The True Story of
Shadrack Boakye* (Series 10) 106

Weird Sports Records (Series 7) 108

When Lisa Met Billy (Series 8 and 12) 110

Yo, Yolanda! Advice About Friends (Series 7) ... 112

Series 13–18 (Lexile® measure 200L–350L)

Ant Attack! (Series 17 and 18) 114

Back From the Grave! (Series 13) 116

Disaster! (Series 14) 118

El Tiburón "The Shark" (Series 13 and 14) 120

Have You Seen My Mummy? (Series 13 and 14) . 122

Killer Plague (Series 15) 124

Left to Die (Series 16) 126

Medical Miracle (Series 14) 128

Music Mash-Up (Series 18) 130

Play Ball! (Series 14) 132

Samurai Fighters (Series 17) 134

The Story of Shi Jin (Series 17) 136

The Sweater Thief (Series 15) 138

Witch Hunt (Series 18) 140

Series 19–25 (Lexile® measure 300L–450L)

Arabian Nights (Series 23 and 24) 142

Beauty and the Geek (Series 19 and 20) 144

Everyday Heroes (Series 23 and 25) 146

*Fire! The Triangle Shirtwaist
Factory Tragedy* (Series 21 and 22) 148

Four Rotten Rulers (Series 19) 150

Hot Jobs (Series 22 and 24) 152

Killer Croc (Series 19 and 20) 154

Lost! Mysteries of the Bermuda Triangle
(Series 24 and 25) 156

Never Give Up (Series 20) 158

The Promise (Series 19 and 20) 160

The Raven (Series 20 and 21) 162

Tragedy at Sea (Series 23) 164

Additional Resources

My Independent Reading Response Log 166

Self-Monitoring Chart 168

Index 172

Using This Book

This guide provides resources to support students' use of *System 44* materials for modeled and independent reading. Use these resources throughout the year to guide students as they read, reread, and respond to Paperbacks, Audiobooks, and eBooks in the *System 44* Library.

What's Inside

System 44 provides a variety of resources for Professional Development, Skills Practice, and Assessment.

- **Professional Development** Resources for Professional Development include research-based background on Building Critical Academic Vocabulary **(pages 22–23)**, Features and Recommended Practice for Paperbacks, Audiobooks, and eBooks **(pages 8–15)**, Instructional Routines **(pages 36–53)**, Lesson Plans **(pages 54–164)** for small group instruction, recommendations for Classroom Management and Organization **(pages 16–17)**, and tips for using the Library to support English Language Development and Special Education **(pages 18–21)**.

- **Skills Practice and Assessment** Graphic Organizers **(pages 55–165)**, My Independent Reading Response Log **(pages 166–167)**, and the Self-Monitoring Chart **(pages 168–171)** guide student reading choice and response during modeled and independent reading. Answer Keys are available through the **Scholastic Achievement Manager (SAM)**.

Resources for Teaching and Practice

System 44 Library teaching resources include the following:

- **Library Overview** The Overview provides at-a-glance information for each book, including Lexile measure, genre, Phonics Focus, and key vocabulary.

- **Lesson Plans** Lesson Plans include a summary of each book; routines for informal assessment and targeted instruction of decoding, vocabulary, and fluency skills; and comprehension questions to guide students' response to text.

- **Text Complexity Measures** Text Complexity, which indicates how accessible or challenging a text is to read, is determined by analyzing three key components: 1) the text's quantitative readability (represented by its Lexile measure); 2) its qualitative measure (based on purpose/levels of meaning, text structure, language, and knowledge demands); and 3) considerations specific to a given reader and task. *System 44* provides the quantitative and qualitative measure for each book in a Text Complexity triangle on Lesson Plan pages.

- **Feature Overviews** Sample pages from Paperbacks, Audiobooks, and eBooks show key features of the books and provide an easy reference for previewing the books. Feature Overviews also include information on how to access Audiobooks and eBooks.

SAM-Only Resources

Additional resources, listed in the chart below, may be downloaded from **SAM**. They are not included in this book.

Resource	SAM Keyword
Summarizing Graphic Organizer	Summarizing 44
Making Inferences Graphic Organizer	Making Inferences 44
Word Sort	Word Sort 44
Fluency Checklist	Fluency Checklist 44
Audiobook MP3 Files Downloading Instructions	MP3 44
Page-and-Track Guides for Audiobook MP3 Files	MP3 44
Answer Key for Library Book Graphic Organizers	GO Answer Key 44
eBook Access Instructions	eBook Access 44

Resources for Students

Students use the following tools with *System 44* Library titles to discuss and write about text and monitor independent reading progress:

Resources in the Book

- **Graphic Organizers** A graphic organizer for each book allows students to demonstrate understanding of individual titles. QuickWrites prompt students to use text evidence to explore language and key ideas in each text.

- **Self-Monitoring Chart** Students use this chart to choose appropriate independent reading books and to track their reading progress.

- **Independent Reading Response Log** This two-page resource guides students to examine key vocabulary and respond to questions in the books. Students complete a response log for each title they read from the *System 44* Library.

Resources on the Student Dashboard

- **My Books** The My Books tab provides at-a-glance information about books students have read, allowing students to track their reading progress and interests and choose appropriate independent reading books.

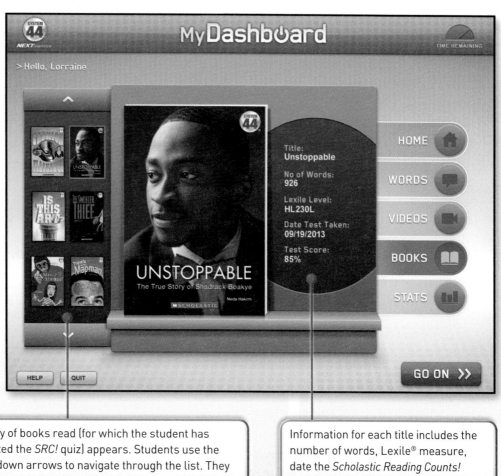

A display of books read (for which the student has completed the *SRC!* quiz) appears. Students use the up and down arrows to navigate through the list. They click on any book to view information about it.

Information for each title includes the number of words, Lexile® measure, date the *Scholastic Reading Counts! (SRC!)* quiz was taken, and quiz score.

Introduction to the System 44 Library

System 44 Paperback Library

The *System 44* Paperback Library is a collection of 56 literary and informational texts that align with the interests and abilities of struggling readers. The books in the Library cover a wide range of text types and topics, with a strong emphasis on nonfiction texts worth reading. Each series' book includes vocabulary that correspond to phonics and word study skills taught in the *System 44* software. Additionally, each book includes a set of highly portable vocabulary words—called Smart Words—that students will encounter in many contexts and that are essential to understanding the text. Through independent reading and targeted instruction using Library books, students practice decoding skills and build fluency, vocabulary, knowledge, and comprehension.

The Library books gradually increase in difficulty, as shown in the chart below.

Software Connection				
Book Feature	**Books Used With Series 1–6**	**Books Used With Series 7–12**	**Books Used With Series 13–18**	**Books Used With Series 19–25**
Lexile® measure	100L–250L	100L–350L	200L–350L	300L–450L
Page Count	8–16 pp.	16 pp.	16–24 pp.	24–32 pp.
Smart Words	3–5	5–6	6	7
Art	Art on every 1–2 pages	Art on every 1–3 pages	Art on approximately every 3 pages	Art on approximately every 4 pages

System 44 eBook Library

The *System 44* Library includes eBook versions of all 56 paperbacks. Students can choose to read eBooks at their proficiency level or above. eBooks offer students visual and auditory support that may be tailored to student needs. eBooks are available anytime, anywhere from Internet-enabled computers and iPads to support and encourage reading outside of the classroom and family involvement. eBooks may also be projected on interactive whiteboards (IWBs) for use during guided practice.

System 44 Audiobook Library

Audio recordings of each book in the *System 44* Library are available on CD and as downloadable MP3 files. Audiobooks promote listening comprehension and provide auditory support to struggling readers as they decode text. As with eBooks, students can choose to read audiobooks at their proficiency level or above.

System 44 Scholastic Reading Counts! Quizzes

Scholastic Reading Counts! quizzes provide computer-based multiple-choice questions for each *System 44* Library book. These quizzes enable students to demonstrate comprehension of the books they read independently. Quiz results can be accessed on the *SRC!* Quiz Manager on **SAM**. Use the Quiz Manager to help students set independent reading goals and find appropriate Library books, to monitor successful book completion, and to create incentives to motivate students during independent reading. See the *Placement, Assessment & Reporting Guide* for additional information.

System 44 Library Features

The *System 44* Library encourages close reading, builds skills, and assesses comprehension.

System 44 Paperback Features

Smart Words
Smart Words are academic vocabulary words that help students understand the text and can be used in a variety of text types across disciplines. Each Smart Word is used at least once in the book.

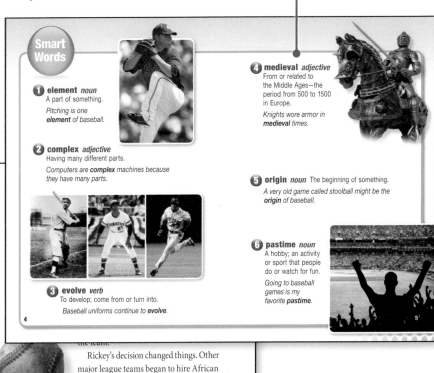

Smart Words

1 element *noun*
A part of something.
*Pitching is one **element** of baseball.*

2 complex *adjective*
Having many different parts.
*Computers are **complex** machines because they have many parts.*

3 evolve *verb*
To develop; come from or turn into.
*Baseball uniforms continue to **evolve**.*

4 medieval *adjective*
From or related to the Middle Ages—the period from 500 to 1500 in Europe.
*Knights wore armor in **medieval** times.*

5 origin *noun* The beginning of something.
*A very old game called stoolball might be the **origin** of baseball.*

6 pastime *noun*
A hobby; an activity or sport that people do or watch for fun.
*Going to baseball games is my favorite **pastime**.*

4

5

Back then, racist laws existed. The laws kept blacks and whites separate. These laws became part of baseball, too. White team owners could no longer hire black players.

So, black players started their own leagues. The Negro Leagues formed in 1920. They were pro leagues for black teams. The Negro Leagues did not have much money. But they had great players.

For years, pro baseball was divided. But two men changed that in 1945.

Rickey's decision changed things. Other major league teams began to hire African Americans. In 1955, Rickey hired Roberto Clemente. Clemente was from Puerto Rico. He became pro baseball's first Latino star. In time, players of all races played together.

Explain
How has baseball changed since 1945? Use evidence from the text to support your answer.

Jackie Robinson swings for the ball! Robinson was the first black major league player in modern baseball.

12

13

During Reading questions
Two types of questions probe students' understanding of the text as they read.

- *Explain* questions: text-based questions that require students to read closely and analyze text. These questions are designed to focus attention on the words, phrases, and events that matter most in advancing the central ideas and theme of a text.
- *React* questions: text-based questions that ask students to respond to, check their understanding of, or predict what will happen next in the text. These questions are designed to focus attention on elements such as character traits and motivations, and key content or plot developments.

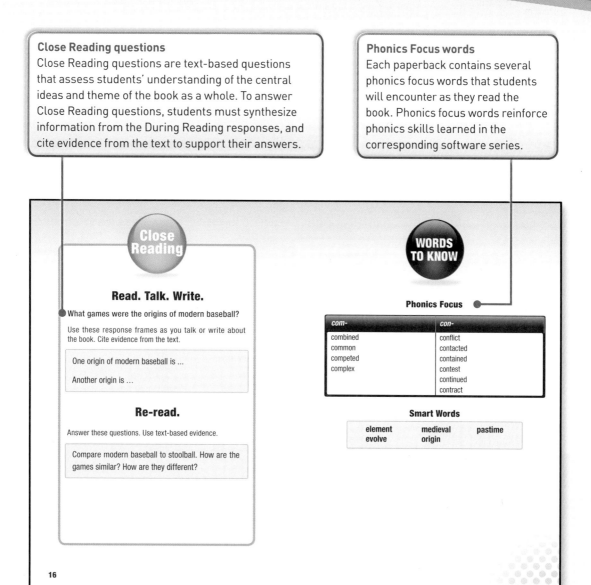

Close Reading questions
Close Reading questions are text-based questions that assess students' understanding of the central ideas and theme of the book as a whole. To answer Close Reading questions, students must synthesize information from the During Reading responses, and cite evidence from the text to support their answers.

Phonics Focus words
Each paperback contains several phonics focus words that students will encounter as they read the book. Phonics focus words reinforce phonics skills learned in the corresponding software series.

Close Reading

Read. Talk. Write.

What games were the origins of modern baseball?

Use these response frames as you talk or write about the book. Cite evidence from the text.

One origin of modern baseball is …

Another origin is …

Re-read.

Answer these questions. Use text-based evidence.

Compare modern baseball to stoolball. How are the games similar? How are they different?

WORDS TO KNOW

Phonics Focus

com-	con-
combined	conflict
common	contacted
competed	contained
complex	contest
	continued
	contract

Smart Words

element	medieval	pastime
evolve	origin	

16

System 44 Audiobook Access and Features

Students have two ways to access *System 44* audiobooks:

1. Play CDs provided with the *System 44* Library.
2. Download MP3 files from SAM. For detailed instructions, go to **SAM** (Keyword: MP3 44).

Each audiobook presents two distinct voices who provide audio supports:

- **The Reading Coach** introduces the book, previews the book's Smart Words and Phonics Focus, and prompts students to respond to text after they have finished reading the book.
- **The Narrator** reads aloud and models fluent reading of the text.

System 44 eBook Access and Features

System 44 eBook features and enhancements support students at every level of reading proficiency. eBooks may be accessed on Internet-enabled computers and iPads. Follow these steps to access the eBook Library:

In class, students enter *System 44* by clicking the *System 44* button on the Student Access page. Once students reach the *System 44* page, they click on the eBook Library button. The eBook Library bookshelf will appear on the screen.

Outside the classroom, you and your students can access the eBook Library through the following URL: **Scholastic.com/System44/MyReading**.

Students use their *System 44* user names and passwords to log in. eBook access instructions are also available on **SAM** (Keyword: eBook Access 44).

The eBook Library Bookshelf
The bookshelf includes easy-to-use features to help students find appropriate books.

To Read
In this view, the bookshelf displays "recommended" eBooks—selected automatically based on the student's current placement in the software. Clicking on any cover opens a pop-up "About the Book" window, which provides details about the selected book.

All Books
In this view, the bookshelf displays all titles in the eBook Library. *SRC!* quiz results and the student's rating show beneath the cover of any books the student has read (and for which the student has taken the *SRC!* quiz).

Search Feature
Search titles by Lexile® range, Author, Fiction, or Nonfiction. When students complete a search, books that meet the search criteria fill the bookshelf.

At the top left of the bookshelf, the student will find the book that he or she opened most recently. A yellow background identifies this book as the book the student is currently reading. The student clicks on the cover of this eBook to open it to the last page read.

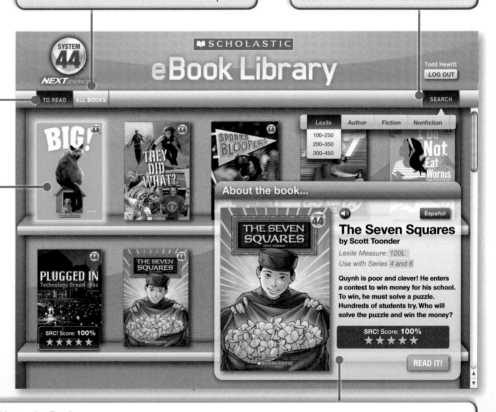

About the Book
Click on any book to view book details, including title, author, Lexile® measure, corresponding Topic Software series, *SRC!* quiz score and book rating (if completed), and a short description of the book. Audio is available in English and Spanish. Click "Read It!" to launch the eBook.

eBook Features

Each eBook contains the following display, reading, and navigation features.

Back to Library
Click on this icon to return to the eBook Library Bookshelf.

Search
Search the eBook for specific words or content by typing a keyword into the search field. Search results show the word or phrase plus five words before and after the selected word and a thumbnail of each page on which the word appears. Click on the "Go" button for a page to navigate to that page. Once the selected pages open, all instances of the keyword appear highlighted.

Bookmark
When you bookmark a specific page, the eBook goes to that page the next time you open it.

Vocabulary Support
Click on any word in the text to hear its pronunciation*. Click on any Smart Word in bold text to open a pop-up window containing the word, part of speech, definition, and context sentence from the Smart Words page. Audio of each Smart Word entry is available in English and Spanish.

Page Navigation
Click on the arrows to navigate forward to the next page or back to the previous page.

Help
Access audio and visual aids to navigate the eBook.

Preview
Click on a thumbnail of any page to navigate to that page.

Page View**
Choose to view either a single page or page spread (two facing pages in the book). Default: Single page.

Rate of Read*
Controls the speed of audio and highlighting. Default: Moderate speed, middle choice.

Audio Scroll
Provides a visual indication of the percentage of text on the page that the student has read. Appears when the student pauses or finishes reading a page. This feature allows students to return to a specific point in the text.

Page Zoom***
Zoom in and out of page.

Read Aloud*
Choose from three modes (Word, Phrase, or Practice), then press Play to begin reading. Word: highlights text word-by-word along with audio. Phrase: highlights text phrase-by-phrase along with audio. Practice: highlights text phrase-by-phrase without audio. Default: Practice mode.

* Available on iPad after August 15, 2013.
** Double Page View not available on iPad.
*** Disabled in landscape mode on iPad.

Using the *System 44* Library in the Classroom

The *System 44* Library aligns with the 25 software series to provide rich materials for use during small-group instruction and independent reading.

Small-Group Differentiated Instruction Use Library books and related Lesson Plans to teach phonics, word study, comprehension, and fluency skills to targeted groups of students. Refer to the Instructional Overview pages in the Phonics and Word Study section of *Resources for Differentiated Instruction* (RDI) to identify books that incorporate phonics skills taught in each Topic Software series.

Independent Reading Guide students to use *System 44* paperbacks, audiobooks, and eBooks—and related student resources (Graphic Organizers, My Independent Reading Response Log, Self-Monitoring Chart)—to read and respond to books.

Use this chart to determine when to use the *System 44* Library for small-group instruction and independent reading:

When to use the Library in the *System 44* Classroom	When to use the Library in classrooms where *System 44* is integrated with *READ 180*
Differentiated Instruction Each Module includes 2 CheckPoint days per week that offer opportunities to differentiate instruction using *System 44* Library books. (See sample Weekly Instruction Plan below.) On those days, the Groupinator will divide Small Group into two smaller groups: one group will read independently while you teach the other group with *RDI* lessons. You may also choose to include 1–3 days of Differentiated Instruction between Modules. See *RDI* page T34 for alternate options for using Library books in small-group instruction.	**Small-Group Rotation** provides daily opportunities to use *System 44* Library books to teach targeted groups of students. **Independent Reading Rotation** offers daily opportunities for independent reading using the *System 44* Library books.

Sample Small-Group Weekly Instruction Plan				
Monday	**Tuesday**	**Wednesday**	**Thursday**	**Friday**
Small-Group Instruction with *44Book*	Small-Group Instruction with *44Book*	Small-Group Instruction with *44Book*	● RDI Code or Word Strategy Lesson ● Independent Reading with *System 44* Library books	● RDI Code or Word Strategy Lesson ● Independent Reading with *System 44* Library books

Recommended Practice for Modeled & Independent Reading

1 Match Students to Books

There are several effective ways to match a student with the appropriate texts. Use your professional judgment and any combination of these supports:

- Use *System 44* **Reports:** Match the Library books to students' current or recently completed software Topics. Run *System 44* reports, such as the Reading Progress Report, to find out a student's current Series and Topic on the Software. If a student is in Topic 6.6, for example, turn to the Series 5–6 Instructional Overview in *RDI* to identify corresponding Library books.

- Direct Students to the **Self-Monitoring Chart**: Make copies of the Self-Monitoring Chart on pages 168–171, and distribute the copies to students. Guide students to use the Chart to select books from the *System 44* Library that correspond to the Topics they are learning on the software.

- Identify **Reading Interests**: Encourage students to read books in the Library that interest them. Students may read summaries of the book on the *System 44* Library Poster and the eBook Library Bookshelf. You may also help students identify their interests by performing a "Book Pass" activity:

  - Place a book on each seat. Separate students into small groups.

  - Have each group select a timekeeper—someone who is good at multitasking and has a watch (preferably with a second hand.) The timekeeper will keep track of time while still participating in the activity.

  - When the timekeeper calls "Book Pass," have students pass their book to the person on their right. Then repeat the process: preview the book, read for two or three minutes, stop and write.

2 Preview Features of the Books

Before reading, preview features of the *System 44* Library. See pages 8–11 for a description of features.

3 Reading 1: Model Fluent Reading

Begin by having students use the read-aloud modes (Word and Phrase) of the eBooks or listen to the Audiobooks. Students should follow the text as the author narrates. The audio features will provide the students with a modeled fluent reading.

4 Reading 2: Reread With Scaffolds

After students listen to a modeled fluent reading, have them reread the books. Encourage students to use the reading supports in the eBooks to help guide them.

5 Reading 3: Read Independently

Tell students to read the books independently. If the students are using the eBooks, have them use Practice mode (no read-aloud.)

6 Assess and Track Progress

Use *Scholastic Reading Counts!* electronic quizzes to assess student comprehension and generate progress reports. For more information, see the Assessment and Reporting Guide.

System 44 Library Lesson Plan Features

As students read, use the *System 44* Library Lesson Plans and Graphic Organizers to help engage them in book discussions and monitor comprehension. Use the guides to focus on content, along with decoding, word study, vocabulary, or fluency instruction and practice.

Phonics Focus
Indicates the Phonics Focus of the book.

Text-Complexity Key
Provides a text complexity measure of the book to help you monitor the range of complexity students are encountering.

Book Summary
Gives a brief book synopsis for teacher reference.

Graphic Organizer
Provides students materials for comprehension and writing practice that may be photocopied or printed from SAM and distributed to students.

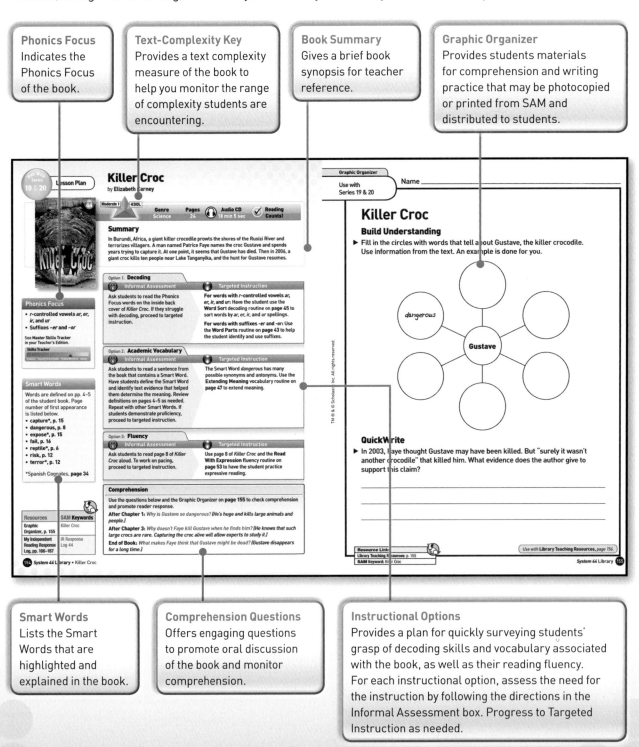

Smart Words
Lists the Smart Words that are highlighted and explained in the book.

Comprehension Questions
Offers engaging questions to promote oral discussion of the book and monitor comprehension.

Instructional Options
Provides a plan for quickly surveying students' grasp of decoding skills and vocabulary associated with the book, as well as their reading fluency. For each instructional option, assess the need for the instruction by following the directions in the Informal Assessment box. Progress to Targeted Instruction as needed.

Recommended Practice for Small-Group Instruction

The *System 44* Library can be used in rotation with the *Resources for Differentiated Instruction*, *Decodable Digest*, and *44 Practice Pages* during Small-Group Instruction. Provide direct instruction by following these steps:

1 Introduce Texts

Before reading, preview features of the *System 44* Library. See pages 8–11 for a description of features.

2 Teach and Discuss

Invite students to read the book with a partner, or with your support as needed. During and after reading, use the book summary and comprehension questions in the Lesson Plan to engage students in discussion and to monitor comprehension. To foster accountable reading and provide comprehension and writing practice, ask students to complete the Graphic Organizer activity provided for each book.

3 Assess

Use the Instructional Options provided in the Lesson Plans to assess students' need for instruction in decoding, vocabulary building, and fluency. Follow the directions in the Informal Assessment box. In cases where there is a need for further instruction, proceed to the Targeted Instruction box.

4 Reinforce

Use the Routines for Comprehension, Decoding, Vocabulary/Word Study, and Fluency provided on pages 36–53 in this book to remediate and reinforce skills.

5 Record Progress

Guide students as they use the following resources, located on **SAM**: Summarizing (Keyword: Summarizing 44), Making Inferences (Keyword: Making Inferences 44), the Vocabulary Builder (Keyword: Vocabulary Builder 44) and the Fluency Checklist (Keyword: Fluency Checklist 44). Also, distribute copies of My Independent Reading Response Log on pages 166–167 of this book to record progress.

Managing Independent Reading

System 44 provides teachers with multiple resources to manage independent reading and promote student accountability for learning, goal setting, and behavior.

Classroom Organization

In an organized classroom, students can easily access materials and use independent reading time efficiently and productively. Follow the guidelines below to set up a Modeled and Independent Reading area of the classroom. For more information, see page T8 of the *44Book* Teacher's Edition.

- Arrange comfortable chairs and tables in a quiet corner of the classroom.
- Place the *System 44* paperbacks and audiobooks in a designated area.
- Organize copies of the *44Book* and the *Decodable Digest* on a nearby shelf.
- Store CD players, laptops, iPads, and headphones near the Library.
- Store copies of reproducible student resources (My Independent Reading Response Log, Graphic Organizers, Self-Monitoring Chart) in a clearly marked and easily accessible place.
- Create a folder for each student in which to store completed materials. Store folders and student notebooks near reproducible student resources.
- Display the *System 44* Library poster.

Student Routines and Accountability

Student Resources Post, discuss, and practice procedures for:

- Handling paperbacks, audiobook CDs, CD players, and MP3 versions of audiobooks
- Using computers and iPads to read eBooks
- Accessing and reading eBooks
- Finding and completing Graphic Organizers and My Independent Reading Response Log
- Using the Self-Monitoring Chart to set independent reading goals and track reading progress
- Using and storing student folders and notebooks

Independent Reading Weekly Calendar Establish and post a schedule for Differentiated Instruction and Independent Reading. Create a weekly calendar so students know when they are scheduled for Differentiated Instruction/Independent Reading.

Student Behavior Post and review the Behavioral Goals Rubric, available on **SAM** (Keyword: Behavioral Rubric) and in the *44Book*. Review and discuss behavior expectations for Responsibility, Respect, and Effort during Independent Reading and when transitioning.

Goals and Incentives

Work with students to set manageable reading goals, create incentives to motivate students during independent reading, and track student progress.

Establishing Goals Use *Scholastic Reading Counts! (SRC!)* to establish and track student goals. Goals can be set for books read or points earned when quizzes are passed. Specific goals depend on student reading level and book length.

Motivation and Incentives Use *SRC!* results to establish an incentive system for words read, books read, quizzes passed, or points earned. Possibilities include the following:

- Highlight the top student each month/grading period for words read, quizzes passed, or points earned.
- Compete for top group or class each grading period.
- Establish increasing goals each quarter or grading period for each student.
- Collaborate with other *System 44* classrooms to set and achieve a goal of total words read.

Student Conferences Establish regular times to conference with students (once a month, once a quarter). Follow these guidelines during conferences:

- Review the *SRC!* Student Reading Report with the student. Discuss the data and also the current book the student is reading.
- Use the Lesson Plan for the book the student is reading to ask specific questions. Students should have the experience of talking to a "friend" about the content of the book.
- Use the *SRC!* data to help students set and track reading goals.
- When conferencing, use the "sandwich" approach: start with the positive, provide targeted feedback on areas to improve, and end with a positive next step.

For more information, see the Student Achievements section in your Teacher's Edition.

Supporting All Students

Support for English Language Development

The 56 books in the *System 44* Library feature multicultural topics and characters and provide a broad range of supports for English language learners.

Multiple Formats of each title (paperbacks, audiobooks, and eBooks) offer multisensory learning opportunities and provide supports that may be released during repeated readings of a book.

- Illustrated text (all versions) provides visual reference to aid comprehension.
- Audio recordings (audiobooks/eBooks) model fluent reading and accurate pronunciation.
- If enabled by the teacher, the Español button (eBooks) allows students to listen to title summaries and Smart Words entries in Spanish.
- Control over the speed of the audio (eBooks) allows students to set the pace of the narration and the highlighting of text.
- Text highlighting (eBooks) helps ELLs develop word recognition and listening comprehension.

Vocabulary Scaffolds within the text of each book support readers who are acquiring English.

- Repetition of words with targeted spelling and phonics patterns helps ELLs build vocabulary and achieve automaticity.
- Repetition of high-utility words, including words from the most common academic word families, helps ELLs achieve comprehension and participation across disciplines.
- Definitions of Smart Words and teacher guidance to help students understand context clues assist students as they expand their vocabulary, clarify meaning, and gain strategies for learning new words.

Instructional Supports include multiple resources to challenge and support ELLs at varying levels of English language proficiency.

- Instructional routines for decoding, vocabulary/word study, fluency, and comprehension may be practiced using books in all Lexile ranges.
- Lesson Plans provide options for assessing and teaching phonics, vocabulary, fluency, and comprehension skills.
- Recommended Practice for Using the *System 44* Library encourages multiple readings of each book to help students build word recognition and fluency.
- Spanish cognates of Smart Words are listed in the Library Overview on pages 24–35. See the English Language Development section of the *Resources for Differentiated Instruction* for suggested routines for Using Spanish Cognates to Teach English.

Family Supports encourage the active participation of family members in students' learning.

- Family Letters share details of the student's reading progress and books read. Family Letters are available in seven languages: English, Spanish, Cantonese, Vietnamese, Haitian-Creole, Hmong, and Filipino.

- The *System 44* Family Portal includes a wide variety of information and resources to support reading and literacy at home for all families, including those of Special Education students and English language learners. Supports include:

  - Research and results
  - Short bilingual videos
  - Bilingual tips
  - Downloadable resources and activities
  - A Family Resource Library that includes helpful tips on Reading at Home, Reading for Information, Reading and Technology, Supporting Reading Success at School, and Motivating Your Child to Read

Visit system44.com/familyportal to learn more about promoting reading at home.

Support for Special Education

Like all components of *System 44*, the Independent Reading Library supports students with special needs and their teachers by applying the most successful, research-proven approaches.

These approaches incorporate Universal Design for Learning (UDL) principles, comprehension support, and leveled text:

Universal Design for Learning

The Library incorporates the three major UDL principles, which make learning universally accessible by creating flexible goals, methods, and materials to accommodate learner differences:

UDL Principle	*System 44* Independent Reading Library Feature
Multiple Means of Representation	• Interactive information delivered in many modes—audio, pictures, and paper and electronic texts—makes sure all students, see it, say it, hear it, read it, and write it. • The Rate of Read feature in the eBooks allows students to customize the information by adjusting the speed of audio and highlighting.
Multiple Means of Action and Expression	• During Small-Group Instruction, students have opportunities to express their knowledge of library content through writing and discussion in one-on-one and small-group settings.
Multiple Means of Engagement	• Independent and small-group activities provide a variety of settings for students to engage with the content. • Paperbacks, eBooks, and audiobooks of graduated lengths focus on subjects relevant to students' lives and subjects. • eBooks and audiobooks encourage playing with sounds and symbols.

Comprehension Support Through Scaffolding and Gradual Release

Students with learning disabilities often struggle to retain new information and store it in their long-term memory. Research shows that teachers can enhance students' comprehension of text by using techniques such as providing a gradual release of responsibility to the student and scaffolding instruction. To address these needs the library includes:

- Reading prompts in the Paperbacks and eBooks help students check for comprehension during and after reading.

- A Reading Coach on the eBooks and audiobooks models fluency and reminds students to look for phonics patterns in the text taught in the Software.

- Graphic Organizers and Comprehension questions in the Lesson Plans scaffold students' understanding of the text during guided and independent reading.

Leveled Text to Match Students' Needs

Students with special needs have experienced academic frustration throughout most of their lives. It is therefore essential that text is individually matched to students' needs:

- All text featured in the eBooks and audiobooks is measured for text complexity. This three-part measure is determined by analyzing the text's quantitative measure and qualitative features. Thus, students are consistently matched to high-interest text appropriate for their particular reading level.

- The Individualized Learning Plan (ILP), accessible via **SAM** and the Teacher Dashboard, provides teachers with a quick and simple way to set and monitor academic goals, including Independent Reading goals.

Vocabulary Development

- The average student learns 2,000 to 3,000 words each year, mostly by reading words in context.
- Instruction for struggling readers should help students learn morphologically connected academic words through repeated in-context encounters.

Students need frequent opportunities for independent reading of texts that contain critical general academic words in context.

Dr. Elfrieda H. Hiebert

Building Critical Academic Vocabulary

What Is Academic Vocabulary?

In the middle grades, students are faced with textbooks that present a vast increase in the amount and complexity of academic vocabulary. This is when students with vocabulary problems begin to struggle (RAND Reading Study Group, 2002).

There are different types of academic vocabulary. One type, technical vocabulary, includes subject-specific words. Usually these words are introduced to students as the focus of content-area instruction (Graves, 2000), so that students will learn terms like *democracy* and *oligarchy* in the social studies classroom and terms like *photosynthesis* and *cytoplasm* in the science classroom as these concepts are being introduced.

Another category of academic vocabulary, sub-technical or general academic vocabulary (Coxhead, 2000), consists of more general words such as *consider*, *system*, *form*, and *structure* that appear across multiple subjects. General academic words vary in meaning in different contexts and act as different parts of speech. For example, a science text may describe the *form* that matter takes, while a social studies text may describe the way in which a government was *formed*.

While general academic words are just as crucial to academic success as technical vocabulary, they are not often deliberately taught. In addition, since they appear infrequently in nonacademic texts, students are less likely to learn these words outside of the classroom.

The Critical Academic Word List (CAWL)

Many of the general academic vocabulary words incorporated throughout the *System 44* Library come from the Critical Academic Word List (CAWL) (Hiebert, 2008). Unlike other lists of general academic words that were developed for university students learning English as a second language (Coxhead, 2000), the CAWL was specifically designed to include the general academic words most critical to the academic success of elementary- and middle-school students.

Determining Which Words Make the List

To compile the CAWL, researchers used the following criteria:

1. **Frequency** The list contains words predicted to appear with at least moderate frequency in elementary- and middle-grade texts, particularly content-area texts.

2 **Morphological Richness** According to Carlisle and Katz (2006), words that appear with some frequency increase the likelihood of recognition of other members of their morphological family. While the word *visualize* is rare, *visual, vision, visible,* and *invisible* occur with moderate frequency in written texts. The CAWL, therefore, includes less commonly occurring words that are part of semantically linked morphological families. This inclusion enables teachers to direct students' attention to similarities and differences between the meanings of words within each family.

3 **Dispersion** This term refers to the degree to which words appear across different subject areas. A word such as *form* appears across many subject areas, while a word such as *adverb* appears mostly in the context of language arts. The CAWL contains words dispersed widely across different subject areas.

The CAWL in Practice: Word Learning Strategies

Research indicates that the average student learns from 2,000 to 3,000 words each year, and that most of this learning is done by reading words in context, not through approaches that attempt to teach words one at a time (Anderson & Nagy, 1992).

Students need frequent opportunities for independent reading of texts that contain critical words in context. The books in the *System 44* Library provide students with repeated exposures to words from the CAWL. Each book contains a list of Smart Words that includes selected general academic vocabulary words as well as content-specific vocabulary words that are essential for book comprehension. Additionally, scaffolded vocabulary support is presented at the back of each book and in this guide.

Differentiating Instruction

✓ **Reinforcing Book Vocabulary** Guide students to review the Smart Words and their definitions provided in each book, and use the audiobooks to build meta-cognitive awareness of these words. Discuss word meaning and have students use words in sentences.

✓ **Morphological Word Families** Foster students' word consciousness by associating Smart Words with related words. Use the Extending Meaning vocabulary routine on **page 46** to guide students to make connections among words.

✓ **Vocabulary Building Practice** Teach strategies to help students unlock word meaning through word analysis and context clues. See the Multiple-Meaning Words routine on **page 47** and the Context Clues Routine on **page 48**.

✓ **Independent Application** Encourage students to use the Vocabulary Builder graphic organizer on **SAM** (Keyword: Vocabulary Builder 44).

References

- Anderson, R., & Nagy, W. (1992). "The Vocabulary Conundrum." *American Educator* 16(4), 14–18.
- Carlisle, J.F. & Katz, L. A. (2006). "Effects of Word and Morpheme Familiarity on Reading of Derived Words." *Reading and Writing, 19,* 669–693.
- Coxhead, A. (2000). "A New Academic Word List." *TESOL Quarterly,* 34(2), 213–238.
- Graves, M. F. (2000). "A Vocabulary Program to Complement and Bolster a Middle-Grade Comprehension Program." *Reading for Meaning: Fostering Comprehension in the Middle Grades.* Teachers College Press.
- Hiebert, E.H. (2008). "Identifying a Critical Form of Vocabulary in Middle-Grade, Content-Area Texts." [Online] Available: http://www.textproject.org
- RAND Reading Study Group (2002). "Reading for Understanding: Toward a Research and Development Program in Reading Comprehension." Washington, DC: RAND.

Library Overview

This chart provides an overview of the Lexile, genre, Phonics Focus, and vocabulary coverage of each book. Vocabulary coverage includes:

- **Smart Words:** Words essential for understanding each book that students should attend to before, during, and after reading.
- **General Academic Words:** Critical general academic words embedded in each book to provide in-context exposures. For more information on general academic words, see "Building Critical Academic Vocabulary" on **pages 22-23**.

Series 1–6, Lexile® Range 100L–250L

Title	Genre	Phonics Focus	Smart Words (With Spanish Cognates)	General Academic Words
Big! Lexile measure 190L **Use with Series 2 and 3**	math	✔ Short vowels *e, i, o* (pet, steps, ten, big, is, in, its, hop, job, on, top) ✔ Consonants *j, w* (job, wins)	height length typical *(típico)*	building, job, number
Bugs That Kill Lexile measure 200L **Use with Series 1 and 2**	science	✔ Short vowels *a, e, i, o, u* (an, at, big, bug, can, get, has, if, in, mad, mob, mantis, nab, not, odd, run, tip, web, yum) ✔ Consonants *b, d, g, p* (big, bug, get, mad, mob, nab, tip, web)	poison spider sting	body
Did You Know? Lexile measure HL170L **Use with Series 1 and 2**	science	✔ Short vowels *a, i, o* (bad, can, has, fit, in, is, it, mix, cops, lot, not) ✔ Consonants *l, x* (lot, mix, six)	fact recall unique *(único)*	adult, nutrients, odd, organ, skin, unique
Fast! The World's Fastest Couch and Other Fast Things Lexile measure 150L **Use with Series 4 and 5**	science	✔ Blends (blast, brisk, desk, fast, glad, grip, must, plan, plant, rest, risk, sprigs, strap, trip, twigs, twins)	limit *(límite)* rate vehicle *(vehículo)*	rate, reach, travel

Title	Genre	Phonics Focus	Smart Words (With Spanish Cognates)	General Academic Words
Messy Jobs Lexile measure 150L **Use with** **Series 1 and 2**	jobs	✔ Short vowels (bags, big, bin, bits, can, cuts, dig, fixes, fun, gets, has, hits, job, lots, man, mixes, rocks, rots, in, is, it, wins) ✔ *-s* and *-es* endings (bits, cuts, digs, dips, fixes, gets, lots, mixes, rocks, rots, wins)	**machine** *(máquina)* **stink** **waste**	machine
Plugged In: Technology Dream Jobs Lexile measure 240L **Use with** **Series 4 and 5**	jobs	✔ Identifying syllables (connect, happens, laptop, tablet) ✔ Beginning blends (craft, slip, still, trend, trip) ✔ Ending blends (ask, best, connect, craft, hand, help, just, king, Kong, list, rock, sing, trend, went)	**entrepreneur** **industry** *(industria)* **launch** **network** **technology** *(tecnología)*	channel, connect, design, designer, grades, icon, information, machine, site, symbols, trend
Poster Power Lexile measure 220L **Use with** **Series 1 and 2**	arts	✔ *-ck* (back, lack, pick, sock) ✔ Short vowels *a, i, o* (an, at, back, bad, can, cans, cats, had, hat, lack, man, sad, bins, in, it, pick, lot, not, sock, top)	**cause** *(causa)* **motive** *(motivo)* **represent** *(representar)*	art, artist, created, reduce, war
Shamila's Goal Lexile measure HL230L **Use with** **Series 4 and 6**	social studies	✔ Closed syllables (class, clinic, clinics, did, fans, fantastic, got, had, help, how, job, kicks, left, lot, net, not, Pakistan, rocks, runs, sent, strict, top) ✔ Ending blends (back, first, kick, left, strict, went)	**adjust** *(ajustar)* **mock** **opportunity** *(oportunidad)* **respect** *(respeto)* **strict** *(estricto)*	academy, aims, attitude, confidence, continued, control, danger, encourage, goal, important, legal, program, team
These Are Not Poems Lexile measure 210L **Use with** **Series 4 and 5**	poetry	✔ Review blends (bring, skull, smells, stick) ✔ *-ng* and *-nk* (bring, hunk, junk, rank, sings, sink) ✔ Double consonants (confess, express, mess, miss, skull, smells, tell, well, will)	**confess** *(confesar)* **express** *(expresar)* **hero** *(héroe)*	express, practice, true

Series 1–6, Lexile Range 100L–250L *(continued)*

Title	Genre	Phonics Focus	Smart Words (With Spanish Cognates)	General Academic Words
They Did What? Lexile measure HL230L **Use with Series 2 and 3**	math	✔ Short vowels (bad, bus, cat, cub, did, had, in, it, on, set, up, zip) ✔ Consonants *q, v, z* (quick, quit, vet, zip)	defy distance *(distancia)* feat	feet, muscles, sense, team, teeth, traveled
Wacky Attractions Lexile measure 180L **Use with Series 1 and 2**	social studies	✔ Short vowels *a, i* (an, at, bad, can, had, hats, man, San, big, did, in, is, it, kids, pin) ✔ Consonants *h, k* (had, has, hats, kids)	attraction *(atracción)* globe *(globo)* visit *(visitar)*	adults, art, artist, attract, attraction, desert, globe, land, odd, paint, place, road, rock, volcanoes
What's New? A History of Invention Lexile measure 230L **Use with Series 6**	science	✔ Closed syllables (actress, biggest, cannot, gimmick, happens, helmet, invent, plastic, problem, products)	date design *(diseñar)* event *(evento)* invent *(inventar)* science *(ciencia)*	invent, invented, invention, inventions, invents, move, order, science, separate
Wonders of the World Lexile measure 240L **Use with Series 4 and 6**	social studies	✔ Blends (act, gift, help, lift, plants, ramp, send, sent, stand, went)	build statue *(estatua)* wonder	act, attacks, moved, united
Yes! Lexile measure 200L **Use with Series 3**	social studies	✔ s- blends (scans, skid, skin, slam, slip, snag, snaps, spills, spin, spots, step, sticks, stop, stuff, stuns) ✔ Double consonants (chill, huffs, mess, miss, puffs, spills, stuff, will, yells)	achieve compete *(competir)* score	achieve, compete

Series 7–12, Lexile Range 100L–350L

Title	Genre	Phonics Focus	Smart Words (With Spanish Cognates)	General Academic Words
African Journey Lexile measure 230L **Use with Series 9**	science	✔ Consonants + -al, -el, or -le (animals, cattle, jungle, little, mammals, middle, rental, simple, single, travel)	local *(local)* **migrate** *(migrar)* **national** *(nacional)* **nature** *(naturaleza)* travel	attack, circle, energy, group, guide, labeled, national, photos, raise, travel
Big Steals Lexile measure HL260L **Use with Series 8 and 9**	social studies	✔ th (months, path, than, that, the, theft, thefts, the, then, this, thugs, with) ✔ -ed, no base change (blasted, drilled, ended, dressed, happened, jumped, locked, rented, vanished, visited) ✔ -ing no base change (happening, missing, standing, traveling) ✔ Review unstressed closed syllables (happen, methods, vanished, visited)	cargo *(carga)* reward signal *(señal)* witness worth	account, ancient, area, art, artists, bank, business, coin, coins, computer, dollars, goal, government, items, method, money, odd, police, rented, reward, sell, signal, tape, taped
Button Your Lip and Other Idioms Lexile measure 210L **Use with Series 9**	language arts	✔ Closed syllables with *schwa* (button, common, finish, gossip, happens, jacket, kitchen, kitten, piglets, problem)	**common** *(común)* **explain** *(explicar)* idiom shake tale	explain, explains, mean, means, need, person, true
Cool Jobs in Basketball Lexile measure 300L **Use with Series 11**	jobs	✔ Words with VCe (advice, athlete, came, collide, combine, compete, desires, dispute, drove, games, grades, hired, hires, hope, huge, inside, Jones, made, name, notes, promote, relate, shape, site, spoke, whole, woke, write) ✔ Prefixes non- and un- (nonathletes, nonstop, unexpected, unpacks)	**athlete** *(atleta)* business **experience** *(experiencia)* hire intern *(interno/a)* rely	able, advice, appear, base, became, combine, combined, confides, decisions, desires, encouraged, exercises, experience, realized, relate, special
Crash! Lexile measure 320L **Use with Series 12 and 13**	science	✔ -ed with no base change (crushed, filled, happened) ✔ -ed with base change (died, excited, exploded, named, placed, raced, sized, slammed, spotted, tugged) ✔ y as a vowel (by, fly, gravity, sky, study, system)	expert *(experto/a)* follow gravity *(gravedad)* orbit *(órbita)* telescope *(telescopio)*	damaged, experts, follow, form, formed, move, need, powerful, ready, reasons, scientists, simple, system, universe

Series 7–12, Lexile Range 100L–350L *(continued)*

Title	Genre	Phonics Focus	Smart Words (With Spanish Cognates)	General Academic Words
DJ Mystery Lexile measure 190L **Use with Series 8**	fiction	✔ *th* (math, path, Seth, thank, Thadd, that, them, then, thin, thing, think, this, with)	crowd **excite** *(excitar)* **invite** *(invitar)* record truth	mean, mystery, truth
Fashion Flashback Lexile measure 220L **Use with Series 8**	social studies	✔ *-ed* ending with no base change (acted, blasted, dressed, ended, expected, fixed, instructed, jazzed, lasted, lifted, limited, matched, missed, packed, shifted, shocked, stacked, stomped, tricked, wished)	**decade** *(década)* fashion **popular** *(popular)* **practical** *(práctico/a)* trend	fashion, history, introduction, popular, rule, simple, trend
Home From War Lexile measure HL210L **Use with Series 11**	fiction	✔ Prefix *de-* (deflated, detach) ✔ Prefix *non-* (nonsense, nonstop) ✔ Prefix *un-* (unsafe, unwilling, unwise)	agree **biology** *(biología)* challenge derail **pursue** *(perseguir)*	buildings, decide, education, expected, figure, focus, job, journal, medical, need, physical, positive, ready support
Is This Art? Lexile measure 230L **Use with Series 7 and 8**	social studies	✔ *ch* and *-tch* (attach, batch, bunch, catch, chat, chip, check, chill, chump, chunks, drenches, lunch, French, match, much, stretches, such)	**artist** *(artista)* change **create** *(crear)* **familiar** *(familiar)* **sculpture** *(escultura)*	created, creates, dangerous, disagree, familiar, simple
The Princess Brat Lexile measure 220L **Use with Series 10**	fiction	✔ Soft *c* and *g* (budge, cage, cell, chance, face, gentle, judge, nice, Princess, rage, spice, twice) ✔ Suffix *-ment* (contentment, excitement)	agreement **famous** *(famoso/a)* raise **reality** *(realidad)* stomp	agreement, gentle, meant, need, relax, simple
Ripped From the Headlines Lexile measure 210L **Use with Series 10**	social studies	✔ Long *a* with final *e* (blaze, brave, came, grade, grave, lane, made, plane, plate, safe, save, tales, waves) ✔ Long *i* with final *e* (alive, crime, fine, fire, five, hike, inside, life, pipe, ride, side, time, wide)	amaze believe brave danger **rescue** *(rescatar)*	act, acted, aid, amaze, amazed, choice, energy, formed, move, normal, protect, survive, true

Title	Genre	Phonics Focus	Smart Words (With Spanish Cognates)	General Academic Words
Survival Guide: How to Keep Your Job Lexile measure 190L **Use with Series 7 and 8**	jobs	✔ *-ing* with no base change (acting, asking, bringing, brushing, catching, checking, fixing, gossiping, happening, listing, messing, picking, punishing, snatching, spilling, sticking, telling, thinking, willing, yelling) ✔ Review *ch, -tch, sh, th* (brushing, catch, chat, checking, chicken, hush, much, punishing, sandwich, shop, snatching, that, them, then, things, think, this, with)	customer fire focus *(enfocar)* reason *(razón)* responsible *(responsable)*	follow, matter, mean, need, nervous, office, raise, reasons, refuse, responsible, rules, sign, supplies, truth
Unstoppable: The True Life Story of Shadrack Boakye Lexile measure HL230L **Use with Series 10**	social studies	✔ Long *a* final *e* (age, came, face, game, grade, made, name, place, safe, state, take) ✔ Long *i* with final *e* (fine, life, like, prize, side, times, twice) ✔ Soft *c* (civil, face, place, twice) ✔ Soft *g* (age, pages) ✔ Suffix *-ment* (puzzlement) ✔ Suffix *-ness* (kindness)	civilian *(civil)* confident potential *(potencial)* rebel *(rebelde)* region *(región)*	announce, challenge, civil war, compete, drama, encouraged, immigration, improved, issues, memories, program, remember, struggled, subject
Weird Sports Records Lexile measure HL190L **Use with Series 7**	social studies	✔ *ch* (bench, champ, chill, much, such) ✔ *-tch* (match) ✔ *sh* (crash, shot, smash, splash, swish)	error *(error)* etiquette *(etiqueta)* exercise *(hacer ejercicio)* foul fine	baseball, basketball, coach, competes, diver, error, errors, exercise, extreme, final, finally, goals, important, kick, loss, mountain, react, relax, score, soccer, sports, survived, team, technical, tennis, volcano
When Lisa Met Billy Lexile measure 220L **Use with Series 8 and 12**	graphic novel/fiction	✔ *-ing* with base change (budding, challenging, chatting, dating, exciting, getting, kidding, liking, quitting, saving, stopping, trembling) ✔ Review *-ing* with no base change (acting, happening, helping, picking, shocking, telling)	director *(director/a)* nervous *(nervioso/a)* quit realize rehearse role *(rol)*	agreed, amazing, challenging, choice, course, director, exciting, family, mean, meant, need, nervous, realize, response, truth, understand
Yo, Yolanda! Advice About Friends Lexile measure 130L **Use with Series 7**	life issues	✔ Digraph *sh* (bash, blush, cash, clash, crush, fresh, gushes, rush, shed, shift, shock, shot, trash, wish)	advice assume forgive mistake problem *(problema)*	advice, assume, borrows, family, mean, moved, moving, need, nervous, usually

Series 13–18, Lexile Range 200L–350L

Title	Genre	Phonics Focus	Smart Words (With Spanish Cognates)	General Academic Words
Ant Attack! Lexile measure 290L **Use with Series 17 and 18**	classic retelling	✔ Prefixes *pre-* and *re-* (prejudge, refill, relight, return) ✔ Long *i igh* (fight, frightened, light, might, night, relight, right, sight, tightly) ✔ Other long *i* spellings (behind, find, kind, wild) ✔ Long *o* spellings (bold, bolted, jolted, told)	attack *(atacar)* drown horror *(horror)* invade *(invadir)* precaution *(precaución)* reassure	approached, attack, became, body, moving, raised, reached, survive, survived, unable, warned
Back From the Grave! Lexile measure 240L **Use with Series 13**	classic retelling	✔ Suffixes *-y* and *-ly* (closely, lucky, quickly, sadly) ✔ Change *y* to *i* (angrily, cried, tried)	bury coffin dream examine *(examinar)* remove worry	agreed, became, body, course, decided, examined, expecting, identify, possibly, raised, servant, treated
Disaster! Lexile measure 330L **Use with Series 14**	science	✔ *com-* and *con-* (combined, common, completely, computed, concrete, construct, contacted, contributed, convinced)	aid damage escape *(escapar)* massive *(masivo)* survivor warning	aid, compared, damage, damaged, decided, deliver, destroyed, determined, family, followed, form, formed, level, natural, needed, power, reached, survive, united, warning
El Tiburón Lexile measure 340L **Use with Series 13 and 14**	social studies	✔ Silent letters *wr-* and *-mb* (numb, wrapped, wreck) ✔ *ph* (phone) ✔ Digraph *wh-* (when, whip, why) ✔ Review endings *-ed, -ing* (asking, completed, crashing, decided, ended, escaped, flipped, getting, helping, hired, jumped, lifted, popping, standing, stopping, swimming, tried, trying, using, waiting, wrapped, yelled)	accident *(accidente)* attempt complete *(completar)* hope purpose *(propósito—* this is closer to "goal"; *fin* is closer to "reason") support	attempt, became, choose, currents, dangerous, decided, disabled, means, moved, purpose, reached, reason, separates, supported
Have You Seen My Mummy? Lexile measure HL320L **Use with Series 13 and 14**	science	✔ *y* as a vowel (body, dry, frosty, happy, mummify, mummy, risky) ✔ Suffixes *-y* and *-ly* (finally, frosty, quickly, recently, risky, swampy) ✔ Open syllables (bacteria, depends, finally, future, he, material, respected) ✔ Unstressed open syllables (amazed, depends, respected) ✔ Silent consonants (knew, know, wrap, wrapped, wrong)	convince *(convencer)* corpse decay preserve *(preservar)* process *(proceso)*	bacteria, chemicals, comforted, cultures, damaged, environments, excited, finally, information, material, produce, release, respected, restored, scientist, success, tradition
Killer Plague Lexile measure GN220L **Use with Series 15**	fiction	✔ *ai* (afraid, contains, fainted, gaining, obtain, remains, strain, wait) ✔ *ay* (anyway, away, day, days, daytime, Layla, may, maybe, mayor, okay, Payton, stay, stayed, way)	contagious *(contagioso)* extinct *(extinto)* inoculate *(inocular)* isolate tissue virus *(virus)*	abandoned, allowed, blood, community, contains, discovered, discovery, disease, examines, examining, exposed, identify, information, job, obvious, protect, recognize, remains, removed, research, results, survive, symptoms, team

Title	Genre	Phonics Focus	Smart Words (With Spanish Cognates)	General Academic Words
Left to Die Lexile measure 350L **Use with Series 16**	science	✔ Long *o* vowel teams *oa* and *ow* (approached, below, blowing, boast, crowed, floating, followed, goal, groaned, grow, know, known, load, moaned, road, show, slow, snow, stow, tow)	approach gear glacier *(glaciar)* struggle summit vertical *(vertical)*	amazing, approached, approaching, base, became, choice, dangerous, determined, difficult, excitement, followed, matter, needed, reached, reason, struggled, survive, survived, view
Medical Miracle Lexile measure 340L **Use with Series 14**	science	✔ Open syllables (baby, even, fatal, final, finally, human, located, open, table, vital) ✔ Unstressed open syllables (adults, capital, confident, medical)	artery *(arteria)* fused *(fusionado/a)* prepare *(preparar)* stretch surgery *(cirugía)* syndrome *(síndrome)*	body, confident, confused, located, need, needed, operate, operates, operating, operation, prepare, prepared, ready, signs, true
Music Mash-Up Lexile measure HL330L **Use with Series 18**	arts	✔ Ending *-ed* with base change (changed, danced, described, dipped, imitated, improvised, inspired, starred) ✔ Ending *-ing* with base change (changing, dancing, exciting, making) ✔ Ending *-y* (crazy, twangy) ✔ Ending *-ly* (wildly) ✔ Prefix *re-* (react, reflect, reflected) ✔ Prefix *pre-* (prevent)	emerge *(emerger)* entertainer imitate *(imitar)* improvise *(improvisar)* perform reflect *(reflejar)*	blues, culture, described, exciting, includes, instrument, invented, isolated, jazz, jobs, muscular, musicians, orchestra, prevent, style, styles, unexpected, unique
Play Ball! Lexile measure 310L **Use with Series 14**	social studies	✔ *com-* (combined, common, competed, complex) ✔ *con-* (conflict, contacted, contained, contest, continued, contract)	complex *(complejo)* element *(elemento)* evolve *(evolucionar)* medieval *(medieval)* origin *(origen)* pastime	civil war, combined, competed, conflict, contacted, defended, divided, existed, formed, impressed, invents, major, series, similar, team, teams

Series 13–18, Lexile Range 200L–350L *(continued)*

Title	Genre	Phonics Focus	Smart Words (With Spanish Cognates)	General Academic Words
Samurai Fighters Lexile measure 300L **Use with Series 17**	social studies	✔ Long *e* vowel teams *ea*, *ee*, and *ie* (beat, defeat, disagree, each, easy, free, greedy, keep, means, need, piece, pleaded, read, see, sneak, teaches, team, thieves, three, weak)	clan *(clan)* defeat emperor *(emperador)* enemy *(enemigo/a)* legend *(leyenda)* samurai *(samurai)*	became, defeat, disagree, enemies, enemy, expert, former, less, loyal, mean, means, need, needed, power, powerful, practice, prepares, respect, respected, rule, ruled, serve, served, sign, special, true
The Story of Shi Jin Lexile measure 220L **Use with Series 17**	world literature	✔ Long *e* spelled *ea* (beat, defeat, each, feast, leads, leaped, plead, please, pleased, read, screamed, sneaked, steal, teach, teaching, weak) ✔ Long *e* spelled *ee* (agree, feel, flee, freed, greeted, meeting, need, needed, needs, see, sleep, teen, teenage, three, weeks) ✔ Long *e* spelled *ie* (believed, thief, thieves)	defend *(defender)* novel *(novela)* offer *(ofrecer)* outlaw revenge villain *(villano)*	action, agree, arrived, charge, defeat, explained, job, margin, mistreat, released, supplies, travel, understand
The Sweater Thief Lexile measure 250L **Use with Series 15**	fiction	✔ Long *a* vowel teams (afraid, away, chain, complain, contained, day, explain, faint, gray, Kayla, main, okay, paid, pay, remain, say, stay, wait, way)	confused *(confundido/a)* employee *(empleado/a)* expensive ignore *(ignorar)* include *(incluir)* praise	acting, confused, contained, counter, course, definitely, employee, entrance, experience, explain, group, ignored, instant, raise, receipt, remain, true, truth, usually
Witch Hunt Lexile measure 300L **Use with Series 18**	social studies	✔ Multiple affixes (bewitched, unlucky) ✔ Ending *-ed* with base change (accused, begged, believed, blamed, changed, cried, disliked, hired, lied, named, released, tried) ✔ Suffixes *-ly* and *-y* (crazy, lucky, quickly, really, strangely, unlucky)	accuse *(acusar)* admit *(admitir)* hearing release rumor *(rumor)* trial	acting, admit, admitted, choices, decide, figure, governor, increase, needed, release, respected, special, strict, truth, unusual

Series 19–25, Lexile Range 300L–450L

Title	Genre	Phonics Focus	Smart Words (With Spanish Cognates)	General Academic Words
Arabian Nights Lexile measure 340L **Use with Series 23 and 24**	graphic novel/ classic retelling	✔ *a, au,* and *aw* (all, awful, called, caused, dawned, fraud, haunted, launch, law, outlaw, saw, small, straw) ✔ Suffixes *-sion* and *-tion* (action, condition, decision, invasion, location) ✔ Root *graph* (graphic)	advisor betray greedy majesty *(majestad)* nightmare supply treasure	accept, acted, action, advisor, agreed, allow, appeared, arrived, attack, become, body, certain, character, course, decision, disappeared, enemy, entered, entering, family, followed, instantly, located, location, mean, need, offered, person, powerful, powers, raised, reach, ready, realized, recognize, servant, special, supply, trade, traded, warning
Beauty and the Geek Lexile measure 380L **Use with Series 19 and 20**	fiction	✔ r-controlled vowels *-air, -are* and *-ear* (care, compare, fair, hair, pair, rare, scared, shared, unfair, upstairs, wears) ✔ Suffixes *-er* and *-est* (biggest, cuter, fastest, finest, happier, happiest, harder, hardest, later, nicer, nicest, older)	compare *(comparar)* impress *(impresionar)* interest *(interés)* introduce *(introducir)* jealous obvious *(obvio)* plan *(plan)*	admit, choice, collection, compare, confused, convinced, course, excited, expected, impress, impressed, introduced, mean, needed, nervous, perfect, perfectly, practice, truth
Everyday Heroes Lexile measure 440L **Use with Series 23 and 25**	social studies	✔ *oo* and *u* (book, Brooklyn, foot, good, hook, looked, misunderstood, onlookers, pull, pushing, put, shook, stood, took, wool) ✔ Prefixes *dis-* and *mis-* (disable, discover, discovery, misunderstood) ✔ Roots *rupt, struct,* and *scrib/script* (abruptly, construction, describe, instructed, instructions, interrupted, script)	discovery distract *(distraer)* distress hesitate instruct *(instruir)* maneuver *(maniobra)* station *(estación)*	able, act, acting, action, appeared, approached, arrived, attack, attacked, balance, body, certain, charge, collection, construction, counter, crime, curve, danger, decided, discover, discovery, discussed, disturbing, enjoyed, family, followed, gently, ignored, instructions, less, location, matter, mattered, meant, memorial, move, moving, need, needed, nervous, nervousness, noticed, occurred, offered, perform, protect, reached, recalling, received, serving, signs, struggled, survive, united, unusual
Fire! The Triangle Shirtwaist Factory Tragedy Lexile measure 440L **Use with Series 21 and 22**	social studies	✔ Diphthongs *oi, oy, ou,* and *ow* (about, avoid, choice, crowded, down, enjoy, ground, joined, now, oil, out, powered, powerful, powerless, shout) ✔ Suffixes *-ful* and *-less* (careful, careless, fearless, hopeful, powerful, powerless, tireless, useless)	factory *(factoría—more commonly "fábrica")* improve labor *(labor—used in the sense of "task" rather than a larger concept of "work")* prevent *(prevenir)* protest *(protestar)* strike tragic *(trágico)*	act, agreed, became, charged, choice, created, danger, dangers, decision, enjoy, family, focus, follow, government, groups, important, improve, investigate, investigating, means, members, moved, movement, moving, need, needed, offices, powered, powerful, powerless, prevent, prevented, protect, protected, protection, reached, ready, refused, remind, respond, responded, rules, support, survive, treated, warn
Four Rotten Rulers Lexile measure HL380L **Use with Series 19**	social studies	✔ /sh/ spelled *ci* (official, officials, politician, special) ✔ /sh/ spelled *ti* (action, attention, civilization, location, motion, nations)	civilization *(civilización)* conquer *(conquistar)* decline explore *(explorar)* foreign fortune tyrant *(tirano)*	action, allowed, area, arranged, arrived, attack, control, decided, defeat, encourage, expanded, greeted, important, job, location, loyal, nations, organized, protect, reacted, region, respect, special, success, violently

Title	Genre	Phonics Focus	Smart Words (With Spanish Cognates)	General Academic Words
Hot Jobs Lexile measure 450L **Use with Series 22 and 24**	jobs	✔ Variant vowel /oo/ and /ew/ (balloon, Baloo, blew, classroom, cool, crew, flew, food, foolish, grew, knew, loomed, moonlight, new, oozing, room, school, shoot, soon, too, tools, zoom) ✔ Prefixes *mid-* and *sub-* (midday, midnight, midsummer, submerged) ✔ Roots *dict* and *port* (important, predict, report, transports)	career *(carrera)* equipment *(equipo)* extreme *(extremo)* handle major *(mayor— means both "of great importance" and "older")* result *(resultado)* train	act, action, aid, become, challenging, communication, current, danger, dangerous, enjoy, equipment, expert, experts, extreme, flows, graduated, important, less, major, mean, means, meant, nature, need, needed, object, observatory, offered, office, possible, practice, protect, resists, result, scientist, special, subjects, survive, warning
Killer Croc Lexile measure 430L **Use with Series 19 and 20**	science	✔ r-controlled vowels *ar, er, ir,* and *ur* (better, car, expert, far, first, hard, large, monster, November, number, return, river, scars, smart, survivors) ✔ Suffixes *-er* and *-or* (hunters, killer, ranger, survivors, swimmers)	capture *(capturar)* dangerous expose *(exponer)* fail reptile *(reptil)* risk terror *(terror)*	attacked, attacking, attacks, body, capture, captured, choice, collects, dangerous, decided, disappeared, disappears, enter, entered, excited, expert, experts, figured, follow, includes, less, move, moved, need, needed, photograph, polluted, possible, ranger, respect, scientist, sense, sign, truth, view
Lost! Mysteries of the Bermuda Triangle Lexile measure 440L **Use with Series 24 and 25**	science	✔ Prefix *tri-* (triangle) ✔ Suffixes *-able* and *-ible* (believable, drinkable, favorable, impassable, inescapable, reasonable, responsible, sensible, unavoidable, unbearable, unexplainable, unfavorable, unforgettable, unpredictable, unsinkable, usable) ✔ Roots *phon, scope, tele,* and *vis/vid* (telephones, telescopes, televisions, visible, visited)	current *(corriente)* disappear *(desaparecer)* panic *(pánico)* surrounded unpredictable *(impredicible)* violent *(violento/a)* visible *(visible)*	attack, attacked, attacks, avoid, base, connect, course, current, currents, danger, dangerous, destroy, destroyed, direction, disappear, disappeared, enter, existed, experts, explain, explains, explanation, explanations, explored, favorable, form, information, located, mean, mysterious, mystery, need, predict, predicting, reasonable, reasons, report, reports, responsible, scientists, sense, signs, surrounded, transport, type, united, usually, violent, visible, warning
Never Give Up Lexile measure HL410L **Use with Series 20**	jobs	✔ *are* (aware, barely, caring, compare, prepare, prepared, rarely, shared) ✔ *air* (airing, airwaves, despair, despaired) ✔ *ear* (wearing)	define *(definir)* dismiss failure obstacle *(obstáculo)* persist *(persistir)* sensation *(sensación)* underestimate *(subestimar)*	ability, actress, adult, attended, aware, basketball, book, channel, coach, compare, computer, computers, control, decided, define, defined, design, device, devices, disagreed, edited, education, farm, featured, finally, focused, health, illustrated, innovative, issues, job, jobs, major, money, persisted, persistence, prepare, prepared, problem, product, products, program, publisher, publishers, rejected, revised, scientists, scored, series, special, sports, struggling, success, successful, support, team, teams, technology, trainer, underestimated, value, visited

Title	Genre	Phonics Focus	Smart Words (With Spanish Cognates)	General Academic Words
The Promise Lexile measure 440L **Use with Series 19 and 20**	social studies	✔ *r*-controlled vowels *or* and *ore* (before, born, forced, forms, more, north, northern, orphan, orphanage, reform, reported, story, torn, Victoria) ✔ */sh/* spellings *ci* and *ti* (direction, inspiration, nation, physician, vacation, vicious)	**accomplish** **activist** *(activista)* **conflict** *(conflicto)* **continue** *(continuar)* **dedicate** *(dedicar)* **mission** *(misión)* **reform** *(reformar)*	able, accomplish, action, actions, affects, agree, aids, attacked, attacks, avoid, became, body, choose, conflict, connection, continue, continued, continues, dangerous, decision, direction, divided, educated, encourages, enemies, enemy, equipment, family, formed, government, group, moved, nation, need, needed, patient, patients, prevent, protects, raised, rates, reason, reported, reporter, resistance, signs, survive, system, tension, treat
The Raven Lexile measure NP **Use with Series 20 and 21**	poetry/ graphic novel	✔ *or* (decorum, for, form, horror, lordly, mortal, or) ✔ *ore* (ashore, before, bore, core, evermore, explore, implore, lore, more, nevermore, shore, store, wore, yore) ✔ *ou* (countenance, doubtless, louder, out) ✔ *ow* (fowl, now) ✔ *oi* (noise, voice) ✔ *oy* (annoys) ✔ Suffix *-less* (nameless) ✔ Suffix *-ful* (fearful)	**beguile** **countenance** **discourse** *(discurso)* **distinctly** **implore** **radiant** *(radiante)* **sorrow**	agreeing, became, borrow, curious, denser, entrance, explore, expressing, following, form, grim, horror, instant, memories, mystery, myths, publish, remember, repeating, separate, truly, uncertain, volume
Tragedy at Sea Lexile measure HL430L **Use with Series 23**	social studies	✔ *a* (almost, also, always, calling, fallen, football, recalled, salty, smaller, water) ✔ *au* (hauling, mauling) ✔ *aw* (awesome, awful, awfully, flawlessly)	**accommodate** *(acomodar)* **crisis** *(crisis)* **injured** **mission** *(misión)* **perilous** **surrender** **warship**	agreed, aid, area, attacks, code, communicate, course, create, dangerous, energy, equipment, eventually, expected, finally, guards, medical, message, military, order, protected, recognize, release, role, supposed, surviving, survivors, target, type, wandering

Why Use a Summarizing Routine?

- This routine helps students better comprehend and communicate about what they read.
- It places students in an active reading and learning role.

Purpose

- Summarizing helps students monitor their comprehension, review what they read, and focus on important concepts.

Summarizing

Use this routine with books in the* System 44 *Library to help students summarize their reading to deepen comprehension.

Summarizing is a process by which students select, organize, and present the most important elements of a text orally or in writing. Summaries tell the key ideas and details of a text.

Summaries are brief, do not contain opinions, and are organized so they start with the most important ideas.

Why Is Teaching Summarizing Important?

Summarizing helps students monitor their comprehension, review what they read, and focus on the "big ideas." By using their own words to briefly state important points, students recognize what they have learned. When they summarize a text, students think about the author's purpose, and practice paraphrasing and analyzing text.

When Should I Teach Summarizing?

Summarizing should be taught after students have significant practice identifying the main topic and key details of a text. It can be used to build and check understanding of texts that contain new concepts and in preparation for a test.

You may want to scaffold the instruction of the routine by doing the following:

- Begin with short passages from a book. Have students provide one- or two-sentence summaries.
- Teach students how to use sticky notes to identify the main topic and key details in a text.
- Have pairs complete each part of the summarizing activity independently and then compare ideas and explain their reasoning.

Summarizing

Guide students to summarize as they read.

1. Share why this skill is important.
   - Explain that summarizing will help them focus on the key ideas in a text.
   - It will also help them better understand their reading.

2. Write *summarize* on the board. Then say:

   You summarize all the time. For example, you may sum up, or summarize, what happened on a TV show for a friend. You say only the most important things that happened. When you summarize a book, you organize the topic and key details of a text to make a short statement in your own words.

3 Explain the following steps to help students summarize a text. State the desired summary length.

Find the topic, or what the book is mostly about.
- Remind students that the topic of a nonfiction text may be stated in a sentence.
- The topic is often at the beginning of a text.

Look for the most important details.
- Remember that the most important details will support the topic.
- The details should appear in order of importance.

Restate the topic and details in a short summary. Use your own words.
- Guide students to write a topic sentence and add details to complete their summaries.

4 Read aloud page 4 from *African Journey* (Series 9). Tell students that you are going to think aloud to show them how to summarize. As you think aloud, use the passage you just read as an example.

I know that the topic is often at the beginning in a nonfiction book or passage.

The topic of African Journey *appears on page 4. It says, "My name is Leslie. Last summer I traveled to Africa."*

Next, I need to find the important details. What information tells me more about the topic? I see that Leslie met many people in Africa. She saw nature and went on a safari. She took photos. She put them in the book.

Now, to summarize the page, I need to combine these ideas in my own words. I will state the topic and details in order of importance.

My summary is "Leslie went to Africa. She met people and saw lots of nature. She put photos from her trip in this book."

5 Then model for students how to complete the **Summarizing** graphic organizer available on **SAM** (Keyword: Summarizing 44).

I'm going to put the topic and important details in the top two boxes. Then I need to put this information in my own words and write my summary in the bottom box.

6 Guide students to complete the **Summarizing** graphic organizer available on **SAM** (Keyword: Summarizing 44) with additional texts. Have them summarize orally first. Then have them write their summaries in their own words.

Suggested Passages for Summarizing

Book	Passage
Plugged In: Technology Dream Jobs (Series 4 and 5)	Page 4
Play Ball! (Series 14)	Pages 6–7
Everyday Heroes (Series 23 and 25)	Pages 6–7

Academic Language for Summarizing

Teach your students these words and phrases to use during discussions.

TERMS

Topic: what a text is mostly about

Details: information that tells more about the topic

Summary: a short statement in your own words that tells the most important ideas in a text

Synthesize: to put ideas together

SENTENCE STARTERS

- *This passage is mostly about . . .*
- *I think . . . is an important detail because . . .*
- *To summarize, . . .*
- *In my own words, . . .*

Why Use a Making Inferences Routine?

- Making inferences promotes questioning of the text.

- When readers make inferences, they combine background knowledge with text clues to improve comprehension.

- Learning how to make inferences helps students comprehend texts in which the author is not always explicit.

Making Inferences

Use this routine with books in the System 44 *Library to help students understand what is not always stated in the text.*

To make inferences, students need to relate what they already know to clues in the text to arrive at one or more possible inferences. Inferences can be estimations, educated guesses, assumptions about how characters feel, or why an event may have occurred.

Why Is Making Inferences Important?

Instruction in making inferences helps students to combine textual information with prior knowledge to make meaning, thereby improving comprehension.

Making inferences can also help in understanding cause and effect, problem and solution, making predictions, and analyzing characters.

When Should I Teach Making Inferences?

Teach students to make inferences whenever they are reading fiction or nonfiction texts. If the author is giving clues but is not explicitly stating what is happening, stop and encourage students to relate prior knowledge of a topic to the reading material.

You can teach making inferences by doing the following:

- Give students meaningful real-world examples of situations when they might make inferences, such as reading someone's body language.
- Then sit with your arms folded. Ask them to infer how you might be feeling (bored, angry, restless).
- Project a passage such as from *They Did What?* (Series 2 and 3). Read page 6 to the whole class.
- Model how you combine prior knowledge and experience about tigers and dentists with text clues to make an inference about the veterinarian dentists' bravery.
- Ask why the author would state, "Those vet dentists are brave." What do you know about tigers? Are they wild or domestic animals? Do they eat meat or plants? Why would the vets need to be brave to stick their hands into a tiger's mouth?
- Explain that the answers to these questions are inferences. You are stating ideas or opinions that are not expressed in the text.

Making Inferences

Guide students to make inferences about their reading.

1 Share why this skill is important. Explain that an author does not always say everything he or she wants you to know or understand.

Making inferences helps you figure out the unstated ideas so you will better understand what you are reading.

2 Write *Making Inferences* on the board. Then say:

> *To make an inference means to combine your experience, or what you already know about a topic, and what you read to figure out something that the author did not state.*

> *Making inferences is an active strategy that requires asking questions, such as, "Why did the person in the text act that way?"*

3 Explain the following steps that will help students make inferences about a text.

Ask yourself what is being stated or is happening in the text.

Think about what you already know from background knowledge or experience.

Combine the text clues with what you already know to make an inference.

Check that the inference makes sense.

4 Read aloud a short passage, such as page 4 from *Poster Power* (Series 1 and 2). Have students draw on background knowledge to make meaning.

> *When I make an inference, I look for text clues and then I think about what I already know about that topic so I can make an inference that makes sense.*

5 Model for students how to complete the **Making Inferences** graphic organizer on **SAM** (Keyword: Making Inferences 44).

What I Learned from Reading: I learned that an artist made a poster that shows a man named Uncle Sam. The man represents the U.S. He wears red, white, and blue, and has a hat with stars.

What I Already Know: The U.S. flag is red, white, and blue with stars.

My Inference: The artist chose to have Uncle Sam wear red, white, and blue with stars because the colors and pattern are the same as those used in the U.S. flag.

6 Guide students by modeling how to identify text clues with additional texts. Then help them complete the **Making Inferences** graphic organizer on **SAM** (Keyword: Making Inferences 44) by using their knowledge and experience to make an inference.

7 Reinforce the skill, gradually introducing more complex texts.

Sample Passages for Making Inferences

Book	What I Learned	What I Know	My Inference
Big! (Series 2 and 3)	You'd have to walk 2,909 steps to reach the top of Burj Khalifa, or you can take the elevator.	Riding an elevator to the top of a building is faster and less tiring than walking up stairs.	Most people probably take the elevator to get to the top of Burj Khalifa.
Did You Know? (Series 1 and 2)	Your femur is stronger than concrete.	Bones can break.	It would be difficult to break your femur.

Academic Language for Making Inferences

Teach your students these words and phrases to use during discussions.

TERMS

Text Clues: key words of details that help a reader figure out the unstated ideas

Inference: a combination of text clues and what you already know about a topic

Experience: something that happened to you or something that you have done

Stated Ideas: information given in the text

Unstated Ideas: information not found in the text

SENTENCE STARTERS

- *The book/passage states . . .*
- *I already know that . . .*
- *When I combine what I know about . . . with the text clue . . . , I can infer . . .*

Why Use Decoding Routines?

- These routines help students match sounds with the symbols used to represent them in words.
- Orally blending words helps students decode words while reading.
- Decoding skills lead to rapid word recognition, greater fluency, and improved comprehension.
- As students develop decoding skills, they become more able to devote their full attention to making meaning from text.

Purpose

Recognizing syllable patterns helps students correctly determine vowel sounds and decode unfamiliar words.

Decoding Routines

Use these brief and playful routines with books in the System 44 *Library to help students grasp sound-symbol relationships.*

Use these routines to provide fast-paced support. To maximize benefits to students be sure to:

- Repeat tasks as often as necessary until students demonstrate success.
- Modify tasks to help students who demonstrate difficulty.
- Informally monitor students during decoding routines and select those who need additional intervention.
- Provide additional support as needed by backtracking to an easier step or providing more cues and examples.

Syllable Strategies

Guide students to read and write multisyllabic words with open and closed syllables.

1 Have students write the Phonics Focus words from the book on a piece of paper. Review key syllable concepts, including:

- Every syllable has just one vowel sound.
- Syllables that end in a consonant are called closed syllables and usually have a short vowel sound.
- Syllables that end in a vowel are called open syllables and usually have a long vowel sound.

2 Guide students to use the Look, Spot, Split, and Read strategy to analyze and read the words. This strategy is available in the *44Book* for students' reference, on page 189 or page 285.

Look for any prefixes, suffixes, or endings you know.
- Remember, the spelling of the base word may have changed when the ending or suffix was added.

Spot the vowels in the base word. The number of vowel spots tells the number of syllables.
- Remember, some vowel sounds are spelled with more than one letter.

Split the word into syllables.
- A good place to split a word is between two consonants.
- If there is only one consonant between syllables, try splitting after it.

Read the word. Does it make a real word? If not, you may need to split the word in a different place or try using a different vowel sound.

Syllable Type Examples

Book	Syllable Type	Phonics Focus Words
What's New? A History of Invention (Series 6)	Closed Syllables	actress, biggest, cannot, gimmick, happens, helmet, invent, plastic, problem, products
Button Your Lip and Other Idioms (Series 9)	Closed Syllables with Schwa	button, common, finish, gossip, happens, jacket, kitchen, kitten, piglets, problem
African Journey (Series 9)	Consonant + *-al*, *-el*, or *-le*	animals, cattle, jungle, little, mammals, middle, rental, simple, single, travel
Medical Miracle (Series 14)	Open Syllables	baby, even, fatal, final, finally, human, located, open, table, vital
	Unstressed Open Syllables	adults, capital, confident, medical

Blends and Digraphs

Guide students to recognize common consonant blends and digraphs.

1 Write a list of words on the board or on a piece of paper, some with consonant blends and some with consonant digraphs, and have students copy the words. Try to pick a sampling of words that shows blends and digraphs in the beginning, middle, and end positions. (Check the charts below for possible examples.)

2 Explain that a consonant blend is two or more consonants that appear together in a word, with each retaining its own sound. Point out an example from the list of words.

3 Explain that a consonant digraph is two consonants that stand for one sound, such as *ch*, *sh*, and *th*. Point out an example from the list of words.

4 Ask students to read each word on the list, circle the consonant blends, and underline the digraphs.

Purpose

Recognition of digraphs and familiarity with common consonant blends lead to improved decoding and automaticity.

Blends Examples

Book	Phonics Focus Words
Yes! (Series 3)	scans, skid, skin, slam, slip, snag, snaps, spills, spin, spots, step, sticks, stop, stuff, stuns
Fast! The World's Fastest Couch and Other Fast Things (Series 4 and 5)	blast, brisk, desk, fast, glad, grip, must, plan, plant, rest, risk, sprigs, strap, trip, twigs, twins
Plugged In: Technology Dream Jobs (Series 4 and 5)	ask, best, craft, hand, help, just, king, list, slip, still, trend, trip
These Are Not Poems (And Other Poems) (Series 4 and 5)	bring, hunk, junk, rank, sink, skull, smells, stick

Digraphs Examples

Book	Phonics Focus Words
These Are Not Poems (and Other Poems) (Series 4 and 5)	bring, sings
Yo, Yolanda! Advice About Friends (Series 7)	bash, blush, cash, clash, crush, fresh, gushes, rush, shed, shift, shock, shot, trash, wish
Is This Art? (Series 7 and 8)	attach, batch, bunch, catch, chat, check, chill, chip, chump, chunks, drenches, French, lunch, match, much, stretches, such
DJ Mystery (Series 8)	math, path, Seth, Thadd, thank, that, them, then, thin, thing, think, this, with
Survival Guide: How to Keep Your Job (Series 7 and 8)	brushing, catch, chat, checking, chicken, hush, much, punishing, sandwich, shop, snatching, that, them, then, things, think, this, with
El Tiburón (Series 13 and 14)	when, whip, why

Word Parts

Students identify and define prefixes, suffixes, inflectional endings, and roots.

Prefixes

1. Review with students that a prefix is a word part that can be added to the beginning of a base word to change its meaning. *For example, the prefix* mis- *means "wrong." The word* misunderstood *means that someone has understood wrongly or incorrectly.*

2. Ask students to list Phonics Focus words with prefixes. Then, ask them to write out the prefix and base word as an addition problem for each word. For example, the word *misunderstood* would be written as follows: *mis- + understood = misunderstood.*

3. Ask students to read each word part separately and then put the parts together to read the whole word.

Prefixes Examples

Book	Prefix	Phonics Focus Words
Cool Jobs in Basketball (Series 11)	non- un-	nonathletes, nonstop, unexpected, unpacks
Disaster! (Series 14)	com- con-	combined, common, completely, computed, concrete, construct, contacted, contributed, convinced
Ant Attack! (Series 17 and 18)	pre- re-	prejudge, refill, relight, return
Witch Hunt (Series 18)	be- un-	bewitched, unlucky
Hot Jobs (Series 22 and 24)	mid- sub-	midday, midnight, midsummer, submerged
Everyday Heroes (Series 23 and 25)	dis- mis-	disable, discover, discovery, misunderstood
Lost! Mysteries of the Bermuda Triangle (Series 24 and 25)	tri-	triangle

Purpose

Recognizing common word parts helps students decode multisyllabic words with greater automaticity. Knowing the meanings of word parts helps students to determine the meanings of unfamiliar words in context.

This routine is best used to practice prefixes, suffixes, inflectional endings, and roots.

Suffixes and Inflectional Endings

1 Explain that suffixes are word parts that can be added to the end of a base word to change the word's meaning or part of speech. *For example, the suffix* -ful *means "full of." The word* hopeful *means "full of hope." Adding* -ful *to the noun* hope *creates the adjective* hopeful. Explain that inflectional endings may make a noun plural, change the tense of a verb, or help a verb agree with its subject.

2 Ask students to list words with suffixes or endings from their current book, leaving room to write beneath each word. Then, ask them to write out the base word and suffix or ending as a math equation for each word. For example, the word *hopeful* would be written as follows: *hope + -ful = hopeful.*

   Note: Remind students that adding suffixes or endings to some base words requires spelling changes. Help them include these changes in their equations (for example: *happy – y + i + -ness = happiness; nice – e + -er = nicer; big + g + -est =* biggest). For words with suffixes *-tion, -sion, -able,* and *-ible,* ask students to divide the word into syllables then create an equation by adding the syllables and suffix or ending (for example: *ac + -tion = action; un- + pre- + dict + -able = unpredictable*).

3 Ask students to read each word part separately and then put the parts together to form the whole word.

Suffixes Examples

Book	Suffix	Phonics Focus Words
The Princess Brat (Series 10)	-ment	contentment, excitement
Back From the Grave! (Series 13)	-y -ly	closely, lucky, quickly, sadly, angrily
Witch Hunt (Series 18)	-y -ly	crazy, lucky, quickly, really, strangely, unlucky
Killer Croc (Series 19 and 20)	-er -or	hunters, killer, ranger, survivors, swimmers
Beauty and the Geek (Series 19 and 20)	-er -est	biggest, cuter, fastest, finest, happier, happiest, harder, hardest, later, nicer, nicest, older
Fire! The Triangle Shirtwaist Factory Tragedy (Series 21 and 22)	-ful -less	careful, careless, fearless, hopeful, powerful, powerless, tireless, useless
Arabian Nights (Series 23 and 24)	-sion -tion	action, condition, decision, invasion, location
Lost! Mysteries of the Bermuda Triangle (Series 24 and 25)	-able -ible	believable, drinkable, favorable, impassable, inescapable, reasonable, responsible, sensible, unavoidable, unbearable, unexplainable, unfavorable, unforgettable, unpredictable, unsinkable, usable

RULES TO KNOW: Suffixes and Endings

Rule 1

VC + ending that begins with a vowel = double the final consonant

EXPLANATION: When a word ends with a short vowel followed by a single consonant, double the final consonant before adding a suffix or ending that begins with a vowel *(hopped, running, muddy).*

Rule 2

silent e + ending that begins with a vowel = drop the silent e

EXPLANATION: When a word ends with a silent *e*, drop the *e* before adding a suffix or ending that starts with a vowel *(racing, finer).*

Rule 3

consonant-y + ending that begins with a vowel = change y to i (except -ing)

EXPLANATION: When a word ends with a consonant and *y*, change the *y* to *i* before adding a suffix or ending that starts with a vowel, except for *-ing (dutiful, luckily, muddier, dried, babies, crying).*

ADDITIONAL ROOTS FOR INSTRUCTION

Greek Roots

hydro (water)

meter (measure)

ology (word or study)

photo (light)

therm (heat)

EXAMPLES

hydrogen, hydroplane
perimeter, thermometer
geology, zoology
photocopy, photography
thermos

Latin Roots

aud (to hear)

ject (to throw)

tract (to draw or pull)

EXAMPLES

audience, audio
eject, inject, reject
attract, extract, tractor

Anglo-Saxon Roots

kno (skill)

lik (similar, to be pleased with)

tru (faithful)

EXAMPLES

know, knowledge
like, likely, likeness
true, truly, truth

Inflectional Endings Examples

Book	Inflectional Ending	Phonics Focus Words
Messy Jobs (Series 1 and 2)	-s -es	bits, cuts, digs, dips, fixes, gets, lots, mixes, rocks, rots, wins
Survival Guide: How to Keep Your Job (Series 7 and 8)	-ing with no base change	acting, asking, bringing, brushing, catching, checking, fixing, gossiping, happening, listing, messing, picking, punishing, snatching, spilling, sticking, telling, thinking, willing, yelling
Fashion Flashback (Series 8)	-ed with no base change	acted, blasted, dressed, ended, expected, fixed, instructed, jazzed, lasted, lifted, limited, matched, missed, packed, shifted, shocked, stacked, stomped, tricked, wished
When Lisa Met Billy (Series 8 and 12)	-ing with base change	budding, challenging, chatting, dating, exciting, getting, kidding, liking, quitting, saving, stopping, trembling
	-ing with no base change	acting, happening, helping, picking, shocking, telling
Crash! (Series 12 and 13)	-ed with no base change	crushed, filled, happened
	-ed with base change	died, excited, exploded, named, placed, raced, sized, slammed, spotted, tugged
Back From the Grave! (Series 13)	-ed with base change	cried, tried
El Tiburón (Series 13 and 14)	-ed and -ing	asking, completed, crashing, decided, ended, escaped, flipped, getting, helping, hired, jumped, lifted, popping, standing, stopping, swimming, tried, trying, using, waiting, wrapped, yelled
Witch Hunt (Series 18)	-ed with no base change	bewitched
	-ed with base change	accused, begged, believed, blamed, changed, cried, disliked, hired, lied, named, released, tried

Roots

Remind students that many words in the English language come from Greek, Latin, and Anglo-Saxon roots. *Knowing the meanings of roots can help you figure out the meanings of words you don't know. For example, the root* tele *means "far off," and the root* scope *means "to see." A telescope lets you see things that are far away.*

Ask students to list words with roots from their current book. Then, ask them to circle all of the roots they can find in each word. Guide students to explain how the root of each word contributes to the word's meaning. Students should use dictionaries as needed.

Roots Examples

Book	Root Words	Phonics Focus Words
Hot Jobs (Series 22 and 24)	*dict, port*	important, predict, report, transports
Everyday Heroes (Series 23 and 25)	*rupt, struct, scrib/script*	abruptly, construction, describe, instructed, instructions, interrupted, script
Arabian Nights (Series 23 and 24)	*graph*	graphic
Lost! Mysteries of the Bermuda Triangle (Series 24 and 25)	*phon, scope, tele, vis/vid*	telephones, telescopes, televisions, visible, visited

Word Sort

Guide students to practice putting familiar words into groups according to their sounds and/or spellings.

This routine can be used with most Phonics Focus elements. The example below uses Phonics Focus words with *r*-controlled vowels from *Killer Croc* (Series 19 and 20).

Have students use the Word Sort graphic organizer on **SAM** (Keyword: Word Sort 44) to sort the Phonics Focus words *better, car, expert, far, first, hard, large, monster, November, number, return, river, scars, smart,* and *survivors* into groups according to their vowel spellings: *ar, ir, er, ur, or.*

Ask students to identify a pattern or principle that is operating and state it aloud. For example, students may conclude that there are three ways to spell the /ûr/ sound as seen in the words *experts, return,* and *first.*

Purpose

Word sorting enhances visual and auditory attention to the internal details of words and helps students remember correct spellings for words with vowel sounds that can be spelled more than one way.

This routine works with a variety of Phonics Focus elements.

Why Use Vocabulary/Word Study Routines?

- These routines give students tools they can use to understand and build vocabulary as they read.
- Vocabulary is fundamental to comprehension. Students cannot understand text without knowing what most of the words mean.
- Having a wide vocabulary is beneficial in building comprehension, as well as achieving overall academic success.

Purpose

Students who practice reading words from different morphological families are more likely to notice familiar base words in longer words.

Associating words with synonyms and antonyms helps students build a larger vocabulary and develop reasoning skills.

Vocabulary/Word Study Routines

Use these routines to help your students build vocabulary.

These routines will equip students with strategies for unlocking unfamiliar words and building vocabulary as they read.

Extending Meaning

Guide students to look for connections among words with the same base, root, or meaning.

Morphological Word Families

Have students write an appropriate Smart Word on a piece of paper. Guide students to notice if the word is formed from a base word, or whether it is a base word itself. Work together to create a list of other words with the same base. For example, the following words share the base *present*: *represent*, *presentation*, *misrepresent*, and *presentable*. Discuss how the base word relates to the meaning of each word.

For words with familiar Greek or Latin roots, ask students to come up with words they know that use the root. For example, the word *telescope* includes the root *tele*, meaning "far off." This root is shared with the words *television*, *telephone*, and *telegraph*. Discuss how the root contributes to the meaning of each word.

Discuss how identifying a familiar word part or base can help students figure out the meaning of an unfamiliar word as they read.

Examples

Book	Smart Word	Word Family
These Are Not Poems (and Other Poems) (Series 4 and 5)	express	expressed, expresses, expressing, expression, expressions, expressive, unexpressive
What's New? A History of Invention (Series 6)	invent	inventing, invented, inventions, inventor, inventive
Button Your Lip and Other Idioms (Series 9)	explain	explained, unexplained, explaining, explains, explainable, unexplainable, explanation, explanatory
The Princess Brat (Series 10)	agreement	agree, agreeable, agreeing, agreements, disagree, disagreement
El Tiburón (Series 13 and 14)	support	supporters, supportive, supporting
The Sweater Thief (Series 15)	employee	employ, employed, employees, employer, employers, employing, employment, employs
The Promise (Series 19 and 20)	activist	act, action, active, activate, activity, actor, actress
Everyday Heroes (Series 23 and 25)	discovery	discover, discovered, discoveries, discovering, discovers
Arabian Nights (Series 23 and 24)	advisor	advice, advised, advises, advisors, advising, advisory, advisable, unadvisable

Synonyms and Antonyms

Have students write an appropriate Smart Word on a piece of paper. Challenge students to make a list of as many synonyms (words with similar meanings) and antonyms (words with opposite meanings) as they can think of, with the aid of a thesaurus if necessary.

Examples

Book	Smart Word	Possible Synonyms	Possible Antonyms
Messy Jobs (Series 1 and 2)	messy	dirty, untidy, filthy, grimy, cluttered, sloppy	clean, tidy, neat
Cool Jobs in Basketball (Series 11)	rely	trust, have faith in, depend on, count on	distrust, doubt, question
When Lisa Met Billy (Series 8 and 12)	quit	cease, end, give up, leave, stop, resign	start, continue, pursue, stick with
Back From the Grave! (Series 13)	remove	subtract, take away, delete	add, remain, keep
Disaster! (Series 14)	aid	help, assist, relieve, support, back	hurt, block, harm, injure
Killer Croc (Series 19 and 20)	dangerous	risky, unsafe, hazardous, perilous, threatening	safe, harmless, secure, protected

Multiple-Meaning Words

Guide students to learn to use context to help determine the correct meaning for multiple-meaning words.

1 **Define Multiple-Meaning Words** Tell students that some words have more than one meaning. To figure out a word's meaning, readers must use clues from the sentence or surrounding sentences.

2 **Identify Multiple-Meaning Words** Introduce students to a multiple-meaning word, and provide at least two alternate meanings. Present the word in context by reading the sentence or sentences in which it appears, and then think aloud to demonstrate how you determine which meaning best fits the context.

This example uses the multiple-meaning word *hearing* from page 13 of *Witch Hunt* (Series 18):

Read the second paragraph aloud. Tell students that the word *hearing* has multiple meanings. *Hearing* can mean "perceiving sound," or "a meeting in a court of law to hear the facts about a case." *The sentences tell about women taken to a courtroom to be asked questions by a judge. These clues help me see that the right meaning for hearing is "a meeting in a court of law to hear the facts about a case."*

3 **Practice** Ask students to use each meaning of the multiple-meaning word in a written sentence.

Purpose

Knowledge of multiple-meaning words helps students develop strategies for identifying correct word meaning to build text comprehension.

Examples of Smart Words with Multiple Meanings

Book	Page and Paragraph	Smart Word	Meanings
Bugs That Kill (Series 1 and 2)	Page 5, paragraph 2	sting	"to bite or stick with something sharp" or "a wound or pain"
Messy Jobs (Series 1 and 2)	Page 3, paragraph 3	waste	"to throw something away before it's used" or "garbage"
Wonders of the World (Series 4 and 6)	Page 3, paragraph 1	wonder	"something that's amazing or surprising" or "to be curious about something"
Is This Art? (Series 7 and 8)	Page 4, paragraph 2	change	"to make something different" or "money in the form of coins"
DJ Mystery (Series 8)	Page 11, paragraph 4	crowd	"a large group of people" or "to not give someone enough room"
Ripped From the Headlines (Series 10)	Page 4, paragraph 1	brave	"not afraid" or "to do something unpleasant and difficult," as in "He braved the storm."
Crash! (Series 12 and 13)	Page 7, bottom paragraph	follow	"to watch or keep track of something" or "to chase or pursue"
Witch Hunt (Series 18)	Page 13, paragraph 2	hearing	"perceiving sound" or "a court trial"
Hot Jobs (Series 22 and 24)	Page 13, paragraph 3	handle	"to deal with or take control" or "the part of an object used to move it"

Context Clues

Students learn strategies to determine the meaning of unfamiliar words based on their context.

1 **Define Context Clues** Explain that when they come across an unfamiliar word, students can sometimes figure out its meaning by looking for clues from other words or sentences around it.

2 **Identify Context Clues** Introduce a Smart Word students are unfamiliar with. Then, read the sentence or paragraph (as needed) in which it appears. Ask students to listen for words that may shed light on the meaning of the unknown Smart Word. Model how to use context clues by thinking aloud for students.

This example uses the Smart Word *strike* from page 14 of *Fire! The Triangle Shirtwaist Factory Tragedy* (Series 21 and 22):

I'll read the last paragraph aloud. As I read, I will look for context clues to figure out the meaning of strike. Explain that the sentences "Workers all over New York went on strike. They refused to go back to work until things improved" suggest that a *strike* has to do with workers not working because of problems at their jobs.

Explain that using context clues does not always lead to determining a word's correct meaning. Students need to reread to confirm their ideas. If students find a definition does not fit the context, they should try again or consult a dictionary.

Purpose

Using context clues helps students determine the meanings of unfamiliar words in context, increasing their comprehension and confidence.

3 Practice Ask students to use the Vocabulary Builder on **SAM** (Keyword: Vocabulary Builder 44) to jot down unfamiliar words they encounter as they read. First, have them use context clues to figure out the meaning. Next, have them look up the word in the dictionary and compare the definitions. Finally, have them record the dictionary definition.

Examples of Context Clues

Book	Page and Paragraph	Smart Word	Context Clues
Survival Guide: How to Keep Your Job (Series 7 and 8)	Page 12, paragraph 2	focus	You are thinking about friends and music. You need to focus on your job.
African Journey (Series 9)	Page 8, paragraph 2	migrate	Some animals migrate . . . . Wildebeests travel really far.
Medical Miracle (Series 14)	Page 9, paragraph 2	artery	An artery carries a lot of blood.
Left to Die (Series 16)	Page 6, paragraph 2	vertical	The mountain's West Face is almost vertical. It goes straight up and down.
Samurai Fighters (Series 17)	Page 12, paragraph 2	legend	One samurai woman became a legend . . . People said she could not be defeated.
Ant Attack! (Series 17 and 18)	Page 9, paragraph 1	precaution	"The ants will not get us," he assured them. "But we must take precautions!"
Fire! The Triangle Shirtwaist Factory Tragedy (Series 21 and 22)	Page 14, paragraph 4	strike	Workers all over New York went on strike. They refused to go back to work until things improved.
Lost! (Series 24 and 25)	Page 17, paragraph 2	current	It's like an invisible river in the ocean.

Idioms

Students learn to identify and understand the meaning of idioms.

1 Define Idioms Tell students that an *idiom* is a phrase or expression that has a meaning that is different from the literal or actual meaning of the words.

2 Identify Idioms Ask students to listen as you read a passage aloud. Identify the idiom and explain its meaning, pointing out how the literal meaning of the words is different from the meaning of the expression. The following example uses the idiom *show off* from page 9 of *Fashion Flashback* (Series 8):

I'll read the second paragraph aloud. As I read, listen for the idiom "show off." Explain to students that *show off* is an idiom that means "to do something to attract attention."

3 Practice Have students use the idiom in a few oral sentences.

Purpose

This routine is particularly helpful for students who are new to English, as they may not be familiar with the idiomatic meaning of an expression.

Why Use Fluency Routines?

- Repeated oral reading with teacher feedback builds fluency and improves comprehension.
- Fluency routines provide varied and engaging ways for students to focus on the qualities of fluent reading.
- The use of routines provides an efficient and familiar way to incorporate regular fluency practice into the classroom.

Student Objectives

- Read aloud fluently, with appropriate tone, phrasing, pacing, and expression.

Fluency Routines

Fluency helps students focus on the purpose of reading—extracting and constructing meaning.

Fluency in the Classroom

Timothy Rasinski, a fluency expert and professor of education, defines fluency as "the ability to read quickly, effortlessly, and efficiently with good, meaningful expression." These routines promote fluency by providing practice exercises to support correct phrasing, speed, and expression.

To create meaningful contexts and authentic purposes for fluency instruction and practice, make fluency routines a familiar and regular part of instruction. Give students daily opportunities to read aloud and to gain confidence. Help students see connections between fluent oral and fluent silent reading, and guide them in using fluency terms such as *expression, tone of voice,* and *phrasing.* Use fluency routines with suggested passages from books in the *System 44* Library, or choose your own passages. Add your own ideas, combine methods, and discover the routines that work best for you.

Phrasing and Punctuation

Students learn to read fluently by "chunking" text, making appropriate pauses, and varying their tone.

1 **Explain Correct Phrasing** Explain that phrases are groups of words, or "chunks" of text, that go together to make meaning. Fluent readers read in meaningful phrases. Point out that reading with good phrasing helps make a text's meaning clear. Briefly discuss the following qualities of phrasing.

- **Pause** Make a slight pause between the parts of a sentence. Stop to take a breath when you see a comma between words. Pause at the end of a sentence.

- **Express the meaning** Stress some words more than others. Raise or lower the tone of your voice. Read some phrases faster or slower. Express excitement when you see an exclamation mark. Read sentences with question marks as questions.

- **Use Phrasing** Consider beginning a new phrase when you see prepositions such as *with, in, to, by, at, on,* and *for,* and transition words such as *then, next, and, but, or,* and *however.*

2 **Model Correct Phrasing** Distribute copies of the Fluency Checklist on **SAM** (Keyword: Fluency Checklist 44). Ask students to turn to the selected passages in their books and follow along as you read a paragraph. Read the paragraph in meaningful phrases, emphasizing and slightly exaggerating the phrases. Read with expression at a varied rate, and pause for punctuation.

Ask students to name one quality of fluency they heard in your reading. Have them refer to the Fluency Checklist. Return to the text and identify examples of your phrasing, pauses, emphasis, and expression. Make a check on the list for each quality as it is mentioned.

3 Practice Have students read through the passage and identify phrasing cues. They should identify punctuation cues, including commas, periods, question marks, and exclamation marks. They should also look for transition words such as *then, next, and, but, or,* and *however* and prepositions such as *with, in, to, by, at, on,* and *for.* Lastly, ask them to choose a few key words that may be important to stress because of meaning.

For partnered reading, ask students to take turns reading the passage while others listen and fill out the Fluency Checklist. Students who listened should then offer constructive feedback about successes and areas for improvement.

For independent practice, have students use a recording device to listen to and to evaluate their reading as they reread the passage, experimenting with different pauses, word stresses, and reading speeds. Offer constructive feedback as needed.

Suggested Passages for Practicing Correct Phrasing

Book	Passage
Messy Jobs (Series 1 and 2)	Pages 4–5
Fashion Flashback (Series 8)	Pages 10–11
Cool Jobs in Basketball (Series 11)	Pages 8–9
Have You Seen My Mummy? (Series 13 and 14)	Pages 10–11
Witch Hunt (Series 18)	Pages 13–15
Fire! The Triangle Shirtwaist Factory Tragedy (Series 21 and 22)	Pages 9–10

Use Natural, Consistent Pace

Students read and reread for skill, pacing, and accuracy.

1 Explain Pacing Briefly discuss how practice makes everything easier—from sports to playing an instrument to cooking. *When people train or rehearse, they practice the same moves, steps, or notes over and over again. Reading is also a skill that can be improved through practice.*

Point out that the best way to make reading automatic is to practice reading the same words again and again. Explain to students that they will practice by reading the same passage several times. Each time they reread the passage, they will begin to recognize more words automatically and will be able to read at a more comfortable pace. They will measure this progress by seeing how much of the passage they can read in one minute. Emphasize that the goal is not to race through the passage, but to read it fluently.

Student Objectives

- Read and reread for speed and accuracy.
- Master unfamiliar words in passages.
- Track fluency progress.

2 **Model Correct Pacing** Ask students to turn to the selected passages in their books. Tell students that you will be timing yourself to see how much of the passage you can read in one minute. Give one student a stopwatch and ask him or her to let you know when one minute is up. Explain that you will be reading for accuracy as well as speed. Ask students to follow along in their books as you read. They should notice where you are at the end of one minute and make note of any words you read incorrectly.

Read the passage at a natural pace. Read a few simple words incorrectly. Stop reading after a minute, and ask students to identify how many words you misread. Explain that the goal of the exercise is to make sure your pace is not too fast or too slow, and to read all of the words correctly.

3 **Practice** Distribute stopwatches to students. Ask students to read the passage silently several times until they feel comfortable with reading all of the words.

For groups of three, ask students to take turns reading the passage from their books. While one student is reading, the second should be timing the exercise, and the third should be noting errors and the last word read. Students who listened should then offer constructive feedback about successes and areas for improvement.

For independent practice, have students use a recording device to record their reading. They should then listen with a stopwatch and make note of errors and the last word read. Periodically check up on their readings and offer constructive feedback as needed.

On subsequent days, provide repeated opportunities to practice the same passage.

Suggested Passages for Practicing Correct Pacing

Book	Passage
Fast! The World's Fastest Couch and Other Fast Things (Series 4 and 5)	Pages 3–5
Wonders of the World (Series 4 and 6)	Pages 3–5
Ripped From the Headlines (Series 10)	Pages 12–13
Medical Miracle (Series 14)	Pages 6–8
Samurai Fighters (Series 17)	Pages 7–9
Everyday Heroes (Series 23 and 25)	Pages 13–15

Read With Expression

Students learn to read in a varied, expressive tone.

1 Explain Expressive Reading Ask students to imagine that they are telling a story to their friends. *What are some things you would do to get your friend more interested in the story? Imagine you're telling a scary story. How would you tell it? Imagine you're telling a story about something funny that happened to you. Would you tell that story in the same way you tell a scary story?* Tell students that when they read out loud, it helps to imagine that they are telling a story to a friend and trying to get that friend interested in the story.

Explain that to read with expression, it helps to understand the story. So, before practicing expressive reading, they should read the entire story to understand what is happening in it.

2 Model Expressive Reading Ask students to turn to the selected passages in their books and follow along as you read. Read the passage twice. During the first reading, demonstrate how a reader's tone of voice and expression can show different feelings and reflect different characters. Ask students to describe your reading. For the second reading, read the passage flatly, without expression. Ask students to describe the difference.

3 Practice Ask students to read the selected text several times until they understand the story and feel comfortable reading all of the words.

For small group practice, distribute copies of the Fluency Checklist on **SAM** (Keyword: Fluency Checklist 44). Students should take turns with one reading while others listen and fill out the Fluency Checklist, with special attention paid to the Expression section. Students who listened should then offer constructive feedback about successes and areas for improvement.

For independent practice, have students use a recording device to listen to and to evaluate their reading as they reread the same passage, experimenting with varying emotions and emphasis. Offer constructive feedback as needed.

Purpose

- Rehearse to improve accuracy, phrasing, and prosody.
- Read for comprehension.
- Read to entertain.

Suggested Passages for Practicing Expressive Reading

Book	Passage
Yes! (Series 3)	Pages 4–5
Button Your Lip and Other Idioms (Series 9)	Pages 10–12
Crash! (Series 12 and 13)	Pages 10–11
Left to Die (Series 16)	Pages 14–15
Killer Croc (Series 19 and 20)	Page 8
Arabian Nights (Series 23 and 24)	Pages 10–12

Lesson Plan
Use With Series **2 & 3**

Big!
by **Kevin Chen**

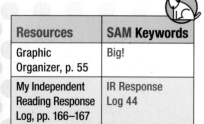

Simple | 190L

| Genre | Pages | Audio CD | Reading |
| Math | 8 | 6 min 55 sec | Counts |

Summary

What makes something big? This book looks at the facts and figures behind the world's tallest roller coaster, tallest building, longest house cat, biggest monster truck, and tallest tree.

Phonics Focus

- **Short** *a, e, i, o*
- **Consonants** *j, w*

See **Master Skills Tracker** in your Teacher's Edition.

Skills Tracker

Preteach | Teach/Practice/Apply | Review/Reinforce | Assess

Smart Words

Words are defined on page 2 of the student book. Page number of first appearance is listed below.

- **height, p. 3**
- **length p. 3**
- **typical*, p. 5**

Spanish Cognates, **page 24*

Option 1: **Decoding**

Informal Assessment

Ask students to read the Phonics Focus words on the inside back cover of *Big!* If they struggle with decoding, proceed to targeted instruction.

Targeted Instruction

For words with short vowels a, e, i, and o: Have the student use the **Word Sort** decoding routine on **page 45** to sort words by their short vowel sounds.

For words with consonants j and w: Have the student use the **Word Sort** decoding routine to sort words by their beginning consonant sounds.

Option 2: **Academic Vocabulary**

Informal Assessment

Ask students to read a sentence from *Big!* that contains a Smart Word from the inside back cover. Have students define the Smart Word and identify evidence in the text that helped them determine the meaning. Review definitions on page 2 as needed. Repeat this procedure with other Smart Words. If students demonstrate proficiency, proceed to targeted instruction.

Targeted Instruction

The Smart Word *typical* has many possible synonyms and antonyms. Use the **Extending Meaning** vocabulary routine on **page 47** to extend meaning.

Option 3: **Fluency**

Informal Assessment

Ask students to read page 3 of *Big!* aloud. To work on reading with correct phrasing, proceed to targeted instruction.

Targeted Instruction

Use pages 3–4 of *Big!* and the **Phrasing and Punctuation** fluency routine on **page 50** to have the student practice correct phrasing.

Comprehension

Use the questions below and the Graphic Organizer on **page 55** to check comprehension and promote reader response.

After Page 3: *How does Burj Khalifa compare to the Empire State Building?* (*Burj Khalifa is almost twice as tall.*)

After Page 6: *How long is a typical cat?* (*A typical cat is 18 inches long.*)

End of Book: *What is the smallest big thing in this book?* (*Stewie the cat is the smallest.*)

Resources	SAM **Keywords**
Graphic Organizer, p. 55	Big!
My Independent Reading Response Log, pp. 166–167	IR Response Log 44

Name _____

Big!

Build Understanding

▶ Details are words, phrases, and sentences that give information about a topic. For each topic below, write a detail from the book that tells how big it is. The first one is done for you.

Topic	Detail
Kingda Ka [Page 3]	*It is 456 feet tall.*
Burj Khalifa [Page 4]	
Stewie [Page 5]	
Bigfoot 5 [Page 6]	
The Tallest Tree [Page 7]	

QuickWrite

▶ Choose one big object from this book. What does the author compare it to? How much bigger is the big object than the one the author compares it to?

_____

_____

_____

_____

Resource Links
Library Teaching Resources: p. 55
SAM Keyword: Big!

Use with Library Teaching Resources, page 54.

System 44 Library   55

Use With Series 1 & 2 **Lesson Plan**

Bugs That Kill
by **Peggy Bresnick Kendler**

Simple 200L

Genre	Pages	Audio CD	Reading Counts!
Science	8	6 min 16 sec	

Summary

Some bugs must kill to eat or to defend themselves. The tarantula is a big spider that kills bugs and even frogs for food. The praying mantis preys on crickets. Killer bees form a mob when they're angry, and kill by stinging all at once. Scorpions kill by stinging with their poisonous tail. Fire ants have a poisonous bite that burns like fire!

Phonics Focus

- **Short vowels** *a, e, i, o, u*
- **Consonants** *b, d, g, p*

See **Master Skills Tracker** in your Teacher's Edition.

Skills Tracker

Preteach Teach/Practice/Apply Review/Reinforce Assess

Smart Words

Words are defined on p. 2 of the student book. Page number of first appearance is listed below.

- **poison, p. 6**
- **spider, p. 3**
- **sting, p. 5**

Option 1: **Decoding**

 Informal Assessment

Ask students to read the Phonics Focus words on the inside back cover of *Bugs That Kill*. If they struggle with decoding, proceed to targeted instruction.

Targeted Instruction

For words with short vowels: Have the student use the **Word Sort** decoding routine on **page 45** to sort words by their short vowel sounds.

For words with consonants *b, d, g, p*: Have students use the **Word Sort** routine to sort words by consonant sounds.

Option 2: **Academic Vocabulary**

 Informal Assessment

Ask students to read a sentence from the book that contains a Smart Word. Have students define the Smart Word and identify text evidence that helped them determine the meaning. Review definitions on page 2 as needed. Repeat with other Smart Words. If students demonstrate proficiency, proceed to targeted instruction.

Targeted Instruction

The Smart Word *sting* can mean "to bite or stick with something sharp" or "a wound or pain." Use the **Multiple-Meaning Words** vocabulary routine on **page 47** with *sting* as an example to help the student use context to determine the correct meaning.

Option 3: **Fluency**

 Informal Assessment

Ask students to read page 4 of *Bugs That Kill* aloud. To work on correct phrasing, proceed to targeted instruction.

 Targeted Instruction

Use pages 4–5 of *Bugs That Kill* and the **Phrasing and Punctuation** fluency routine on **page 50** to have the student practice correct phrasing.

Comprehension

Use the questions below and the Graphic Organizer on **page 57** to check comprehension and promote reader response.

After Page 3: *What does a tarantula eat?* (It eats other bugs and even frogs.)

After Page 4: *What does a praying mantis look like?* (It has big eyes and a small head, a green body, and long legs.)

End of Book: *Why should people avoid killer bees, scorpions, and fire ants?* (They can all kill people.)

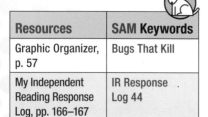

Resources	SAM Keywords
Graphic Organizer, p. 57	Bugs That Kill
My Independent Reading Response Log, pp. 166–167	IR Response Log 44

Name _____

Bugs That Kill

Build Understanding

▶ Details are words, phrases, and sentences that give information about a topic. Write two details about each bug from the book. The first one is done for you.

Topic	Detail
Tarantula *(Page 3)*	• This bug is a big spider. • It even eats frogs!
Praying Mantis *(Page 4)*	
Killer Bee *(Page 5)*	
Scorpion *(Page 6)*	
Fire Ant *(Page 7)*	

QuickWrite

▶ Why do these bugs kill? Explain your answer. Use evidence from the book.

_____

_____

_____

Did You Know?
by **Inez Prieto**

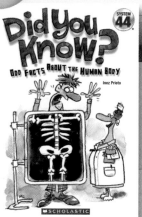

Simple | HL170L

Genre	Pages	Audio CD	Reading
Science	8	6 min 6 sec	Counts

Summary

This book discusses five interesting and unusual facts about the human body: an individual sheds almost 50 pounds of dead skin in a lifetime, the small intestine is 23 feet long, the brain can recall 50,000 smells, everyone's tongue print is unique, and the femur is stronger than concrete.

Phonics Focus

- Short *a*
- Short *i*
- Short *o*
- Consonants *l*, *x*

See **Master Skills Tracker** in your Teacher's Edition.

Skills Tracker

Preteach Teach/Practice/Apply Review/Reinforce Assess

Smart Words

Words are defined on page 2 of the student book. Page number of first appearance is listed below.

- fact, p. 4
- recall, p. 5
- unique*, p. 6

*Spanish Cognates, **page 24**

Option 1: Decoding

Informal Assessment

Ask students to read the Phonics Focus words on the inside back cover of *Did You Know?*. If they struggle with decoding, proceed to targeted instruction.

Targeted Instruction

For words with short vowels *a*, *i*, and *o*: Have the student use the **Word Sort** decoding routine on **page 45** to sort words by their short vowel sounds. **For words with consonant *l*:** Use the **Word Sort** decoding routine on **page 45** to sort words by their beginning consonant sounds. **For words with consonant *x*:** Use the **Word Sort** decoding routine on **page 45** to sort words by their ending consonant sounds.

Option 2: Academic Vocabulary

Informal Assessment

Ask students to read a sentence from *Did You Know?* that contains a Smart Word from the inside back cover. Have students define the Smart Word and identify evidence in the text that helped determine the meaning. Review definitions on page 2 as needed. Repeat this procedure with other Smart Words. If students demonstrate proficiency, proceed to targeted instruction.

Targeted Instruction

The Smart Word *recall* can mean "to remember something" or "to order someone or something to return." Use the **Multiple Meanings** vocabulary routine on **page 47** with *recall* as an example to help the student use context to determine the correct meaning.

Option 3: Fluency

Informal Assessment

Ask students to read page 4 of *Did You Know?* aloud. To work on reading with correct phrasing, proceed to targeted instruction.

Targeted Instruction

Use pages 4–5 of *Did You Know?* and the **Use Natural, Consistent Pace** fluency routine on **page 51** to have the student practice correct phrasing.

Comprehension

Use the questions below and the Graphic Organizer on **page 59** to check comprehension and promote reader response.

After Page 3: *What happens to dead skin after your body sheds it?* (The skin flakes become dust.)

After Page 5: *How many smells can your brain recall?* (It can recall about 50,000 smells.)

End of Book: *Why does the picture on page 6 show one guy karate kicking another in the thigh?* (The picture illustrates that the femur, or thigh bone, is very strong.)

Resources	SAM Keywords
Graphic Organizer, p. 59	Did You Know?
My Independent Reading Response Log, pp. 166-167	IR Response Log 44

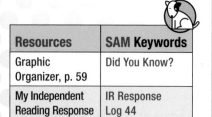

Name _____

Did You Know?

Build Understanding

Details are words, phrases, and sentences that give information about a topic. Write a detail about each topic below. The first topic is done for you.

Topic	Detail
skin *(Page 3)*	A human body sheds 48.5 pounds of dead skin in a lifetime.
small intestine *(Page 4)*	
tongue *(Page 5)*	
brain *(Page 6)*	
femur *(Page 7)*	

QuickWrite

▶ Pick one topic from the book. Write an email to a friend telling all about the topic in your own words. Use text evidence in your email.

_____

_____

_____

Resource Links
Library Teaching Resources: p. 59
SAM Keyword: Did You Know?

Use with **Library Teaching Resources,** *page 58.*

System 44 Library 59

Fast!

by Juliette Caggiano

Simple ◀ ▲ 150L

Genre	Pages	Audio CD	✓ Reading
Science	8	5 min 45 sec	Counts!

Summary

Some things are fast—very fast! This book features fast-growing bamboo, high-speed elevators, cheetahs that run 71 miles per hour, a speedy couch you can drive, and space probes that are the fastest vehicles in the sky.

Phonics Focus

- Blends

See **Master Skills Tracker** in your Teacher's Edition.

Skills Tracker

Preteach Teach/Practice/Apply Review/Reinforce Assess

Smart Words

Words are defined on p. 2 of the student book. Page number of first appearance is listed below.

- limit*, p. 5
- rate, p. 3
- vehicle*, p. 6

*Spanish Cognates, **page 24**

Option 1: **Decoding**

 Informal Assessment

Ask students to read the Phonics Focus words on the inside back cover of *Fast!* If they struggle with decoding, proceed to targeted instruction.

 Targeted Instruction

For words with blends: Use the **Blends and Digraphs** decoding routine on **page 41** to help the student build accuracy.

Option 2: **Academic Vocabulary**

 Informal Assessment

Ask students to read a sentence from the book that contains a Smart Word. Have students define the Smart Word and identify text evidence that helped them determine the meaning. Review definitions on page 2 as needed. Repeat with other Smart Words. If students demonstrate proficiency, proceed to targeted instruction.

Targeted Instruction

The idiom *check this out* used in the first paragraph of page 3 means "look at this." Build understanding of idioms using the **Idioms** vocabulary routine on **page 49** with this expression as an example.

Option 3: **Fluency**

 Informal Assessment

Ask students to read page 3 of *Fast!* aloud. To work on pacing, proceed to targeted instruction.

 Targeted Instruction

Use pages 3–5 of *Fast!* and the **Use Natural, Consistent Pace** fluency routine on **page 51** to have the student practice reading at a natural pace.

Comprehension

Use the questions below and the Graphic Organizer on **page 61** to check comprehension and promote reader response.

After Page 3: *How tall would you be if you grew as fast as bamboo?* (miles tall)

After Page 5: *How do visitors reach the top of Taipei 101?* (Visitors ride up in the world's fastest elevator.)

End of Book: *What are Helios I and Helios II?* (They are space probes, and the fastest vehicles in the sky.)

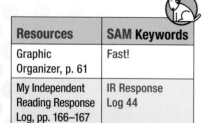

Resources	SAM Keywords
Graphic Organizer, p. 61	Fast!
My Independent Reading Response Log, pp. 166–167	IR Response Log 44

Name _____

Fast!

Build Understanding

▶ Fill in the circles with words or phrases that tell about the cheetah. Use details from the text. An example is done for you.

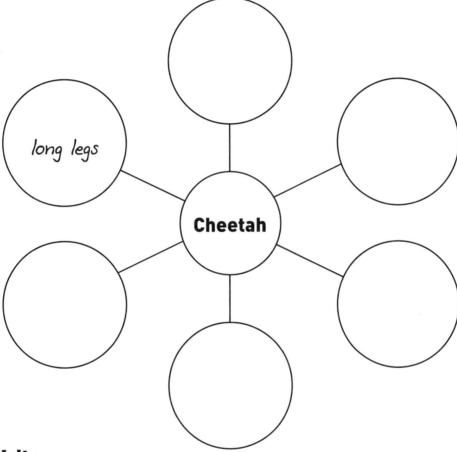

long legs

Cheetah

QuickWrite

▶ Why is the cheetah able to run so fast? Use details from the text.

_____

_____

_____

Lesson Plan

Messy Jobs
by **Alan Takamura**

Simple   150L

Genre	Pages	Audio CD	Reading
Jobs	**8**	**7 min 12 sec**	**Counts!**

Summary

Some jobs are messy. Worm farmers dig up worms. Ship painters get covered in paint. Podiatrists handle feet. Clean-up workers mop up oil spills. Motocross bikers race through dirt. Read about the messes people in these jobs face at work.

Phonics Focus

- **Short vowels**
- **-s, -es**

See **Master Skills Tracker** in your Teacher's Edition.

Skills Tracker

Preteach   Teach/Practice/Apply   Review/Reinforce   Assess

Smart Words

Words are defined on p. 2 of the student book. Page number of first appearance is listed below.

- **machine***, p. 4
- **stink**, p. 3
- **waste**, p. 3

*Spanish Cognates, **page 25**

Option 1: Decoding

Informal Assessment

Ask students to read the Phonics Focus words on the inside back cover of *Messy Jobs*. If they struggle with decoding, proceed to targeted instruction.

Targeted Instruction

For words with short vowels: Have students use the **Word Sort** decoding routine on **page 45** to sort words by their short vowel sounds.

For words with -s and -es: Use the **Word Parts** decoding routine on **page 43** to help students identify and use inflectional endings.

Option 2: Academic Vocabulary

Informal Assessment

Ask students to read a sentence from the book that contains a Smart Word. Have students define the Smart Word and identify text evidence that helped them determine the meaning. Review definitions on page 2 as needed. Repeat with other Smart Words. If students demonstrate proficiency, proceed to targeted instruction.

Targeted Instruction

The Smart Word *waste* can mean "to throw something away before it's used" or "junk or garbage." Use the **Multiple-Meaning Words** vocabulary routine on **page 47** with *waste* as an example to help students use context to determine correct meaning.

Option 3: Fluency

Informal Assessment

Ask students to read page 4 of *Messy Jobs* aloud. To work on reading with correct phrasing, proceed to targeted instruction.

Targeted Instruction

Use pages 4–5 of *Messy Jobs* and the **Phrasing and Punctuation** fluency routine on **page 50** to have students practice correct phrasing.

Comprehension

Use the questions below and the Graphic Organizer on **page 63** to check comprehension and promote reader response.

After Page 3: *What do farmers do with the worms and droppings?* (They sell the worms as fishing bait. They sell the droppings as plant fertilizer.)

After Page 5: *What is the job of a podiatrist?* (A podiatrist's job is to take care of feet.)

End of Book: *Why is motocross racing a messy job?* (It's messy because racers ride in the dirt and get covered in mud.)

Resources	SAM Keywords
Graphic Organizer, p. 63	Messy Jobs
My Independent Reading Response Log, pp. 166–167	IR Response Log 44

Name _____

Messy Jobs

Build Understanding

▶ What would each person below say is the messiest part of his or her job? Write what each would say, using details from the text. The first one is done for you.

The messiest thing I do is get old paint off a ship. Paint bits fly all over! They get on me.

Ship Painter
(Page 4)

Podiatrist
(Page 5)

Motocross Racer
(Page 7)

QuickWrite

▶ Which messy jobs help people or animals stay healthy? How? Cite evidence from the book.

_____

_____

_____

Plugged In
by Jared Williams

Simple	240L	**Genre** Jobs	**Pages** 16	**Audio CD** 10 min 48 sec	**Reading Counts!**

Summary

Meet six people who have jobs in the technology industry. Prerna Gupta makes music apps. Kathy Cano-Murillo sells her arts and crafts on a Web site. Shigeru Miyamoto designs video games. Michael Seibel makes video-sharing apps. Alexa Andrzejewski created a Web site where people share their favorite dishes. Louie Mantia designs icons.

Phonics Focus

- Identifying syllables
- Beginning blends
- Ending blends

See **Master Skills Tracker** in your Teacher's Edition.

Skills Tracker

Preteach Teach/Practice/Apply Review/Reinforce Assess

Smart Words

Words are defined on pages 2–3 of the student book. Page number of first appearance is listed below.

- entrepreneur, p. 5
- industry*, p. 4
- launch, p. 5
- network, p. 5
- technology*, p. 4

*Spanish Cognates, **page 25**

Option 1: Decoding

Informal Assessment

Ask students to read the Phonics Focus words on the inside back cover of *Plugged In*. If they struggle with decoding, proceed to targeted instruction.

Targeted Instruction

For words with two syllables: Use the **Syllable Strategies** decoding routine on **page 40** to Look, Spot, Split, and Read words with multiple syllables.

For words with beginning and ending blends: Use the **Blends and Digraphs** decoding routine on **page 41** to help the student identify common consonant blends.

Option 2: Academic Vocabulary

Informal Assessment

Ask students to read a sentence from *Plugged In* that contains a Smart Word. Have them define the Smart Word and cite evidence in the text that helped them determine the meaning. Review definitions on pages 2–3 as needed. Repeat this procedure with other Smart Words. If students demonstrate proficiency, proceed to targeted instruction.

Targeted Instruction

The idiom *plugged in*, as used in the title and in the second paragraph on page 4, means "attuned to and knowledgeable about something, such as an industry or social environment." Build understanding of idioms using the **Idioms** vocabulary routine on **page 49** with the expression *plugged* in as a model.

Option 3: Fluency

Informal Assessment

Ask students to read page 4 of *Plugged In* aloud. To work on reading with correct phrasing, proceed to targeted instruction.

Targeted Instruction

Use pages 4–5 of *Plugged In* and the **Phrasing and Punctuation** fluency routine on **page 50** to have the student practice correct phrasing.

Comprehension

Use the questions below and the Graphic Organizer on **page 65** to check comprehension and promote reader response.

After Page 5: *How does Prerna Gupta's music app work?* (When you sing into your phone, it adds background music.)

After Page 8: *What were Shigeru Miyamoto's first video games like?* (They were arcade games played on big machines.)

End of Book: *What are some jobs and businesses in technology?* (Running Web sites, making apps, designing video games and icons)

Resources	SAM Keywords
Graphic Organizer, p. 65	Plugged In
My Independent Reading Response Log, pp. 166–167	IR Response Log 44

Use with
Series 4 & 5

Name ______________________________

Plugged In

Build Understanding

▶ How might the people in *Plugged In* answer these questions about their work? Use details from the text to write their responses. The first one is done for you.

My job bored me. So I quit, and started my own business.

Question to Prerna:
Why did you become an entrepreneur?

Question to Kathy:
What is the purpose of your Web site?

Question to Shigeru:
How long have you been designing video games?

Question to Alexa:
How does travel inspire you?

Question to Louie:
Why are icons important?

QuickWrite

▶ Choose two people in this book. How does technology help them with their jobs? Use evidence from the text in your response.

____

____

____

Resource Links
Library Teaching Resources: p. 65
SAM Keyword: Plugged In

Use with **Library Teaching Resources,** *page 64.*

Poster Power
by Lamar Jones

Simple   220L

Genre	Pages	Audio CD	Reading Counts!
Arts	8	6 min 24 sec	✓

Summary

Posters are often used to rally people around a cause. Shepard Fairey's ADOPT poster urges people to bring home shelter pets. James Flagg's Uncle Sam poster helped recruit soldiers. Smokey Bear reminds people to practice fire safety. "Reduce, Reuse, Recycle" posters ask people to make less trash and recycle what they can. A "Hands Across America" poster alerted Americans to a fund-raising event to help the homeless.

Phonics Focus

- Short *a*
- Short *i*
- Short *o*
- *-ck*

See **Master Skills Tracker** in your Teacher's Edition.

Skills Tracker

Preteach Teach/Practice/Apply Review/Reinforce Assess

Smart Words

Words are defined on page 2 of the student book. Page number of first appearance is listed below.

- **cause*, p. 3**
- **motivate*, p. 3**
- **represent*, p. 4**

*Spanish Cognates, **page 25**

Option 1: Decoding

 Informal Assessment

Ask students to read the Phonics Focus words on the inside back cover of *Poster Power*. If they struggle with decoding, proceed to targeted instruction.

 Targeted Instruction

For words with short vowels *a*, *i*, and *o*: Have the student use the **Word Sort** decoding routine on **page 45** to sort words by their short vowel sounds.

For words with *-ck*: Use the **Word Sort** decoding routine to sort words by their ending consonant sounds.

Option 2: Academic Vocabulary

 Informal Assessment

Ask students to read a sentence from *Poster Power* that contains a Smart Word from the inside back cover. Have students define the word and identify evidence in the text they used to determine the meaning. Review definitions on page 2 as needed. Repeat this procedure with other Smart Words. If students demonstrate proficiency, proceed to targeted instruction.

 Targeted Instruction

The Smart Word *cause* can mean "a goal or belief for which people work," "the reason something happened," or "to make something happen." Use the **Multiple Meaning Words** vocabulary routine on **page 47** with *cause* as an example to help the student use context to determine correct meaning.

Option 3: Fluency

 Informal Assessment

Ask students to read page 3 of *Poster Power* aloud. To work on reading with correct phrasing, proceed to targeted instruction.

 Targeted Instruction

Use pages 3–4 of *Poster Power* and the **Phrasing and Punctuation** fluency routine on **page 50** to have the student practice correct phrasing.

Comprehension

Use the questions below and the Graphic Organizer on **page 67** to check comprehension and promote reader response.

After Page 4: *Why did the army need men in 1917? (The U.S. was at war.)*

After Page 6: *What does the poster encourage people to "reduce"? (Trash)*

End of Book: *Select one poster in this book that was successful. What evidence does the author give for its success? (The "I Want You" poster was successful because it inspired many men to join the army. The "Hands Across America" poster spread the word about the event; as a result, millions of people went to the event.)*

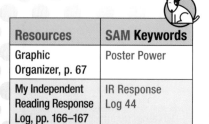

Resources	SAM Keywords
Graphic Organizer, p. 67	Poster Power
My Independent Reading Response Log, pp. 166–167	IR Response Log 44

Use with
Series 1 & 2

Name ____________________

Poster Power

Build Understanding

▶ Each poster in *Poster Power* was created to help solve a problem. Fill in the problem that each poster helps solve with information from the text.

Poster	Problem
Adopt *(Page 3)*	Homeless pets
I Want You *(Page 4)*	
Smokey Bear *(Page 5)*	
Reduce, Reuse, Recycle *(Page 6)*	
Hands Across America *(Page 7)*	

QuickWrite

▶ Pick one poster. Write 3–4 sentences that explain its message. Use details from the book.

____

____

____

____

Resource Links
Library Teaching Resources: p. 67
SAM Keyword: Poster Power

Use with **Library Teaching Resources,** *page 66.*

Shamila's Goal
by **Jaleesa Miles**

 Moderate 1   HL230L

Genre	Pages	Audio CD	Reading Counts
Social Studies	16	11 min 13 sec	

Summary

Shamila Kohestani grew up in Afghanistan when the Taliban was in power. At this time, Shamila could not go to school or play sports. When the Taliban left power, Shamila became interested in soccer, and was chosen to attend a U.S. soccer clinic for Afghan girls. This opportunity led to many more, including prep school and college in the United States, and a spot on the first Afghan National Women's soccer team.

Phonics Focus

- **Ending blends**
- **Closed syllables**

See **Master Skills Tracker** in your Teacher's Edition.

Skills Tracker

Preteach   Teach/Practice/Apply   Review/Reinforce   Assess

Smart Words

Words are defined on pp. 2–3 of the student book. Page number of first appearance is listed below.

- **adjust*, p. 7**
- **mock, p. 10**
- **opportunity*, p. 9**
- **respect*, p. 10**
- **strict*, p. 6**

*Spanish Cognates, **page 25**

Option 1: **Decoding**

 Informal Assessment

Ask students to read the Phonics Focus words on the inside back cover of *Shamila's Goal*. If they struggle with decoding, proceed to targeted instruction.

 Targeted Instruction

For words with ending blends: Have the student use the **Blends and Digraphs** decoding routine on **page 41** to identify common consonant blends.

For words with closed syllables: Use the **Syllable Strategies** decoding routine on **page 40** to Look, Spot, Split, and Read words with closed syllables.

Option 2: **Academic Vocabulary**

Informal Assessment

Ask students to read a sentence from *Shamila's Goal* that contains a Smart Word. Have students define the Smart Word and identify evidence in the text that helped them determine the meaning. Repeat with other Smart Words. If students demonstrate proficiency, proceed to targeted instruction.

Targeted Instruction

The Smart Word *respect* is the base of the words *respected, respecting, respectful, respectable,* and *disrespect*. Use the **Extending Meaning** vocabulary routine on **page 46** to build student familiarity with morphological word families.

Option 3: **Fluency**

 Informal Assessment

Ask students to read page 4 of *Shamila's Goal* aloud. To work on reading with correct phrasing, proceed to targeted instruction.

 Targeted Instruction

Use pages 4–5 of *Shamila's Goal* and the **Read With Expression** fluency routine on **page 53** to have the student practice correct phrasing.

Comprehension

Use the questions below and the Graphic Organizer on **page 69** to check comprehension and promote reader response.

After Page 7: *How did Shamila's life change when the Taliban took over her country?* (She could no longer go to school and had to study at home in secret.)

After Page 13: *Why did some people mock Shamila and her teammates?* (Although it was now legal for girls and women to play soccer, some people still didn't think they should.)

End of Book: *Why does Shamila plan to move back to Afghanistan?* (She wants to help create opportunities for other Afghan girls.)

Resources	SAM Keywords
Graphic Organizer, p. 69	Shamila
My Independent Reading Response Log, pp. 166–167	IR Response Log 44

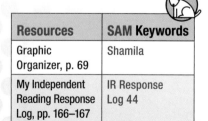

Name ______________________________

Shamila's Goal

Build Understanding

▶ All of the events below are discussed in the book, but they are out of order. List the events in the correct order. The first event is done for you.

Events
Shamila goes to a soccer clinic in the United States.
Shamila has to study at home in secret.
Shamila joins the first Afghan Women's soccer team.
Shamila gets a scholarship to a U.S. college.
The Taliban loses control of Afghanistan.

First Shamila has to study at home in secret.

↓

Second

↓

Next

↓

Then

↓

Last

QuickWrite

▶ How did soccer change Shamila's life? Explain, using evidence from the text.

____

____

____

____

Resource Links
Library Teaching Resources: p. 69
SAM Keyword: Shamila

Use with **Library Teaching Resources,** *page 68.*

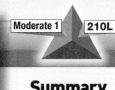

These Are Not Poems
by Tina Posner

Moderate 1 ◄▲► 210L

Genre	Pages	Audio CD	Reading
Poetry	8	6 min 14 sec	Counts!

Summary

This book is as much a journal as a collection of poems, as the introductory poem explains. The four other poems focus on themes such as being more than meets the eye, having a secret crush, learning to be the boss in the kitchen, and living a real life versus a movie life.

Phonics Focus

- **Review blends**
- **Double consonants**
- **-ng and -nk**

See **Master Skills Tracker** in your Teacher's Edition.

Skills Tracker

Preteach   Teach/Practice/Apply   Review/Reinforce   Assess

Smart Words

Words are defined on p. 2 of the student book. Page number of first appearance is listed below.

- **confess***, p. 5
- **express***, p. 3
- **hero***, p. 7

*Spanish Cognates, **page 25**

Option 1: Decoding

 Informal Assessment

Ask students to read the Phonics Focus words on the inside back cover of *These Are Not Poems*. If they struggle with decoding, proceed to targeted instruction.

 Targeted Instruction

For words with blends, and -ng and -nk: Use the **Blends and Digraphs** decoding routine on **page 41** to build accuracy.

For words with double consonants: Have the student use the **Word Sort** routine on **page 45** to sort words by double consonant sounds. Supplement words as needed.

Option 2: Academic Vocabulary

 Informal Assessment

Ask students to read a sentence from the book that contains a Smart Word. Have students define the Smart Word and identify text evidence that helped them determine the meaning. Review definitions on page 2 as needed. Repeat with other Smart Words. If students demonstrate proficiency, proceed to targeted instruction.

Targeted Instruction

The Smart Word *express* is the base of the words *expressed, expresses, expressing, expression, expressions, expressive,* and *unexpressive*. Use the **Extending Meaning** vocabulary routine on **page 46** to build student familiarity with morphological word families.

Option 3: Fluency

 Informal Assessment

Ask students to read page 6 of *These Are Not Poems* aloud. To work on correct phrasing, proceed to targeted instruction.

 Targeted Instruction

Use page 6 of *These Are Not Poems* and the **Phrasing and Punctuation** fluency routine on **page 50** to have the student practice correct phrasing.

Comprehension

Use the questions below and the Graphic Organizer on **page 71** to check comprehension and promote reader response.

After Page 3: *Why does this poet write poems? (She writes to express her thoughts and feelings, and to deal with hard times.)*

After Page 6: *When is the poet the boss in the kitchen? (when her mother isn't home)*

End of Book: *In what ways is real life different from the movies? (Movies can make things look easy, but real life is hard work.)*

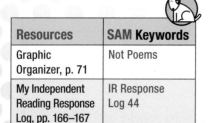

Resources	SAM Keywords
Graphic Organizer, p. 71	Not Poems
My Independent Reading Response Log, pp. 166–167	IR Response Log 44

Name _____

These Are Not Poems

Build Understanding

▶ The girl writes poems to express her feelings. Write what she might say to answer each question below. Use details from the text. The first one is done for you.

Poems are corny.

1. "These Are Not Poems"
What might the reader think about poems?

2. "The Me Inside Me"
Who knows the girl best?

3. "My Secret"
What do people love to guess?

4. "The Boss in the Kitchen"
What has the girl learned from her mother?

5. "Real Life"
What do real-life heroes have to do?

QuickWrite

▶ In "Real Life" the girl contrasts her life with the lives of movie heroes. List one way she is different from a movie hero. Use words and phrases from the poem in your answer.

_____

_____

_____

They Did What?

by **Nesar Aman**

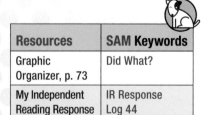

Simple HL230L

Genre	Pages	Audio CD	Reading Counts
Math	8	6 min 17 sec	✓

Summary

Some people perform feats that are hard to believe. *They Did What?* presents facts and figures about five amazing feats. Read about a woman who walked 220 feet over hot coals, a man who crossed Niagara Falls on a tightrope 200 feet high, a skater who landed a double back flip, dentists who removed a tooth from a 300-lb. tiger, and a man who pulled a bus 70 feet—with his ponytail!

Phonics Focus

- **Short** *a, e, i, o, u*
- **Consonants** *q, v, z*

See **Master Skills Tracker** in your Teacher's Edition.

Skills Tracker

Preteach Teach/Practice/Apply Review/Reinforce Assess

Smart Words

Words are defined on page 2 of the student book. Page number of first appearance is listed below.
- **defy**, p. 3
- **distance***, p. 3
- **feat**, p. 3

*Spanish Cognates, **page 26**

Option 1: **Decoding**

 Informal Assessment

Ask students to read the Phonics Focus words on the inside back cover of *They Did What?* If they struggle with decoding, proceed to targeted instruction.

 Targeted Instruction

For words with short vowels: Use the **Word Sort** decoding routine on **page 45** to sort words by their short vowel sounds.

For words with consonants *q, v,* and *z*: Have the student use the **Word Sort** decoding routine on **page 45** to sort words by their beginning consonant sounds.

Option 2: **Academic Vocabulary**

 Informal Assessment

Ask students to read a sentence from *They Did What?* that contains a Smart Word from the inside back cover. Have students define the Smart Word and identify evidence in the text that helped them determine the meaning. Review definitions on page 2 as needed. Repeat this procedure with other Smart Words. If students demonstrate proficiency, proceed to targeted instruction.

 Targeted Instruction

The Smart Word *feat* has many possible synonyms. Use the **Extending Meaning** vocabulary routine on **page 47** to extend meaning.

Option 3: **Fluency**

 Informal Assessment

Ask students to read page 4 of *They Did What?* aloud. To work on expressive reading, proceed to targeted instruction.

 Targeted Instruction

Use pages 4–5 of *They Did What?* and the **Read With Expression** fluency routine on **page 53** to have the student practice expressive reading.

Comprehension

Use the questions below and the Graphic Organizer on **page 73** to check comprehension and promote reader response.

After Page 3: *How far is 220 feet in terms of city blocks? (It is less than one block.)*

After Page 4: *Who walked farther—Amanda Dennison or Nik Wallenda? How many feet farther did she/he walk? (Nik Wallenda walked 1,570 feet farther than Amanda Dennison.)*

End of Book: *How is Manjit Singh like the other risk takers in this book? (He likes the thrill of taking a risk.)*

Resources	SAM Keywords
Graphic Organizer, p. 73	Did What?
My Independent Reading Response Log, pp. 166–167	IR Response Log 44

Name _____

They Did What?

Build Understanding

▶ What might each person below say is the toughest thing about the feat he or she did? Fill in the speech bubbles. Write something that each person might say. Use details from the text to help you write your answers.

Amanda Dennison
(Page 3)

Fabiola da Silva
(Page 5)

Manjit Singh
(Page 7)

QuickWrite

▶ Rename this book! Think of a new title. Then write 1–3 sentences explaining why it is a good title. Use text evidence to support your choice.

_____

_____

_____

_____

_____

Resource Links
Library Teaching Resources: p. 73
SAM Keyword: Did What?

*Use with **Library Teaching Resources,** page 72.*

System 44 Library **73**

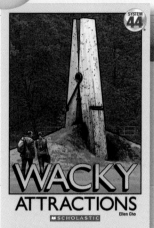

Wacky Attractions
by **Ellen Cho**

Simple — **HL180L**

| Genre | Pages | | Audio CD | | Reading |
| Social Studies | 8 | | 6 min 42 sec | | Counts! |

Summary

The five attractions in this book are amazing in unusual ways. A giant clothes pin in Belgium appears to pinch the earth. A huge, stone hand in Chile seems to reach right out of the sand. In California, a place called Bubblegum Alley is completely covered with chewed-up gum. In Turkey, some ancient caves have been turned into hotels! And a field in Ohio is full of giant corn—that's made from concrete.

Phonics Focus

- **Short vowels *a* and *i***
- **Consonants *h* and *k***

See **Master Skills Tracker** in your Teacher's Edition.

Skills Tracker

Preteach   Teach/Practice/Apply   Review/Reinforce   Assess

Smart Words

Words are defined on page 2 of the student book. Page number of first appearance is listed below.

- **attraction*, p. 3**
- **globe*, p. 5**
- **visit*, p. 3**

Spanish Cognates, **page 26*

Option 1: **Decoding**

 Informal Assessment

Ask students to read the Phonics Focus words on the inside back cover of *Wacky Attractions*. If they struggle with decoding, proceed to targeted instruction.

Targeted Instruction

For words with short vowels *a* and *i*: Have the student use the **Word Sort** decoding routine on **page 45** to sort words by their short vowel sounds.

For words with consonants *h* and *k*: Have the student use the **Word Sort** decoding routine to sort words by their beginning consonant sounds.

Option 2: **Academic Vocabulary**

 Informal Assessment

Ask students to read a sentence from the book that contains a Smart Word. Have students define the Smart Word and identify evidence in the text that helped them determine the meaning. Review definitions on page 2 as needed. Repeat this procedure with other Smart Words. If students demonstrate proficiency, proceed to targeted instruction.

Targeted Instruction

The Smart Word *visit* is the base of the words *visited, visiting, visitor,* and *revisit.* Use the **Extending Meaning** vocabulary routine on **page 46** to build student familiarity with morphological word families.

Option 3: **Fluency**

 Informal Assessment

Ask students to read page 3 of *Wacky Attractions* aloud. To work on reading with correct phrasing, proceed to targeted instruction.

Targeted Instruction

Use pages 3–4 of *Wacky Attractions* and the **Phrasing and Punctuation** fluency routine on **page 50** to have the student practice correct phrasing.

Comprehension

Use the questions below and the Graphic Organizer on **page 75** to check comprehension and promote reader response.

After Page 3: *Where is the big clothes pin? (It is in Belgium.)*

After Page 6: *What are the cave hotels made from? (They are made from rock that comes from volcanoes.)*

End of Book: *Why did an artist make giant, concrete corn? (He wanted to show that farms are important.)*

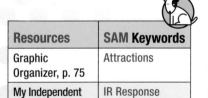

Resources	SAM **Keywords**
Graphic Organizer, p. 75	Attractions
My Independent Reading Response Log, pp. 166–167	IR Response Log 44

Name ______________________________

Wacky Attractions

Build Understanding

▶ Details are words, phrases, and sentences that give information about a topic. Write a detail about each attraction that describes how the attraction is wacky. The first one is done for you.

Topic	Details
Giant Clothes Pin *(Page 3)*	It is 50 feet tall.
Hand of the Desert *(Page 4)*	
Bubblegum Alley *(Page 5)*	
Cave Hotels *(Page 6)*	
Cadillac Ranch *(Page 7)*	

QuickWrite

▶ How do visitors change Bubblegum Alley? Write one sentence. Cite evidence from the text.

____

____

____

____

____

____

____

Resource Links
Library Teaching Resources: p. 75
SAM Keyword: Attractions

Use with **Library Teaching Resources,** *page 74.*

What's New? A History of Invention

by Peter Gutiérrez

Moderate 1   230L

Genre	Pages	Audio CD	Reading
Science	16	9 min 58 sec	Counts!

Summary

The time lines in this book show when cool things were invented. These time lines mark scientific milestones in movies, beauty products, sports equipment, transportation, and medicine.

Phonics Focus

- **Closed syllables**

See **Master Skills Tracker** in your Teacher's Edition.

Skills Tracker

Preteach   Teach/Practice/Apply   Review/Reinforce   Assess

Smart Words

Words are defined on pp. 2–3 of the student book. Page number of first appearance is listed below.

- **date**, p. 4
- **design***, p. 10
- **event***, p. 4
- **invent***, p. 5
- **science***, p. 8

*Spanish Cognates, **page 26**

Option 1: **Decoding**

 Informal Assessment

Ask students to read the Phonics Focus words on the inside back cover of *What's New?* If they struggle with decoding, proceed to targeted instruction.

Targeted Instruction

For words with closed syllables: Have students use the **Syllable Strategies** decoding routine on **page 40** to help the student determine the correct sound for vowels in closed syllables.

Option 2: **Academic Vocabulary**

 Informal Assessment

Ask students to read a sentence from the book that contains a Smart Word. Have students define the Smart Word and identify text evidence that helped them determine the meaning. Review definitions on pages 2–3 as needed. Repeat with other Smart Words. If students demonstrate proficiency, proceed to targeted instruction.

Targeted Instruction

The Smart Word *invent* is the base of the words *inventing, invented, inventions, inventor,* and *inventive.* Use the **Extending Meaning** vocabulary routine on **page 46** with *invention* as an example to build student familiarity with morphological word families.

Option 3: **Fluency**

 Informal Assessment

Ask students to read page 6 of *What's New?* aloud. To work on correct pacing, proceed to targeted instruction.

Targeted Instruction

Use pages 6–7 of *What's New?* and the **Use Natural, Consistent Pace** fluency routine on **page 51** to have the student practice reading at a natural pace.

Comprehension

Use the questions below and the Graphic Organizer on **page 77** to check comprehension and promote reader response.

After Page 7: *What is Smell-O-Vision?* (an invention that lets people smell movies)

After Page 9: *Name two inventions on the beauty time line.* (Possible answers include: the perm, false eyelashes, tanning lotion, shaving cream, a drug that makes hair grow.)

End of Book: *Who performed the first open-heart surgery?* (Dr. Daniel Hale Williams)

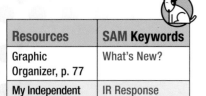

Resources	SAM **Keywords**
Graphic Organizer, p. 77	What's New?
My Independent Reading Response Log, pp. 166–167	IR Response Log 44

What's New? A History of Invention

Build Understanding

▶ All of the events listed below are from the book, but they are out of order. Rewrite the events in the correct order. The first one is done for you.

Events

Thomas Edison shows movies.

An actress wears false eyelashes.

Doctors test the first fake heart.

A man invents a baseball bat.

Someone invents the first motorcycle.

First
Someone invents the first motorcycle.

Second

Next

Then

Last

QuickWrite

▶ Select one time line in the book. Then explain how the object described in the time line changed from past to present.

_____

_____

_____

Resource Links
Library Teaching Resources: p. 77
SAM Keyword: What's New?

Use with **Library Teaching Resources,** *page 76.*

System 44 Library 77

Wonders of the World
by **Joshua Davis**

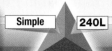

Simple	240L			
		Genre Social Studies	**Pages** 8	**Audio CD** 6 min 51 sec	**Reading Counts!**

Summary

The world is full of many wonders. Some, like the Egyptian pyramids, are ancient wonders of the past. Others, like the Internet, are modern-day wonders. This book features seven well-known wonders from near and far.

Phonics Focus

- Blends

See **Master Skills Tracker** in your Teacher's Edition.

Skills Tracker

Preteach | Teach/Practice/Apply | Review/Reinforce | Assess

Smart Words

Words are defined on p. 2 of the student book. Page number of first appearance is listed below.
- build, p. 4
- statue*, p. 6
- wonder, p. 3

*Spanish Cognates, **page 26**

Option 1: **Decoding**

 Informal Assessment

Ask students to read the Phonics Focus words on the inside back cover of *Wonders of the World*. If they struggle with decoding, proceed to targeted instruction.

 Targeted Instruction

For words with blends: Use the **Blends and Digraphs** decoding routine on **page 41** to help students build accuracy.

Option 2: **Academic Vocabulary**

 Informal Assessment

Ask students to read a sentence from the book that contains a Smart Word. Have students define the Smart Word and identify text evidence that helped them determine the meaning. Review definitions on page 2 as needed. Repeat with other Smart Words. If students demonstrate proficiency, proceed to targeted instruction.

 Targeted Instruction

The Smart Word *wonder* can mean "something that is amazing or surprising" or "to be curious about something." Use the **Multiple-Meaning Words** vocabulary routine on **page 47** with *wonder* as an example to help students use context to determine the correct meaning.

Option 3: **Fluency**

 Informal Assessment

Ask students to read page 3 of *Wonders of the World* aloud. To work on pacing, proceed to targeted instruction.

 Targeted Instruction

Use pages 3–5 of *Wonders of the World* and the **Use Natural, Consistent Pace** fluency routine on **page 51** to have students practice reading at a natural pace.

Resources	SAM Keywords
Graphic Organizer, p. 79	World Wonders
My Independent Reading Response Log, pp. 166–167	IR Response Log 44

Comprehension

Use the questions below and the Graphic Organizer on **page 79** to check comprehension and promote reader response.

After Page 5: *How many years did it take to build the Great Wall of China? (It took more than 2,000 years.)*

End of Book: *Why did France give the Statue of Liberty to the United States? (France gave it to the United States as a hundred-year birthday present.)*

Name _____

Wonders of the World

Build Understanding

▶ Summarize information about each wonder below. Use the most important details from the book. An example is done for you.

Internet *(Page 3)*

The Internet connects people. People use it to find news.

They use it to send emails.

Pyramids of Giza *(Page 4)*

_____

_____

Great Wall of China *(Page 5)*

_____

_____

Statue of Liberty *(Page 7)*

_____

_____

QuickWrite

▶ Choose one wonder from the book. What makes it wonderful? Use evidence from the text in your response.

_____

_____

Lesson Plan

Yes!
by **Ellen Lebrecque**

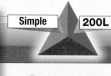

Simple ◄ ► **200L**

Genre **Social Studies**	**Pages** **16**	**Audio CD** **5 min 47 sec**	✓ **Reading** **Counts!**

Summary

Sports players have their shining moments. When they do, they shout, "Yes!" From scoring a point to winning a gold medal, victory on the soccer field, ball field, racetrack, or basketball court is sweet.

Phonics Focus

- **s-blends**
- **Double consonants**

See **Master Skills Tracker** in your Teacher's Edition.

Skills Tracker

Preteach | Teach/Practice/Apply | Review/Reinforce | Assess

Smart Words

Words are defined on p. 2 of the student book. Page number of first appearance is listed below.

- **achieve, p. 3**
- **compete,* p. 4**
- **score, p. 3**

*Spanish Cognates, **page 26**

Option 1: **Decoding**

 Informal Assessment

Ask students to read the Phonics Focus words on the inside back cover of *Yes!* If they struggle with decoding, proceed to targeted instruction.

 Targeted Instruction

For words with s-blends: Use the **Blends and Digraphs** decoding routine on **page 41** to help the student build accuracy.

For words with double consonants: Have the student use the **Word Sort** decoding routine on **page 45** to sort words by their double consonant spellings.

Option 2: **Academic Vocabulary**

 Informal Assessment

Ask students to read a sentence from the book that contains a Smart Word. Have students define the Smart Word and identify text evidence that helped them determine the meaning. Review definitions on page 2 as needed. Repeat with other Smart Words. If students demonstrate proficiency, proceed to targeted instruction.

 Targeted Instruction

The idiom *hot stuff* on page 5 means "someone who is really good at something." Build understanding of idioms using the **Idioms** vocabulary routine on **page 49** with this expression as an example.

Option 3: **Fluency**

 Informal Assessment

Ask students to read page 4 of *Yes!* aloud. To work on expressive reading, proceed to targeted instruction.

 Targeted Instruction

Use pages 4–5 of *Yes!* and the **Read With Expression** fluency routine on **page 53** to have the student practice expressive reading.

Comprehension

Use the questions below and the Graphic Organizer on **page 81** to check comprehension and promote reader response.

After Page 4: *What does Shaun White achieve? (the gold medal)*

End of Book: *Why isn't Coach Pete upset when water is dumped on him? (He isn't upset because his team has just won.)*

Resources	SAM **Keywords**
Graphic Organizer, p. 81	Yes!
My Independent Reading Response Log, pp. 166–167	IR Response Log 44

Name _____

Yes!

Build Understanding

▶ Explain why each player shouts, "Yes!" An example is done for you.

Shaun White *(Page 4)*

Shaun shouts, "Yes!" because he wins the gold medal.

_____

Chantal Petitclerc *(Page 5)*

_____

_____

Dwight Howard *(Page 6)*

_____

_____

Pete Carroll *(Page 7)*

_____

_____

QuickWrite

▶ Choose two athletes in this book. How are their "Yes!" moments alike? Use evidence from the text to support your answer.

_____

_____

_____

Resource Links
Library Teaching Resources: p. 81
SAM Keyword: Yes!

Use with **Library Teaching Resources,** *page 80.*

System 44 Library 81

Lesson Plan

African Journey
by Leslie Bakke and Susan O'Connor

Moderate 1 | 230L

| Genre | Pages | Audio CD | Reading |
| Science | 16 | 8 min 33 sec | ✓ Counts! |

Summary

Leslie Bakke journeys to Tanzania, where she climbs Mount Kilimanjaro, the tallest mountain in Africa. She also goes on a nature safari in the Serengeti, a huge national park teeming with wildlife, and visits the Maasai, a local tribe. Her journey is recorded through a collection of vivid photos with commentary.

Phonics Focus

- **Consonant + -al, -el, or -le**

See **Master Skills Tracker** in your Teacher's Edition.

Skills Tracker
Preteach Teach/Practice/Apply Review/Reinforce Assess

Smart Words

Words are defined on pp. 2–3 of the student book. Page number of first appearance is listed below.

- **local*, p. 7**
- **migrate*, p. 8**
- **national*, p. 5**
- **nature*, p. 4**
- **travel, p. 4**

*Spanish Cognates, **page 27**

Option 1: **Decoding**

 Informal Assessment

Ask students to read the Phonics Focus words on the inside back cover of *African Journey*. If they struggle with decoding, proceed to targeted instruction.

 Targeted Instruction

For words with consonants + -al, -el, or -le: Use the **Syllable Strategies** decoding routine on **page 40** to help the student determine the correct vowel sounds for -al, -el, and -le.

Option 2: **Academic Vocabulary**

 Informal Assessment

Ask students to read a sentence from the book that contains a Smart Word. Have students define the Smart Word and identify text evidence that helped them determine the meaning. Review definitions on pages 2–3 as needed. Repeat with other Smart Words. If students demonstrate proficiency, proceed to targeted instruction.

 Targeted Instruction

Use the **Context Clues** vocabulary routine on **page 48** with the Smart Word *migrate* to help the student use context clues to determine meaning.

Option 3: **Fluency**

 Informal Assessment

Ask students to read page 8 of *African Journey* aloud. To work on correct phrasing, proceed to targeted instruction.

 Targeted Instruction

Use pages 8–11 of *African Journey* and the **Phrasing and Punctuation** fluency routine on **page 50** to have the student practice correct phrasing.

Comprehension

Use the questions below and the Graphic Organizer on **page 83** to check comprehension and promote reader response.

After Page 7: *How long does it take Leslie to climb Mount Kilimanjaro? (one week)*

After Page 10: *The zebras look like they're hugging, but they are not. What are they doing? (They are resting and helping each other by looking out for lions.)*

End of Book: *What is the name of the tribe that Leslie visits and what do they raise? (The tribe is called the Maasai. They raise cattle.)*

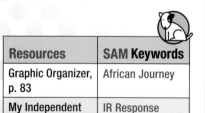

Resources	SAM Keywords
Graphic Organizer, p. 83	African Journey
My Independent Reading Response Log, pp. 166–167	IR Response Log 44

Graphic Organizer

Use with Series 9

Name ____________________

African Journey

▶ Build Understanding

Details are words, phrases, and sentences that give information about a topic. Write two details about each topic from the book. The first one is done for you.

Topic	Details
Mount Kilimanjaro *(Pages 6–7)*	• *Mount Kilimanjaro is the tallest mountain in Africa.* • *There is a glacier at the top of the mountain.*
Going on Safari *(Pages 8–9)*	
Animal Buddies *(Pages 10–11)*	
On the Hunt *(Pages 12–13)*	
Visiting the Maasai *(Pages 14–15)*	

QuickWrite

Describe how the land and weather changed as the author climbed up Mount Kilimanjaro. Cite evidence from the text to support your answer.

____

____

____

Resource Links
Library Teaching Resources: p. 83
SAM Keyword: African Journey

Use with **Library Teaching Resources,** *page 82.*

Lesson Plan

Big Steals
by **Syed Basher**

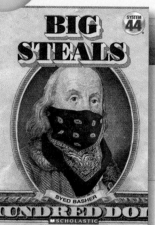

Simple ◄ ► HL260L

| Genre | Pages | | Audio CD | | Reading |
| Social Studies | 16 | | 11 min 39 sec | | Counts! |

Summary

These thefts were big! Thieves used computers to steal 7 million dollars from South African banks. An ancient treasure disappeared from Libya. Thieves in Holland took diamonds worth millions. Robbers tunneled into a bank in Brazil. Famous art was stolen from a Boston museum. Thieves took 20 bags of cash from a British train.

Phonics Focus

- **Digraph *th***
- ***-ing* and *-ed*, no base change**
- **Unstressed closed syllables**

See **Master Skills Tracker** in your Teacher's Edition.

Skills Tracker

Preteach · Teach/Practice/Apply · Review/Reinforce · Assess

Smart Words

Words are defined on pages 2–3 of the student book. Page number of first appearance is listed below.

- **cargo*, p. 8**
- **reward, p. 13**
- **signal*, p. 14**
- **witness, p. 4**
- **worth, p. 7**

Spanish Cognates, **page 27*

Option 1: **Decoding**

 Informal Assessment

Ask students to read the Phonics Focus words on the inside back cover of *Big Steals*. If they struggle with decoding, proceed to targeted instruction.

 Targeted Instruction

For words with *th*: Use the **Blends and Digraphs** decoding routine on **page 41**.

For words with *-ed*, *-ing*: Use the **Word Parts** routine on **page 43**.

For words with unstressed closed syllables: Use the **Syllable Strategies** decoding routine on **page 40**.

Option 2: **Academic Vocabulary**

 Informal Assessment

Ask students to read a sentence from the book that contains a Smart Word. Have students define the Smart Word and identify text evidence that helped them determine the meaning. Review definitions on pages 2–3 as needed. Repeat with other Smart Words. If students demonstrate proficiency, proceed to targeted instruction.

 Targeted Instruction

The Smart Word *signal* has two possible meanings. Use the **Multiple Meaning** vocabulary routine on **page 47** with *signal* as an example to help the student determine the correct meaning.

Option 3: **Fluency**

 Informal Assessment

Ask students to read page 10 of *Big Steals* aloud. To work on pacing, proceed to targeted instruction.

 Targeted Instruction

Use pages 10–11 of *Big Steals* and the **Use Natural, Consistent Pace** fluency routine on **page 51** to have the student practice correct pacing.

Comprehension

Use the questions below and the Graphic Organizer on **page 85** to check comprehension and promote reader response.

After Page 7: *What historical event helped thieves get away with the treasure of Benghazi? (Rebels were fighting the government, and Benghazi was in chaos.)*

After Page 11: *Why did the tunnel thieves pretend they were running a lawn-care business? (They wanted people to think they were hauling dirt as part of their job—not taking it from a tunnel they were digging to a bank.)*

End of Book: *Which stolen items in this book were worth the most money? (The treasure of Benghazi was the biggest theft. The stolen treasure is worth billions of dollars.)*

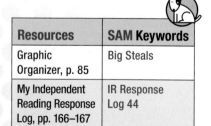

Resources	SAM Keywords
Graphic Organizer, p. 85	Big Steals
My Independent Reading Response Log, pp. 166–167	IR Response Log 44

Graphic Organizer

Use with Series 8 & 9

Name ____________________

Big Steals

Build Understanding

▶ What did each thief or group of thieves in this book steal? How did they do it? Summarize each theft. Include the most important details from the book.

Cyber Swipe *(Page 5)*

Thieves stole almost 7 million dollars from a South African bank. They broke into the bank's computer system and took money from customer accounts.

The Treasure of Benghazi *(Page 6)*

____

Diamond Heist *(Page 8)*

____

The Great Tunnel Heist *(Page 10)*

____

Art Theft *(Page 12)*

____

The Great Train Robbery *(Page 14)*

____

QuickWrite

▶ What was daring about the diamond theft at Schiphol Airport? Use text evidence to support your answer.

____

____

____

Resource Links
Library Teaching Resources: p. 85
SAM Keyword: Big Steals

Use with **Library Teaching Resources,** *page 84.*

Lesson Plan

Button Your Lip and Other Idioms
by Polly Downes

Moderate 1   210L

| | Genre | Pages | Audio CD | Reading |
| | Language Arts | 16 | 9 min 48 sec | Counts! |

Summary

Idioms are expressions that seem to mean one thing, but really mean another. This book explains what people really mean when they say, "shake a leg," "hold your horses," "put on your thinking cap," and eight other idioms.

Phonics Focus

- **Closed syllables with schwa**

See **Master Skills Tracker** in your Teacher's Edition.

Skills Tracker

Preteach Teach/Practice/Apply Review/Reinforce Assess

Smart Words

Words are defined on pp. 2–3 of the student book. Page number of first appearance is listed below.
- common*, p. 4
- explain*, p. 4
- idiom, p. 4
- shake, p. 4
- tale, p. 6

*Spanish Cognates, **page 27**

Option 1: **Decoding**

 Informal Assessment

Ask students to read the Phonics Focus words on the inside back cover of *Button Your Lip and Other Idioms*. If they struggle with decoding, proceed to targeted instruction.

 Targeted Instruction

For words with closed syllables with schwa: Use the **Syllable Strategies** decoding routine on **page 40** to help students decode multisyllabic words.

Option 2: **Academic Vocabulary**

 Informal Assessment

Ask students to read a sentence from the book that contains a Smart Word. Have students define the Smart Word and identify text evidence that helped them determine the meaning. Review definitions on pages 2–3 as needed. Repeat with other Smart Words. If students demonstrate proficiency, proceed to targeted instruction.

 Targeted Instruction

The Smart Word *explain* is the base of the words *explained, unexplained, explaining, explains, explainable, unexplainable, explanation,* and *explanatory.* Use the **Extending Meaning** vocabulary routine on **page 46** to build student familiarity with morphological word families.

Option 3: **Fluency**

 Informal Assessment

Ask students to read page 10 of *Button Your Lip and Other Idioms* aloud. To work on expressive reading, proceed to targeted instruction.

 Targeted Instruction

Use pages 10-12 of *Button Your Lip and Other Idioms* and the **Read With Expression** fluency routine on **page 53** to have students practice expressive reading.

Comprehension

Use the questions below and the Graphic Organizer on **page 87** to check comprehension and promote reader response.

After Page 6: *Where does the idiom "saved by the bell" come from? (Hundreds of years ago, coffins had bells so that people who were buried alive could let others know.)*

After Page 10: *What does the idiom "hold your horses" mean? (Slow down and wait.)*

End of Book: *Which idiom means to say the wrong thing at the wrong time? (the idiom "put your foot in your mouth")*

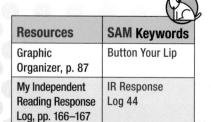

Resources	SAM Keywords
Graphic Organizer, p. 87	Button Your Lip
My Independent Reading Response Log, pp. 166–167	IR Response Log 44

Name ____________________

Button Your Lip and Other Idioms

Build Understanding

▶ Match each idiom to its meaning. The first one is done for you.

1. Backseat Driver	Hurry
2. Button Your Lip	A bossy person
3. Do Not Let the Cat Out of the Bag	Think about a problem
	Do not talk
4. Hit the Nail on the Head	To be right
5. Hold Your Horses	Slow down
6. Put on Your Thinking Cap	Say the wrong thing at the wrong time
7. Put Your Foot in Your Mouth	
8. Shake a Leg	Do not tell a secret

QuickWrite

▶ Choose one idiom that comes from an old story. Tell the story in your own words.

____

____

____

Resource Links
Library Teaching Resources: p. 87
SAM Keyword: Button Your Lip

Use with **Library Teaching Resources,** *page 86.*

Use With Series 11 · Lesson Plan

Cool Jobs in Basketball
by Peter Gutiérrez

Simple ◆ 300L

Genre	Pages	Audio CD	Reading Counts!
Jobs	16	9 min 51 sec	✓

Summary

Jobs in professional basketball aren't only for athletes. Yvonne Nelson is an intern who plans events for basketball teams. Tony Mejia is a reporter who writes about basketball. Keith Jones helps injured athletes and makes important team decisions. These individuals have found ways to use their skills and be part of basketball.

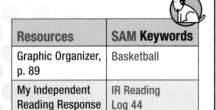

Phonics Focus

- Words with VC*e*
- Prefixes *non-* and *un-*

See **Master Skills Tracker** in your Teacher's Edition.

Skills Tracker

Preteach Teach/Practice/Apply Review/Reinforce Assess

Smart Words

Words are defined on pp. 4–5 of the student book. Page number of first appearance is listed below.

- athlete*, p. 6
- business, p. 6
- experience*, p. 7
- hire, p. 6
- intern*, p. 8
- rely, p. 9

*Spanish Cognates, **page 27**

Option 1: **Decoding**

 Informal Assessment

Ask students to read the Phonics Focus words on the inside back cover of *Cool Jobs in Basketball*. If they struggle with decoding, proceed to targeted instruction.

 Targeted Instruction

For words with VC*e*: Have the student use the **Word Sort** decoding routine on **page 45** to sort by long *i*, *o*, and *u* sounds.

For words with prefixes *non-* and *un-*: Use the **Word Parts** decoding routine on **page 42** to help the student identify and use prefixes.

Option 2: **Academic Vocabulary**

 Informal Assessment

Ask students to read a sentence from the book that contains a Smart Word. Have students define the Smart Word and identify text evidence that helped them determine the meaning. Review definitions on pages 4–5 as needed. Repeat with other Smart Words. If students demonstrate proficiency, proceed to targeted instruction.

 Targeted Instruction

The Smart Word *rely* has many possible synonyms and antonyms. Use the **Extending Meaning** vocabulary routine on **page 47** to extend meaning.

Option 3: **Fluency**

 Informal Assessment

Ask students to read page 8 of *Cool Jobs in Basketball* aloud. To work on correct phrasing, proceed to targeted instruction.

 Targeted Instruction

Use pages 8–9 of *Cool Jobs in Basketball* and the **Phrasing and Punctuation** fluency routine on **page 50** to have the student practice correct phrasing.

Comprehension

Use the questions below and the Graphic Organizer on **page 89** to check comprehension and promote reader response.

After Chapter 1: *Why isn't professional basketball only for athletes?* (There are jobs in professional basketball for people with all kinds of experience.)

After Chapter 3: *What jobs do Yvonne and Tony have?* (Yvonne is an intern who promotes the teams and plans events. Tony writes about basketball for a Web site.)

End of Book: *How does Keith help the players he works with?* (Keith helps injured athletes by teaching them exercises to make them better.)

Resources	SAM Keywords
Graphic Organizer, p. 89	Basketball
My Independent Reading Response Log, pp. 166–167	IR Reading Log 44

Name _____

Cool Jobs in Basketball

Build Understanding

▶ How might Yvonne, Tony, and Keith describe their jobs? In the speech bubbles below, write what they might say. Use details from the book. The first one is done for you.

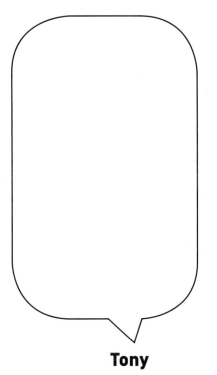

I'm an intern. I make sure the athletes look good for ads. I also plan events. I love all the friends I've made.

Yvonne

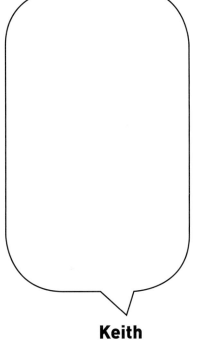

Tony

Keith

QuickWrite

▶ How was Yvonne's job as an intern similar to being an athlete? Support your answer with information from the text.

_____

_____

_____

Crash!

by **Steph Smith**

Moderate 1   320L

Genre	Pages	Audio CD	Reading
Science	**16**	**10 min 12 sec**	**Counts!**

Summary

Scientists are keeping track of asteroids, especially one named Apophis. Experts tracking Apophis know that in the future it will fly by Earth. If Apophis crashes into Earth, it will create tremendous damage. Scientists have some ideas about how to knock an asteroid off its path. They just hope it won't get too close!

Phonics Focus

- *-ed* with no base change
- *-ed* with base change
- *y* as a vowel

See **Master Skills Tracker** in your Teacher's Edition.

Skills Tracker

Preteach   Teach/Practice/Apply   Review/Reinforce   Assess

Smart Words

Words are defined on pp. 4–5 of the student book. Page number of first appearance is listed below.

- expert*, p. 7
- follow, p. 7
- gravity*, p. 12
- orbit*, p. 10
- telescope*, p. 10

*Spanish Cognates, **page 27**

Option 1: **Decoding**

 Informal Assessment

Ask students to read the Phonics Focus words on the inside back cover of *Crash!* If they struggle with decoding, proceed to targeted instruction.

 Targeted Instruction

For words with *-ed* with and without base change: Use the **Word Parts** decoding routine on **page 43** to help students identify and use inflectional endings.

For words with *y* as a vowel: Have students use the **Word Sort** decoding routine on **page 45** to sort words by long *e*, long *i*, and short *i* sounds.

Option 2: **Academic Vocabulary**

 Informal Assessment

Ask students to read a sentence from the book that contains a Smart Word. Have students define the Smart Word and identify text evidence that helped them determine the meaning. Review definitions on pages 4–5 as needed. Repeat with other Smart Words. If students demonstrate proficiency, proceed to targeted instruction.

 Targeted Instruction

The Smart Word *follow* can mean "to watch or keep track of something as it moves" or "to chase or pursue." Use the **Multiple-Meaning Words** vocabulary routine on **page 47** with *follow* as an example to help students determine the correct meaning.

Option 3: **Fluency**

 Informal Assessment

Ask students to read page 10 of *Crash!* aloud. To work on expressive reading, proceed to targeted instruction.

 Targeted Instruction

Use pages 10–11 of *Crash!* and the **Read With Expression** fluency routine on **page 53** to have students practice expressive reading.

Comprehension

Use the questions below and the Graphic Organizer on **page 91** to check comprehension and promote reader response.

After Chapter 1: *What is an asteroid? (It is a big rock that flies around in space.)*

After Chapter 2: *What ideas do experts have about how to stop an asteroid from hitting Earth? (The asteroid can be pushed away by a spaceship that crashes into it. Or, it can be pulled away using the force of gravity from a big ship.)*

End of Book: *When Apophis flies by Earth again in 2029, where will be the best place to see it? (The best place to see it will be in Europe.)*

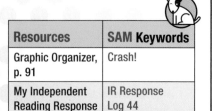

Resources	SAM Keywords
Graphic Organizer, p. 91	Crash!
My Independent Reading Response Log, pp. 166–167	IR Response Log 44

Name _____

Crash!

Build Understanding

▶ Identify the most important ideas in each chapter. Then, summarize the chapter in your own words. One has been done for you as an example.

Chapter 1: "Look! An Asteroid!"

_____

_____

Chapter 2: "On the Right Track"

An asteroid named Apophis could hit Earth. Scientists are studying it and tracking it. Experts have ideas about how to throw an asteroid off track to prevent it from slamming into Earth.

Chapter 3: "Out of This World"

_____

_____

QuickWrite

▶ Describe two ways scientists try to stop an asteroid from hitting Earth. Cite text evidence.

_____

_____

_____

Resource Links
Library Teaching Resources: p. 91
SAM Keyword: Crash!

*Use with **Library Teaching Resources,** page 90.*

System 44 Library **91**

DJ Mystery

by **Michael Leviton**

Moderate 1 · 190L

Genre	Pages	Audio CD	Reading
Fiction	16	9 min 15 sec	Counts!

Summary

Everyone at Thorn High listens to DJ Mystery's music, but nobody knows that he's really Keith. Seth, the coolest kid at school, wants DJ Mystery to play at his party. Keith decides to go. Everyone is shocked when they learn who the real Keith is. With Seth's help, they learn to see Keith in a whole different light.

Phonics Focus

• *th*

See **Master Skills Tracker** in your Teacher's Guide.

Skills Tracker

Preteach Teach/Practice/Apply Review/Reinforce Assess

Smart Words

Words are defined on pp. 2–3 of the student book. Page number of first appearance is listed below.

• **crowd, p. 11**
• **excite*, p. 4**
• **invite*, p. 9**
• **record, p. 4**
• **truth, p. 5**

*Spanish Cognates, **page 28**

Option 1: Decoding

 Informal Assessment

Ask students to read the Phonics Focus words on the inside back cover of *DJ Mystery*. If they struggle with decoding, proceed to targeted instruction.

 Targeted Instruction

For words with *th*: Use the **Blends and Digraphs** decoding routine on **page 41** to help the student build accuracy.

Option 2: Academic Vocabulary

 Informal Assessment

Ask students to read a sentence from the book that contains a Smart Word. Have students define the Smart Word and identify text evidence that helped them determine the meaning. Review definitions on pages 2–3 as needed. Repeat with other Smart Words. If students demonstrate proficiency, proceed to targeted instruction.

 Targeted Instruction

The Smart Word *crowd* can mean "a large group of people" or "to not give someone enough room." Use the **Multiple-Meaning Words** vocabulary routine on **page 47** with *crowd* as an example to help the student use context to determine correct meaning.

Option 3: Fluency

 Informal Assessment

Ask students to read page 6 of *DJ Mystery* aloud. To work on expressive reading, proceed to targeted instruction.

 Targeted Instruction

Use pages 6–8 of *DJ Mystery* and the **Read With Expression** fluency routine on **page 53** to have the student practice expressive reading.

Comprehension

Use the questions below and the Graphic Organizer on **page 93** to check comprehension and promote reader response.

After Page 5: *What do students know about DJ Mystery?* (They know he is a fellow student at Thorn High and that he makes cool records.)

After Page 13: *Why do people have a hard time believing that Keith is DJ Mystery?* (They have a hard time believing it because DJ Mystery's music is really cool. Keith, on the other hand, is not popular and some kids call him a loser.)

End of Book: *What does Seth realize about Keith?* (He realizes that no one got to know who Keith really was, and kids judged him unfairly.)

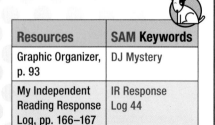

Resources	SAM Keywords
Graphic Organizer, p. 93	DJ Mystery
My Independent Reading Response Log, pp. 166–167	IR Response Log 44

Name ____________________

DJ Mystery

Build Understanding

▶ All of the events listed below are from the book, but they are out of order. Rewrite each event in the correct order. The first one is done for you.

Events

Jen makes fun of Keith at lunchtime.

Seth invites DJ Mystery to his party.

Seth stops Keith at the door.

Keith dances with Trina.

Trina and Keith talk about going to the party.

Jen asks Keith to dance with her.

First
Seth invites DJ Mystery to his party.

Second

Third

Fourth

Next

Last

QuickWrite

▶ Why does Keith choose to dance with Trina instead of Jen? Explain your answer with evidence from the book.

____

____

____

Resource Links
Library Teaching Resources: p. 93
SAM Keyword: DJ Mystery

Use with **Library Teaching Resources,** *page 92.*

Fashion Flashback
by Richard Camden

 Moderate 1 | 220L

Genre	Pages	Audio CD	Reading Counts!
Social Studies	16	10 min 23 sec	

Summary

Fashion is always changing. In the 1920s, women have fun in flapper dresses, but in the 1940s, they're serious in slacks. In the 1970s people are outrageous in platforms and wide lapels, but prefer preppy styles in the 1980s and go grunge in the 1990s. As long as people continue to enjoy wearing clothing, styles will continue to come and go.

Phonics Focus

- -ed with no base change

See **Master Skills Tracker** in your Teacher's Edition.

Skills Tracker

Preteach Teach/Practice/Apply Review/Reinforce Assess

Smart Words

Words are defined on pp. 2–3 of the student book. Page number of first appearance is listed below.

- decade* p. 9
- fashion, p. 4
- popular*, p. 4
- practical*, p. 7
- trend, p. 5

*Spanish Cognates, **page 28**

Option 1: Decoding

 Informal Assessment

Ask students to read the Phonics Focus words on the inside back cover of *Fashion Flashback*. If they struggle with decoding, proceed to targeted instruction.

 Targeted Instruction

For words with -ed with no base change: Have the student use the **Word Parts** decoding routine on **page 43** to help the student identify and use inflectional endings.

Option 2: Academic Vocabulary

 Informal Assessment

Ask students to read a sentence from the book that contains a Smart Word. Have students define the Smart Word and identify text evidence that helped them determine the meaning. Review definitions on pages 2–3 as needed. Repeat with other Smart Words. If students demonstrate proficiency, proceed to targeted instruction.

 Targeted Instruction

The idiom *show off* used in the second paragraph of page 9 means "to do something to get attention." Build understanding of idioms using the **Idioms** vocabulary routine on **page 49** with this expression as an example.

Option 3: Fluency

Informal Assessment

Ask students to read page 10 of *Fashion Flashback* aloud. To work on correct phrasing, proceed to targeted instruction.

Targeted Instruction

Use pages 10–11 of *Fashion Flashback* and the **Phrasing and Punctuation** fluency routine on **page 50** to have the student practice correct phrasing.

Comprehension

Use the questions below and the Graphic Organizer on **page 95** to check comprehension and promote reader response.

After Page 7: *What event makes women of the 1920s wear lighter, more fun dresses?* (A big war ends in 1918, and women switch to lighter dresses so they can dance and have fun.)

After Page 11: *What are some fashion trends in the 1970s?* (long skirts, short skirts, suits with wide lapels, wide collars, high boots, platform shoes, bell-bottom jeans, skinny jeans, sparkles, bright colors, and lots of hair)

End of Book: *What is the look of the 1990s called?* (grunge)

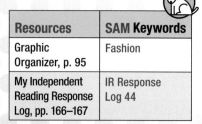

Resources	SAM Keywords
Graphic Organizer, p. 95	Fashion
My Independent Reading Response Log, pp. 166–167	IR Response Log 44

Fashion Flashback

Build Understanding

▶ Many styles have come and gone. Fill in the circles with some of the fashions described in the book. An example is done for you.

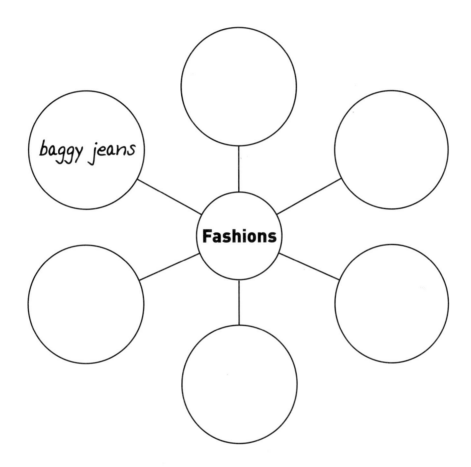

QuickWrite

▶ How did attitudes about fashion in the 1980s differ from attitudes about fashion in the 1990s? Use details from the book to support your answer.

_____

_____

_____

Lesson Plan

Home From War
by **Kimberly Feltes Taylor**

Moderate 1 | HL210L

Genre	Pages	Audio CD	Reading
Fiction	16	11 min 08 sec	Counts!

Summary

Nicole is a military veteran who lost her leg in an attack in Iraq. Now, she's back home, taking classes at a local community college and hoping to pursue a career in medicine. School is harder than Nicole expected. With a prosthetic leg, she tires easily and feels different from other students. But members of her veterans support group encourage her to "stick with it." Eventually, Nicole befriends another struggling student and begins to feel better about college.

Phonics Focus

- **Prefixes** *non-*, *de-*, and *un-*

See **Master Skills Tracker** in your Teacher's Edition.

Skills Tracker

Preteach | Teach/Practice/Apply | Review/Reinforce | Assess

Smart Words

Words are defined on pages 4–5 of the student book. Page number of first appearance is listed below.

- **agree**, p. 14
- **biology***, p. 9
- **challenge**, p. 12
- **derail**, p. 14
- **pursue***, p. 8

*Spanish Cognates, **page 28**

Option 1: **Decoding**

 Informal Assessment

Ask students to read the Phonics Focus words on the inside back cover of *Home From War*. If they struggle with decoding, proceed to targeted instruction.

Targeted Instruction

For prefixes *non-*, *de-*, **and** *un-*: Use the **Word Parts** decoding routine on **page 42** to help the student identify and use these prefixes.

Option 2: **Academic Vocabulary**

 Informal Assessment

Ask students to read a sentence from the book that contains a Smart Word from the inside back cover. Have students define the Smart Word and identify text evidence that helped them determine the meaning. Review definitions on pages 4–5 as needed. Repeat with other Smart Words. If students demonstrate proficiency, proceed to targeted instruction.

 Targeted Instruction

Use the **Context Clues** vocabulary routine on **page 48** with the Smart Word *pursue* as an example to help the student use context clues to determine meaning.

Option 3: **Fluency**

 Informal Assessment

Ask students to read page 9 of *Home From War* aloud. To work on expressive reading, proceed to targeted instruction.

 Targeted Instruction

Use pages 9 and 11 of *Home From War* and the **Read With Expression** fluency routine on **page 53** to have the student practice reading with expression.

Comprehension

Use the questions below and the Graphic Organizer on **page 97** to check comprehension and promote reader response.

After Page 8: *Why does Nicole want to pursue a job in medicine?* (She wants to help others the way Army doctors helped her when she lost her leg.)

After Page 11: *What challenges does Nicole face on her first day of college?* (She feels different from the other students, has to walk a lot, and notices many people staring at her.)

End of Book: *Why does Shane think it might be "unsafe" to talk to Nicole?* (She scowled at him in the first biology class, so Shane wonders if she will be unfriendly now, too.)

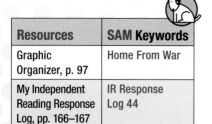

Resources	SAM Keywords
Graphic Organizer, p. 97	Home From War
My Independent Reading Response Log, pp. 166–167	IR Response Log 44

Name ____________________

Home From War

Build Understanding

▶ Read the list of events below. Then write the events in the order they happen in the book. The first one is done for you.

Events
Nicole starts writing in a journal.
Nicole is hurt in a bombing.
Nicole's veterans group advises her to stick with college.
Nicole makes friends with Shane.
Nicole has a difficult first day of college.

First *Nicole is hurt in a bombing.*

↓

Second

↓

Third

↓

Fourth

↓

Last

QuickWrite

▶ How does the veterans group help Nicole? Explain two ways. Cite text evidence to support your response.

____

____

____

____

Resource Links
Library Teaching Resources: p. 97
SAM Keyword: Home From War

Use with **Library Teaching Resources,** *page 96.*

Lesson Plan

Is This Art?
by **Grace Nguyen**

Simple — 230L

Genre	Pages	Audio CD	Reading
Social Studies	16	9 min 46 sec	Counts!

Summary

Art can be quite out of the ordinary. Artists create it in all shapes, styles, and sizes—such as a building wrapped in cloth, and a sculpture made from a stool and bicycle wheel. Just what is art and what isn't? That's for every person to decide.

Phonics Focus

- **ch, -tch**

See **Master Skills Tracker** in your Teacher's Edition.

Skills Tracker

Preteach   Teach/Practice/Apply   Review/Reinforce   Assess

Smart Words

Words are defined on pp. 2–3 of the student book. Page number of first appearance is listed below.

- **artist***, p. 5
- **change**, p. 4
- **create***, p. 6
- **familiar***, p. 5
- **sculpture***, p. 4

*Spanish Cognates, **page 28**

Option 1: Decoding

 Informal Assessment

Ask students to read the Phonics Focus words on the inside back cover of *Is This Art?* If they struggle with decoding, proceed to targeted instruction.

 Targeted Instruction

For words with *ch* and *-tch*: Use the **Blends and Digraphs** decoding routine on **page 41** to help the student build accuracy.

Option 2: Academic Vocabulary

 Informal Assessment

Ask students to read a sentence from the book that contains a Smart Word. Have students define the Smart Word and identify text evidence that helped them determine the meaning. Review definitions on pages 2–3 as needed. Repeat with other Smart Words. If students demonstrate proficiency, proceed to targeted instruction.

 Targeted Instruction

The Smart Word *change* can mean "to make something be different or new" or "money in the form of coins." Use the **Multiple-Meaning Words** vocabulary routine on **page 47** with *change* as an example to help the student use context to determine the correct meaning.

Option 3: Fluency

 Informal Assessment

Ask students to read page 8 of *Is This Art?* aloud. To work on correct phrasing, proceed to targeted instruction.

 Targeted Instruction

Use pages 8–9 of *Is This Art?* and the **Phrasing and Punctuation** fluency routine on **page 50** to have the student practice correct phrasing.

Comprehension

Use the questions below and the Graphic Organizer on **page 99** to check comprehension and promote reader response.

After Page 7: *What do artists do for Cow Parade? (They paint cow sculptures and put them on display.)*

After Page 10: *What did Andy Warhol paint pictures of? (He painted pictures of simple and familiar things.)*

End of Book: *Why does Rodney McMillian think that old stuff can be art? (Old stuff tells an important story about the people who used it.)*

Resources	SAM Keywords
Graphic Organizer, p. 99	Is This Art?
My Independent Reading Response Log, pp. 166–167	IR Response Log 44

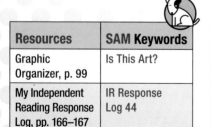

Name _____

Is This Art?

Build Understanding

▶ The artists in this book use all sorts of materials to make their art. Fill in the circles with the names of the different materials or objects they use. An example is done for you.

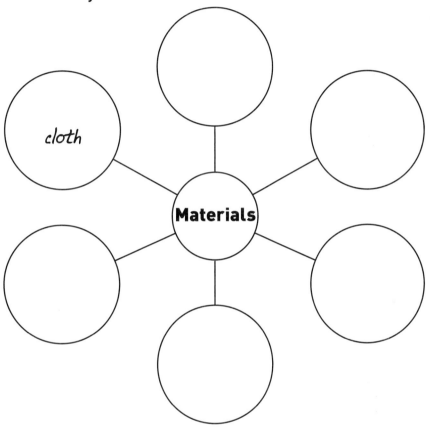

QuickWrite

▶ How are Stan Woodward and Marcel Duchamp alike? Use details from the book to support your answer.

_____

_____

_____

_____

Resource Links
Library Teaching Resources: p. 99
SAM Keyword: Is This Art?

Use with **Library Teaching Resources,** *page 98.*

System 44 Library 99

The Princess Brat
by Jennifer Johnson

Moderate 1 ▲ **220L**

Genre Fiction	**Pages** 16	🎧	**Audio CD** 8 min 35 sec	✓ **Reading Counts!**

Summary

Princess is a famous, rich brat who stars in a reality show on a ranch. For the show, she has to do chores like feeding pigs, cutting grass, and fixing lunch. She fails miserably at every job and finally quits. Back at home, she loves watching herself on TV, and her fans love to see how bratty she is.

Phonics Focus

- Soft *c* and *g*
- Suffix *-ment*

See **Master Skills Tracker** in your Teacher's Edition.

Skills Tracker

Preteach Teach/Practice/Apply Review/Reinforce Assess

Smart Words

Words are defined on pp. 2–3 of the student book. Page number of first appearance is listed below.

- agreement, p. 6
- famous*, p. 5
- raise, p. 4
- reality*, p. 6
- stomp, p. 8

*Spanish Cognates, **page 28**

Option 1: **Decoding**

 Informal Assessment

Ask students to read the Phonics Focus words on the inside back cover of *The Princess Brat*. If they struggle with decoding, proceed to targeted instruction.

Targeted Instruction

For words with soft *c* and *g*: Have the student use the **Word Sort** decoding routine on **page 45** to sort words with soft *c* and *g* spellings.

For words with suffix *-ment*: Use the **Word Parts** decoding routine on **page 43** to help identify and use suffixes.

Option 2: **Academic Vocabulary**

 Informal Assessment

Ask students to read a sentence from the book that contains a Smart Word. Have students define the Smart Word and identify text evidence that helped them determine the meaning. Review definitions on pages 2–3 as needed. Repeat with other Smart Words. If students demonstrate proficiency, proceed to targeted instruction.

Targeted Instruction

Agree is the base of the Smart Word *agreement* and the words *agreeable*, *agreeing*, *agreements*, *disagree*, *disagreement*, and others. Use the **Extending Meaning** vocabulary routine on **page 46** to build student familiarity with morphological word families.

Option 3: **Fluency**

 Informal Assessment

Ask students to read page 13 of *The Princess Brat* aloud. To work on natural, expressive reading proceed to targeted instruction.

Targeted Instruction

Use pages 13–14 of *The Princess Brat* and the **Read With Expression** fluency routine on **page 53** to have the student practice expressive reading.

Comprehension

Use the questions below and the Graphic Organizer on **page 101** to check comprehension and promote reader response.

After Page 5: *Why is Princess famous? (Nobody knows.)*

After Page 12: *Why doesn't Princess cut the grass? (It's a nice day, and she wants to relax. She feels she is working too hard.)*

End of Book: *Why do the TV fans love Princess? (They love her because she is so bratty.)*

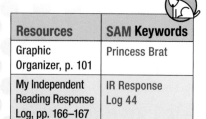

Resources	SAM Keywords
Graphic Organizer, p. 101	Princess Brat
My Independent Reading Response Log, pp. 166–167	IR Response Log 44

Name _____

The Princess Brat

Build Understanding

▶ Fill in the circles with words that describe Princess. Use details from the book.
An example is done for you.

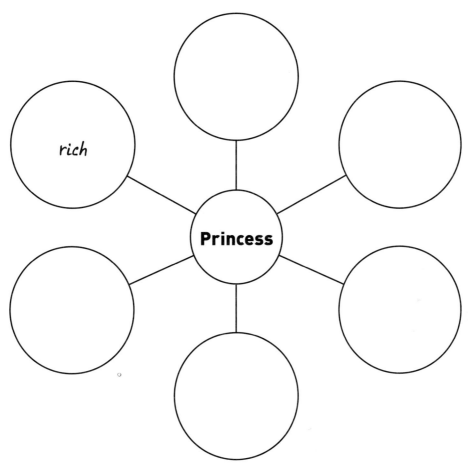

QuickWrite

▶ How did Princess feel about her time on the ranch? Use evidence from the text
to explain your answer.

_____

_____

_____

Ripped From the Headlines
by **Peter Gutiérrez**

Moderate 1	210L

Genre	Pages	Audio CD	Reading
Social Studies	**16**	**10 min 28 sec**	**Counts!**

Summary

Wild stories make the headlines. Bethany makes the news after a shark bites off her arm. Felix catches a baby thrown out the window of a burning building. A hiker named Aron cuts off his own arm to save his life. These stories and others are featured in this book about brave heroes and amazing circumstances.

Phonics Focus

- **Long _a_ with final _e_**
- **Long _i_ with final _e_**

See **Master Skills Tracker** in your Teacher's Edition.

Skills Tracker

Preteach   Teach/Practice/Apply   Review/Reinforce   Assess

Smart Words

Words are defined on pp. 2–3 of the student book. Page number of first appearance is listed below.

- amaze, p. 4
- believe, p. 4
- brave, p. 4
- danger, p. 5
- rescue*, p. 6

*Spanish Cognates, **page 28**

Option 1: Decoding

 Informal Assessment

Ask students to read the Phonics Focus words on the inside back cover of _Ripped From the Headlines_. If they struggle with decoding, proceed to targeted instruction.

 Targeted Instruction

For words with long _a_ and _i_ with final _e_: Have the student use the **Word Sort** decoding routine on **page 45** to sort words by long vowel sound. Point out that a final _e_ can control a long vowel sound to make it long.

Option 2: Academic Vocabulary

 Informal Assessment

Ask students to read a sentence from the book that contains a Smart Word. Have students define the Smart Word and identify text evidence that helped them determine the meaning. Review definitions on pages 2–3 as needed. Repeat with other Smart Words. If students demonstrate proficiency, proceed to targeted instruction.

 Targeted Instruction

The Smart Word _brave_ can mean "not afraid" or "to do something unpleasant and difficult," as in "He braved the storm." Use the **Multiple-Meaning Words** vocabulary routine on **page 47** with _brave_ as an example to help the student use context to determine the correct meaning.

Option 3: Fluency

 Informal Assessment

Ask students to read page 12 of _Ripped From the Headlines_ aloud. To work on pacing, proceed to targeted instruction.

 Targeted Instruction

Use pages 12–13 of _Ripped From the Headlines_ and the **Use Natural, Consistent Pace** fluency routine on **page 51** to have the student practice reading at a natural pace.

Comprehension

Use the questions below and the Graphic Organizer on **page 103** to check comprehension and promote reader response.

After Page 7: _What happens to Muhammet? (He survives after being trapped for five days under the rubble of a building.)_

After Page 9: _What happens to Palmira and who saves her? (A strange man grabs her while her gym class is outside in a park. Her friends attack the man and save her.)_

End of Book: _How does Aron's brave act save his life? (Cutting off his own arm allows him to get out from under the rock and find help.)_

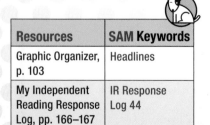

Resources	SAM Keywords
Graphic Organizer, p. 103	Headlines
My Independent Reading Response Log, pp. 166–167	IR Response Log 44

Name _____

Ripped From the Headlines

Build Understanding

▶ Summarize each story below in your own words. One has been done for you as an example.

"Shark Attack!" *(Page 5)*

Bethany is surfing when a shark bites off her arm. A friend helps save Bethany's life. Today, Bethany is still surfing.

"Stranger Danger!" *(Pages 8–9)*

_____

_____

"Falling Baby!" *(Pages 12–13)*

_____

_____

"Trapped!" *(Pages 14-15)*

_____

_____

QuickWrite

▶ The author writes on page 5 that "Bethany did not let a shark bite stop her dream." How did she follow her dream after the attack?

_____

_____

_____

Survival Guide: How to Keep Your Job

by **Chris Kensler**

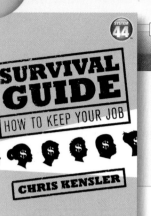

 Simple — 190L

Genre	Pages	 Audio CD	Reading
Jobs	**16**	**10 min 58 sec**	**Counts!**

Summary

People who want to keep their jobs need to know how to deal with problems. What's the best way to deal with a difficult boss? Is it okay to call in sick to have a day off? The advice in this book explains how to deal with these real-life job issues.

Phonics Focus

- **-ing with no base change**
- Review **ch, -tch, sh, th**

See **Master Skills Tracker** in your Teacher's Guide.

Skills Tracker

Preteach | Teach/Practice/Apply | Review/Reinforce | Assess

Smart Words

Words are defined on pp. 2–3 of the student book. Page number of first appearance is listed below.

- **customer, p. 9**
- **fire, p. 4**
- **focus*, p. 12**
- **reason*, p. 9**
- **responsible*, p. 7**

*Spanish Cognates, **page 29**

Option 1: **Decoding**

 Informal Assessment

Ask students to read the Phonics Focus words on the inside back cover of *Survival Guide*. If they struggle with decoding, proceed to targeted instruction.

 Targeted Instruction

For words with -ing with no base change: Use the **Word Parts** decoding routine on **page 43** to help the student identify and use inflectional endings.

For words with ch, -tch, sh, and th: Use the **Blends and Digraphs** decoding routine on **page 41** to help build accuracy.

Option 2: **Academic Vocabulary**

 Informal Assessment

Ask students to read a sentence from the book that contains a Smart Word. Have students define the Smart Word and identify text evidence that helped them determine the meaning. Review definitions on pages 2–3 as needed. Repeat with other Smart Words. If students demonstrate proficiency, proceed to targeted instruction.

 Targeted Instruction

Use the **Context Clues** vocabulary routine on **page 48** with the Smart Word *focus* to help the student use context clues to determine meaning.

Option 3: **Fluency**

Informal Assessment

Ask students to read page 4 of *Survival Guide* aloud. To work on pacing, proceed to targeted instruction.

Targeted Instruction

Use pages 4–6 of *Survival Guide* and the **Use Natural, Consistent Pace** fluency routine on **page 51** to have the student practice reading at a natural pace.

Comprehension

Use the questions below and the Graphic Organizer on **page 105** to check comprehension and promote reader response.

After Page 6: *What does the person who works in the deli wonder about? (whether it's okay to take sandwiches and supplies from work)*

After Page 11: *What advice is given about applying for a job you have no experience doing? (Tell the truth. Explain you are willing to learn or be trained.)*

End of Book: *Why is it important to work hard during a summer job? (You may need the job next summer, or you may want your boss to help you get another job.)*

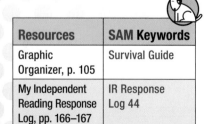

Resources	SAM Keywords
Graphic Organizer, p. 105	Survival Guide
My Independent Reading Response Log, pp. 166–167	IR Response Log 44

Graphic Organizer

Use with
Series 7 & 8

Name ____________________

Survival Guide

Build Understanding

▶ Fill in the chart below with the solution to each problem. An example has been done for you.

Problem	Solution
1. You want to call in sick, but you would be telling a lie. *(Page 7)*	
2. A customer is mean to you every day. *(Page 9)*	Be nice to the customer. This will make your boss happy. It might make the customer happy, too.
3. Your boss is a jerk, and you want to yell at him. *(Page 13)*	
4. You want a raise, but you're too nervous to ask for one. *(Page 15)*	

QuickWrite

▶ Describe one way to "be responsible on the job." Explain your answer using details from the book.

____

____

____

Resource Links
Library Teaching Resources: p. 105
SAM Keyword: Survival Guide

Use with **Library Teaching Resources,** *page 104.*

Unstoppable
by **Neda Hakimi**

Simple   ▲   HL230L

 Genre Social Studies | **Pages** 16 | **Audio CD** 10 min 35 sec | ✓ **Reading Counts!**

UNSTOPPABLE
The True Story of Shadrack Boakye
Neda Hakimi
SCHOLASTIC

Summary

Shadrack Boakye was born in Liberia just before a bloody civil war began. His mother escaped with him to Ghana, where Shadrack's grandmother lived. Shadrack later joined his father in the United States, but he spoke little English and couldn't read. With the help of a teacher who believed in him, he learned to read and discovered his talent for writing. Today, he is an award-winning playwright who runs his own theater company.

Phonics Focus

- Long *a* and *i* with final *e*
- Soft *c* and *g*
- Suffixes *-ment* and *-ness*

See **Master Skills Tracker** in your Teacher's Edition.

Skills Tracker

Preteach | Teach/Practice/Apply | Review/Reinforce | Assess

Smart Words

Words are defined on pages 2–3 of the student book. Page number of first appearance is listed below.

- civilian*, p. 6
- confident, p. 12
- potential*, p. 12
- rebel*, p. 6
- region*, p. 6

*Spanish Cognates, **page 29**

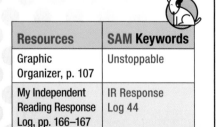

Resources	SAM **Keywords**
Graphic Organizer, p. 107	Unstoppable
My Independent Reading Response Log, pp. 166–167	IR Response Log 44

Option 1: **Decoding**

 Informal Assessment

Ask students to read the Phonics Focus words on the inside back cover of *Unstoppable*. If they struggle with decoding, proceed to targeted instruction.

Targeted Instruction

For words with long *a* and *i* with final *e*, and words with soft *c* and *g*: Have the student use the **Word Sort** decoding routine on **page 45** to sort words by vowel sound, and by soft *c* and *g* spellings.

For words with suffixes *-ment* and *-ness*: Use the **Word Parts** decoding routine on **page 43** to help the student identify and use suffixes.

Option 2: **Academic Vocabulary**

Informal Assessment

Ask students to read a sentence from the book that contains a Smart Word. Have students define the Smart Word and identify text evidence that helped them determine the meaning. Review definitions on pages 2–3 as needed. Repeat this procedure with other Smart Words. If students demonstrate proficiency, proceed to targeted instruction.

Targeted Instruction

The Smart Word *rebel* is the base of the words *rebelled*, *rebelling*, *rebellion*, *rebellious*, and *rebelliously*. Use the **Extending Meaning** vocabulary routine on **page 46** to build student familiarity with morphological word families.

Option 3: **Fluency**

 Informal Assessment

Ask students to read page 12 of *Unstoppable* aloud. To work on pacing, proceed to targeted instruction.

 Targeted Instruction

Use pages 12–13 of *Unstoppable* and the **Use Natural, Consistent Pace** fluency routine on **page 51** to have the student practice correct pacing.

Comprehension

Use the questions below and the Graphic Organizer on **page 107** to check comprehension and promote reader response.

After Page 7: *Why did Shadrack and his mother leave Liberia? (A civil war was going on, and rebels were killing civilians like Shadrack and his family.)*

After Page 10: *How did Shadrack use his imagination in his grandmother's village? (He made up stories about people who passed through on buses.)*

End of Book: *How did Ms. Murphy help Shadrack to change his life? (She helped him learn to read and write, which helped give him confidence to pursue acting and writing.)*

Graphic Organizer

Use with
Series 10

Name ______________________________

Unstoppable

Build Understanding

▶ The book describes many challenges faced by Shadrack and others. Fill in the solution to each problem below. The first one is done for you.

Problem	Solution
1. Rebels were killing civilians in Shadrack's region. *(Page 6)*	Shadrack's mother fled Liberia with Shadrack.
2. Shadrack and his mother needed a new place to live. *(Page 8)*	
3. In the United States, Shadrack struggled to learn English and catch up in school. *(Pages 11–12)*	
4. Many minority and immigrant students continue to struggle in school today. *(Page 15)*	

QuickWrite

▶ The title of this book is *Unstoppable*. How has Shadrack shown that he is "unstoppable"? Cite text evidence in your response.

Resource Links
Library Teaching Resources: p. 107
SAM Keyword: Unstoppable

Use with **Library Teaching Resources,** *page 106.*

Weird Sports Records
by **Daniel Sanchez**

Simple | HL190L

Genre	Pages	Audio CD	✓ Reading
Social Studies	16	10 min 50 sec	Counts!

Summary

Some sports records are weird records. They're not won for being the best at a sport. They're earned for being extreme in other ways. Some teams set records for being the biggest losers in their sport. Other weird records include the longest tennis match, the most ejections from professional baseball games, the biggest NASCAR pile-up—even the most dogs on a surfboard and the fastest racing snail.

Phonics Focus

- Digraph *sh*
- *ch* and *-tch*

See **Master Skills Tracker** in your Teacher's Edition.

Skills Tracker

Preteach Teach/Practice/Apply Review/Reinforce Assess

Smart Words

Words are defined on pages 2–3 of the student book. Page number of first appearance is listed below.

- error*, p. 6
- etiquette*, p. 6
- exercise*, p. 12
- fine, p. 7
- foul, p. 7

*Spanish Cognates, **page 29**

Option 1: Decoding

 Informal Assessment

Ask students to read the Phonics Focus words on the inside back cover of *Weird Sports Records*. If they struggle with decoding, proceed to targeted instruction.

 Targeted Instruction

For words with *sh*, *ch*, and *-tch*: Have the student use the **Word Sort** decoding routine on **page 45** to sort words by spellings *sh*, *ch*, and *-tch*.

Option 2: Academic Vocabulary

 Informal Assessment

Ask students to read a sentence from the book that contains a Smart Word. Have students define the Smart Word and identify text evidence that helped them determine the meaning. Review definitions on pages 2–3 as needed. Repeat this procedure with other Smart Words. If students demonstrate proficiency, proceed to targeted instruction.

Targeted Instruction

The Smart Word *fine* has several possible meanings. Use the **Multiple-Meaning Words** vocabulary routine on **page 47** with *fine* as an example to help the student determine the correct meaning.

Option 3: Fluency

 Informal Assessment

Ask students to read page 10 of *Weird Sports Records* aloud. To work on reading with correct phrasing, proceed to targeted instruction.

 Targeted Instruction

Use pages 10–11 of *Weird Sports Records* and the **Phrasing and Punctuation** fluency routine on **page 50** to have the student practice correct phrasing.

Comprehension

Use the questions below and the Graphic Organizer on **page 109** to check comprehension and promote reader response.

After Page 5: *How did fans "lose" at the Australia vs. American Samoa soccer game?* (Fans "lost" because the game was too lopsided to be exciting.)

After Page 7: *What is a technical foul?* (A technical foul is a foul for bad behavior.)

End of Book: *How fast did Archie the snail travel to set his record?* (Archie the snail raced 13 inches in 2 minutes, 20 seconds.)

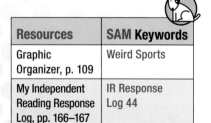

Resources	SAM Keywords
Graphic Organizer, p. 109	Weird Sports
My Independent Reading Response Log, pp. 166–167	IR Response Log 44

Name ______________________________

Weird Sports Records

Build Understanding

▶ Details are words, phrases, and sentences that give information about a topic. Write a detail about each topic from *Weird Sports Records*. The first one is done for you.

Topic	Details
Biggest Losers *(Pages 4–5)*	Slovakia beat Bulgaria 82-0 in hockey.
Hall of Shame *(Pages 6–7)*	
So Long! *(Pages 8–9)*	
Out of Control *(Pages 10–11)*	
Oldest and Youngest *(Pages 12–13)*	
Weird and Wacky *(Pages 14–15)*	

QuickWrite

▶ Choose one sports record from the section "So Long!" What is "weird" about the record? Explain, using text evidence in your response.

____

____

____

____

____

____

Resource Links
Library Teaching Resources: p. 109
SAM Keyword: Weird Sports

Use with **Library Teaching Resources,** *page 108.*

When Lisa Met Billy
by Jorge Ramaldo

Moderate 1 | 220L

| Genre Graphic Novel | Pages 16 | Audio CD 9 min 22 sec | Reading Counts! |

Summary

Lisa gets the female lead in the school play. Billy, a boy Lisa likes, gets the male lead. Unfortunately, Lisa has to drop out of the play to help out at her parents' store, and Angie is given Lisa's role. Billy visits Lisa at work, and the two rehearse. When Angie gets sick, Lisa steps in to save the play and her romance with Billy.

Phonics Focus

- *-ing* with base change
- Review *-ing* with no base change

See **Master Skills Tracker** in your Teacher's Edition.

Skills Tracker

Preteach   Teach/Practice/Apply   Review/Reinforce   Assess

Smart Words

Words are defined on pp. 2–3 of the student book. Page number of first appearance is listed below.

- director*, p. 5
- nervous*, p. 5
- quit, p. 9
- realize, p. 9
- rehearse, p. 5
- role*, p. 4

*Spanish Cognates, **page 29**

Option 1: Decoding

 Informal Assessment

Ask students to read the Phonics Focus words on the inside back cover of *When Lisa Met Billy*. If they struggle with decoding, proceed to targeted instruction.

 Targeted Instruction

For words with *-ing* with and without base change: Use the **Word Parts** decoding routine on **page 43** to help the student identify and use inflectional endings.

Option 2: Academic Vocabulary

 Informal Assessment

Ask students to read a sentence from the book that contains a Smart Word. Have students define the Smart Word and identify text evidence that helped them determine the meaning. Review definitions on pages 2–3 as needed. Repeat with other Smart Words. If students demonstrate proficiency, proceed to targeted instruction.

Targeted Instruction

The Smart Word *quit* has many possible synonyms and antonyms. Use the **Extending Meaning** vocabulary routine on **page 47** to extend meaning.

Option 3: Fluency

 Informal Assessment

Ask students to read page 6 of *When Lisa Met Billy* aloud. To work on expressive reading, proceed to targeted instruction.

 Targeted Instruction

Use pages 6–9 of *When Lisa Met Billy* and the **Read With Expression** fluency routine on **page 53** to have the student practice expressive reading.

Comprehension

Use the questions below and the Graphic Organizer on **page 111** to check comprehension and promote reader response.

After page 7: *What role does Lisa get in the play? (She gets the part of Rosita, the lead role.)*

After page 10: *What two things is Lisa upset about? (She is upset because she can't be in the play. She's also upset because she won't get to spend time with Billy.)*

End of Book: *Why does Lisa get another chance to be in the play? (Angie gets sick and Lisa knows Rosita's lines because she has been practicing with Billy.)*

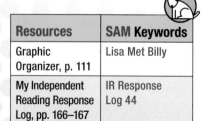

Resources	SAM Keywords
Graphic Organizer, p. 111	Lisa Met Billy
My Independent Reading Response Log, pp. 166–167	IR Response Log 44

Graphic Organizer

Use with Series 8 & 12

Name ______________________________

When Lisa Met Billy

Build Understanding

▶ Fill in the solution to each problem below. Use details from the book. One has been done for you.

Problem	Solution
1. Lisa gets a part in the play, but her parents tell her they need her help in the store.	*Lisa quits the play.*
2. Lisa has to work, but she wants to find a way to see Billy.	
3. Angie gets sick. She can't be in the play.	

QuickWrite

▶ Why does Lisa want to rehearse with Billy when she's not even in the play? Support your answer with evidence from the story.

____

____

____

Resource Links
Library Teaching Resources: p. 111
SAM Keyword: Lisa Met Billy

Use with **Library Teaching Resources,** *page 110.*

Yo, Yolanda! Advice About Friends
by **Kim Feltes and Elsa Reyes**

Moderate 1 ▲ **130L**

| | Genre | Pages | | Audio CD | | Reading |
| | **Life Issues** | **16** | | **8 min 21 sec** | | **Counts!** |

Summary

What do you do when friends talk about you behind your back, a pal borrows money but doesn't return it, or a friend has a crush on your brother? How do you make friends at a new school, or make amends for something you did wrong? Teens write to Yolanda looking for help. Yolanda gives advice about dealing with friends.

Phonics Focus

- **Digraph *sh***

See **Master Skills Tracker** in your Teacher's Edition.

Skills Tracker

Preteach   Teach/Practice/Apply   Review/Reinforce   Assess

Smart Words

Words are defined on pp. 2–3 of the student book. Page number of first appearance is listed below.
- advice, p. 4
- assume, p. 8
- forgive, p. 6
- mistake, p. 4
- problem*, p. 4

*Spanish Cognates, **page 29**

Option 1: **Decoding**

 Informal Assessment

Ask students to read the Phonics Focus words on the inside back cover of *Yo, Yolanda! Advice About Friends*. If they struggle with decoding, proceed to targeted instruction.

 Targeted Instruction

For words with digraph *sh*: Use the **Blends and Digraphs** decoding routine on **page 41** to help the student build accuracy.

Option 2: **Academic Vocabulary**

 Informal Assessment

Ask students to read a sentence from the book that contains a Smart Word. Have students define the Smart Word and identify text evidence that helped them determine the meaning. Review definitions on pages 2–3 as needed. Repeat with other Smart Words. If students demonstrate proficiency, proceed to targeted instruction.

 Targeted Instruction

The idiom *give them another shot* used in the last paragraph of page 6 means "give them another chance," or "let them try again." Build understanding of idioms using the **Idioms** vocabulary routine on **page 49** with this expression as an example.

Option 3: **Fluency**

Informal Assessment

Ask students to read page 14 of *Yo, Yolanda! Advice About Friends* aloud. To work on expressive reading, proceed to targeted instruction.

Targeted Instruction

Use page 14 of *Yo, Yolanda!* and the **Read With Expression** fluency routine on **page 53** to have the student practice expressive reading.

Comprehension

Use the questions below and the Graphic Organizer on **page 113** to check comprehension and promote reader response.

After Page 6: *What does Yolanda say Feeling Trashed should do if her friends say that talking about her was no big deal?* (She advises Feeling Trashed to find new friends.)

After Page 10: *Why is Feeling Used upset at her friend who has a crush on her brother?* (She's upset because her friend comes over all the time, but only wants to see her brother, not her.)

End of Book: *What's Yolanda's advice to the girl who stole her friend's ring?* (Yolanda recommends that she give it back and apologize.)

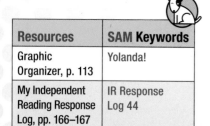

Resources	SAM Keywords
Graphic Organizer, p. 113	Yolanda!
My Independent Reading Response Log, pp. 166–167	IR Response Log 44

Name _____

Yo, Yolanda! Advice About Friends

Build Understanding

▶ The teens in this book write to Yolanda for advice. Fill in the spaces below with the solution that Yolanda suggests. The first one is done for you.

The Teen's Problem	Yolanda's Solution
1. A girl's friends make fun of her clothes and shoes behind her back. [Page 6]	Yolanda says that the girl should tell her friends that they hurt her feelings.
2. A boy's best pal keeps borrowing money but doesn't pay him back. [Page 8]	
3. A girl doesn't like that her friend wants to come over all the time just to see her brother. [Page 10]	
4. A shy girl moves to a new school and needs to make new friends. [Page 12]	
5. A girl feels bad about stealing her friend's ring. [Page 14]	

QuickWrite

▶ *Feeling Used* believes her friend likes her brother. What evidence does she give to support her claim?

_____

_____

_____

Resource Links
Library Teaching Resources: p. 113
SAM Keyword: Yolanda!

Use with **Library Teaching Resources,** *page 112.*

System 44 Library 113

Lesson Plan

Ant Attack!

Based on the short story "Leiningen Versus the Ants" by Carl Stephenson
Adapted by **Michael Leviton**

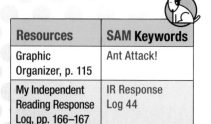

Moderate 1	290L

Genre	Pages	Audio CD	Reading
Classic Retelling	24	16 min	Counts!

Summary

Rodriguez is warned that killer ants will invade his farm. Instead of leaving, he digs two ditches. He fills one with water and the other with fire. The ants find a way to cross the water and wait out the fire, so Rodriguez decides to open a dam and flood his farm to drown the ants. Although Rodriguez stops the invasion, the ants nearly kill him.

Phonics Focus

- Prefixes *pre-* and *re-*
- Long *i igh*
- Other long *i* spellings
- Other long *o* spellings

See **Master Skills Tracker** in your Teacher's Edition.

Skills Tracker

Preteach Teach/Practice/Apply Review/Reinforce Assess

Smart Words

Words are defined on pp. 4–5 of the student book. Page number of first appearance is listed below.

- attack*, p. 8
- drown, p. 10
- horror*, p. 10
- invade*, p. 6
- precaution*, p. 9
- reassure, p. 9

*Spanish Cognates, **page 30**

Option 1: Decoding

 Informal Assessment

Ask students to read the Phonics Focus words on the inside back cover of *Ant Attack!* If they struggle with decoding, proceed to targeted instruction.

Targeted Instruction

For words with prefixes *pre-* and *re-*: Use the **Word Parts** decoding routine on **page 42** to help the student identify and use prefixes.

For words with long *i* and *o* spellings: Have the student use the **Word Sort** decoding routine on **page 45** to sort words by long *i* and long *o* sounds.

Option 2: Academic Vocabulary

 Informal Assessment

Ask students to read a sentence from the book that contains a Smart Word. Have students define the Smart Word and identify text evidence that helped them determine the meaning. Review definitions on pages 4–5 as needed. Repeat with other Smart Words. If students demonstrate proficiency, proceed to targeted instruction.

 Targeted Instruction

Use the **Context Clues** vocabulary routine on **page 48** with the Smart Word *precaution* as an example to help the student use context clues to determine meaning.

Option 3: Fluency

 Informal Assessment

Ask students to read page 18 of *Ant Attack!* aloud. To work on expressive reading, proceed to targeted instruction.

 Targeted Instruction

Use pages 18–19 of *Ant Attack!* and the **Read With Expression** fluency routine on **page 53** to have the student practice expressive reading.

Comprehension

Use the questions below and the Graphic Organizer on **page 115** to check comprehension and promote reader response.

After Chapter 1: *Why doesn't Rodriguez listen to the man who comes to warn him?* (Rodriguez thinks it's ridiculous to be afraid of ants.)

After Chapter 4: *Why don't the two ditches keep the ants away?* (The ants cross the first ditch by walking on each other. The fire in the second ditch will eventually burn out.)

End of Book: *Which of Rodriguez's plans is the most effective? Why?* (Opening the dam is the most effective because it floods the farm and kills the ants.)

Resources	SAM Keywords
Graphic Organizer, p. 115	Ant Attack!
My Independent Reading Response Log, pp. 166–167	IR Response Log 44

Name _____

Ant Attack!

Build Understanding

▶ Read the list of events below. Then write the events in the order in which they happen in the book. The first one is done for you.

Events
Rodriguez runs to open up the dam.
A man on a boat warns Rodriguez about the killer ants.
Workers pick the ants off Rodriguez and carry him to the barn roof.
The workers build two ditches.
Rodriguez ignites the gas to make a wall of fire.

First *A man on a boat warns Rodriguez about the killer ants.*

⬇

Second

⬇

Third

⬇

Fourth

⬇

Last

QuickWrite

▶ When does Rodriguez begin to feel afraid? Why? Explain your answer with evidence from the text.

_____

_____

_____

_____

Resource Links
Library Teaching Resources: p. 115
SAM Keyword: Ant Attack!

Use with Library Teaching Resources, page 114.

System 44 Library 115

Back From the Grave!
Based on a Story by **Guy de Maupassant**
Adapted by **Michael Leviton**

Moderate 1 ◄ **240L**

Genre	Pages	Audio CD	Reading
Classic Retelling	16	9 min 45 sec	Counts!

Summary

After Juliet dies, her father is awakened by the doorbell and finds her at the door. A grave robber had cut off her fingers to steal her rings and woken her from her death-like sleep. Their servant, the robber, drops dead at the sight of Juliet. Juliet is grateful to him, for otherwise she would still be in the coffin.

Phonics Focus

- Suffixes *-y* and *-ly*
- Change *y* to *i*

See **Master Skills Tracker** in your Teacher's Edition.

Skills Tracker

Preteach   Teach/Practice/Apply   Review/Reinforce   Assess

Smart Words

Words are defined on pp. 4–5 of the student book. Page number of first appearance is listed below.

- **bury**, p. 9
- **coffin**, p. 10
- **dream**, p. 11
- **examine***, p. 8
- **remove**, p. 9
- **worry**, p. 8

*Spanish Cognates, **page 30**

Option 1: **Decoding**

 Informal Assessment

Ask students to read the Phonics Focus words on the inside back cover of *Back From the Grave!* If they struggle with decoding, proceed to targeted instruction.

 Targeted Instruction

For words with suffixes *-y* and *-ly*, and words in which *y* changes to *i*: Use the **Word Parts** decoding routine on **page 43** to help the student identify and use suffixes and inflectional endings.

Option 2: **Academic Vocabulary**

 Informal Assessment

Ask students to read a sentence from the book that contains a Smart Word. Have students define the Smart Word and identify text evidence that helped them determine the meaning. Review definitions on pages 4–5 as needed. Repeat with other Smart Words. If students demonstrate proficiency, proceed to targeted instruction.

 Targeted Instruction

The Smart Word *remove* has many possible synonyms and antonyms. Use the **Extending Meaning** vocabulary routine on **page 47** to extend meaning.

Option 3: **Fluency**

 Informal Assessment

Ask students to read page 14 of *Back From the Grave!* aloud. To work on expressive reading, proceed to targeted instruction.

 Targeted Instruction

Use pages 14–15 of *Back From the Grave!* and the **Read With Expression** fluency routine on **page 53** to have the student practice expressive reading.

Comprehension

Use the questions below and the Graphic Organizer on **page 117** to check comprehension and promote reader response.

After Chapter 1: *What gift does Juliet receive from her father? (She receives four rings with red stones.)*

After Chapter 3: *What happens the night after Juliet is buried? (Juliet's father has a dream in which Juliet is crying that she isn't dead. Then the doorbell rings, and standing at the door is a bloody girl who claims to be Juliet.)*

End of Book: *Why is Juliet grateful to Prosper? (She says that if he hadn't robbed her, she'd still be buried alive.)*

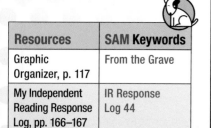

Resources	SAM Keywords
Graphic Organizer, p. 117	From the Grave
My Independent Reading Response Log, pp. 166–167	IR Response Log 44

Graphic Organizer

Use with Series 13

Name ____________________

Back From the Grave!

Build Understanding

▶ Answer the questions below using details from the story. The first one is done for you.

Chapter 1: "Juliet's Death"
What does Juliet die from?

She dies from a weak heart.

Chapter 2: "Sad Good-Byes"
What does Juliet's best friend say about Juliet?

Chapter 3: "The Visitor"
What does Juliet's father see when he opens the door in the middle of the night?

Chapter 4: "Dead or Alive?"
What does Prosper do to Juliet?

QuickWrite

▶ Prosper does a shocking thing. But something good comes out of it. Write at least two sentences to explain how this happens.

____

____

____

Resource Links
Library Teaching Resources: p. 117
SAM Keyword: From the Grave

Use with **Library Teaching Resources,** *page 116.*

Disaster!
by **Sean Price**

Moderate 1 ▲ 330L

Genre Science	**Pages** 24	🎧 **Audio CD** 13 min 35 sec	✓ **Reading Counts!**

Summary

When tornadoes, tsunamis, and hurricanes strike, the result is often disaster. In 1999, tornadoes roar through Oklahoma and other states. In 2004, a tsunami in the Indian Ocean kills over 280,000 people. In 2005, Hurricane Katrina causes the New Orleans levees to break, flooding the city. Read how survivors of these disasters rebuild their homes and their lives.

Phonics Focus

• *com-* and *con-*

See **Master Skills Tracker** in your Teacher's Edition.

Skills Tracker
Preteach | Teach/Practice/Apply | Review/Reinforce | Assess

Smart Words

Words are defined on pp. 4–5 of the student book. Page number of first appearance is listed below.

• aid, p. 16
• damage, p. 6
• escape*, p. 14
• massive*, p. 12
• survivor, p. 16
• warning, p. 10

*Spanish Cognates, **page 30**

Option 1: **Decoding**

 Informal Assessment

Ask students to read the Phonics Focus words on the inside back cover of *Disaster!* If they struggle with decoding, proceed to targeted instruction.

 Targeted Instruction

For words with *com-* and *con-*: Use the **Word Parts** decoding routine on **page 42** to help the student identify and use prefixes.

Option 2: **Academic Vocabulary**

 Informal Assessment

Ask students to read a sentence from the book that contains a Smart Word. Have students define the Smart Word and identify text evidence that helped them determine the meaning. Review definitions on pages 4–5 as needed. Repeat with other Smart Words. If students demonstrate proficiency, proceed to targeted instruction.

Targeted Instruction

The Smart Word *aid* has many possible synonyms and antonyms. Use the **Extending Meaning** vocabulary routine on **page 47** to extend meaning.

Option 3: **Fluency**

 Informal Assessment

Ask students to read page 6 of *Disaster!* aloud. To work on pacing, proceed to targeted instruction.

 Targeted Instruction

Use pages 6–8 of *Disaster!* and the **Use Natural, Consistent Pace** fluency routine on **page 51** to have the student practice correct pacing.

Comprehension

Use the questions below and the Graphic Organizer on **page 119** to check comprehension and promote reader response.

After Chapter 1: *What happens to Kaci's home during the tornado?* (The power goes out, the outer walls shake apart, and then the roof flies off.)

After Chapter 2: *What kind of damage does the 2004 tsunami cause?* (It kills at least 280,000 people and leaves survivors homeless.)

End of Book: *Why did some people remain in New Orleans after they got the hurricane warning?* (Some people were too old. Some were sick. Some had no car.)

Resources	SAM Keywords
Graphic Organizer, p. 119	Disaster!
My Independent Reading Response Log, pp. 166–167	IR Response Log 44

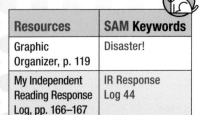

Name _____

Disaster!

Build Understanding

▶ Kaci, Fitri, and Troy all survive disasters. Imagine that they can all speak to each other. What would they tell each other about their experiences? Write what they would say. Use details from the book.

1. Kaci *(Chapter 1)*　　　**2. Fitri** *(Chapter 2)*　　　**3. Troy** *(Chapter 3)*

QuickWrite

▶ Describe two ways that people around the world respond to the tsunami disaster. Use evidence from the text to support your answer.

_____

_____

_____

El Tiburón, "The Shark"
by Patrick Daley

 Simple 340L

	Genre	Pages	🎧	Audio CD	✓	Reading
	Social Studies	16		9 min 57 sec		Counts!

Summary

Sergio is paralyzed after a terrible car accident. At first he is depressed, but he finds purpose for his life by training to be a long-distance swimmer. With determination and support from his brother Marcos, he swims the Strait of Gibraltar and becomes famous.

Phonics Focus

- Silent letters *wr-* and *-mb*
- *ph*
- Digraph *wh-*
- Review endings *-ed, -ing*

See **Master Skills Tracker** in your Teacher's Edition.

Skills Tracker

Preteach   Teach/Practice/Apply   Review/Reinforce   Assess

Smart Words

Words are defined on pp. 4–5 of the student book. Page number of first appearance is listed below.

- accident*, p. 6
- attempt, p. 9
- complete*, p. 12
- hope, p. 8
- purpose*, p. 9
- support, p. 9

*Spanish Cognates, **page 30**

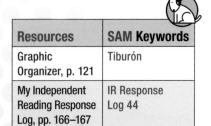

Resources	SAM Keywords
Graphic Organizer, p. 121	Tiburón
My Independent Reading Response Log, pp. 166–167	IR Response Log 44

Option 1: **Decoding**

 Informal Assessment

Ask students to read the Phonics Focus words on the inside back cover of *El Tiburón*. If they struggle with decoding, proceed to targeted instruction.

 Targeted Instruction

For words with digraph *wh-*: Use the **Blends and Digraphs** decoding routine on **page 41** to help the student build accuracy.

For words with *-ed* and *-ing*: Use the **Word Parts** decoding routine on **page 43** to help students identify and use inflectional endings.

Option 2: **Academic Vocabulary**

Informal Assessment

Ask students to read a sentence from the book that contains a Smart Word. Have students define the Smart Word and identify text evidence that helped them determine the meaning. Review definitions on pages 4–5 as needed. Repeat with other Smart Words. If students demonstrate proficiency, proceed to targeted instruction.

Targeted Instruction

The Smart Word *support* is the base of the words *supporters*, *supportive*, and *supporting*. Use the **Extending Meaning** vocabulary routine on **page 46** to build the student's familiarity with morphological word families.

Option 3: **Fluency**

 Informal Assessment

Ask students to read page 8 of *El Tiburón* aloud. To practice correct phrasing, proceed to targeted instruction.

 Targeted Instruction

Use pages 8–9 of *El Tiburón* and the **Phrasing and Punctuation** fluency routine on **page 50** to have the student practice correct phrasing.

Comprehension

Use the questions below and the Graphic Organizer on **page 121** to check comprehension and promote reader response.

After Chapter 1: *What happens to Sergio? (He becomes paralyzed in a car accident and can't walk.)*

After Chapter 2: *What makes Sergio happy again? (He becomes a long-distance swimmer and feels he has a purpose again.)*

End of Book: *Why does Sergio become famous? (He is the first disabled person to swim the Strait of Gibraltar.)*

Name _____

El Tiburón, "The Shark"

Build Understanding

▶ Events from the story are listed in the box. Write each event in the order it occurs in the story. The first one is done for you.

Events	
Sergio hires a swimming coach.	
Sergio swims for 24 hours in Marcos's honor.	
Sergio breaks his spine.	
Sergio swims the Strait of Gibraltar.	
Sergio dreams that the ocean speaks to him.	

First
Sergio breaks his spine.

Second

Next

Then

Last

QuickWrite

▶ Sergio faced many challenges. Pick one challenge and explain how Sergio was able to overcome it. Use details from the book to support your answer.

_____

_____

_____

_____

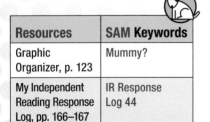

Have You Seen My Mummy?
by **Sara Singh**

| Simple | HL320L |

| | Genre
Science | Pages
16 | Audio CD
10 min 44 sec | Reading
Counts |

Summary

Until 1950, the Anga people of Papua, New Guinea mummified their dead. The last Anga made into a mummy was the father of Gemtasu, the current Anga chief. Recently, the mummy had begun to decay. With help from a mummy expert, Gemtasu restored his father's mummy. This books tells the story, and explains how Anga mummies were made.

Phonics Focus

- *y* as a vowel
- Suffixes –*y* and –*ly*
- Silent consonants
- Open syllables
- Unstressed open syllables

See **Master Skills Tracker** in your Teacher's Edition.

Skills Tracker

Preteach Teach/Practice/Apply Review/Reinforce Assess

Smart Words

Words are defined on pages 4–5 of the student book. Page number of first appearance is listed below.

- convince*, p. 7
- corpse, p. 9
- decay, p. 8
- preserve*, p. 10
- process*, p. 13

*Spanish Cognates, **page 30**

Option 1: **Decoding**

 Informal Assessment

Ask students to read the Phonics Focus words on the inside back cover of *Have You Seen My Mummy?* If they struggle with decoding, proceed to targeted instruction.

 Targeted Instruction

For words with suffixes –*ly* and -*y*: Use the **Word Parts** decoding routine on **page 43** to help identify and use suffixes.

For words with open syllables and unstressed open syllables: Use the **Syllable Strategies** routine on **page 40** to help determine the correct vowel sounds in open and unstressed open syllables.

Option 2: **Academic Vocabulary**

Informal Assessment

Ask students to read a sentence from *Have You Seen My Mummy?* that contains a Smart Word. Have students define the Smart Word and identify text evidence that helped them determine the meaning. Review definitions on pages 4–5 as needed. Repeat with other Smart Words. If students demonstrate proficiency, proceed to targeted instruction.

Targeted Instruction

The idiom "pay respect" on page 8 means "to express admiration and respect." Build understanding of idioms using the **Idioms** vocabulary routine on **page 49** with this expression as an example.

Option 3: **Fluency**

Informal Assessment

Ask students to read page 10 of *Have You Seen My Mummy?* aloud. To work on reading with correct phrasing, proceed to targeted instruction.

Targeted Instruction

Use pages 10–11 of *Have You Seen My Mummy?* and the **Use Natural, Consistent Pace** fluency routine on **page 51** to have the student practice correct phrasing.

Comprehension

Use the questions below and the Graphic Organizer on **page 123** to check comprehension and promote reader response.

After Page 8: *Why did Gemtasu get upset when he saw his father's mummy?* (The mummy was decaying and falling apart.)

After Page 9: *What always needs to happen to stop a corpse from decaying?* (Bacteria must be stopped from living and multiplying on the corpse.)

End of Book: *How might the Anga use Ron Beckett's knowledge in the future?* (The Anga might use Ron's process to restore other decaying mummies.)

Resources	SAM Keywords
Graphic Organizer, p. 123	Mummy?
My Independent Reading Response Log, pp. 166–167	IR Response Log 44

Name _____

Have You Seen My Mummy?

Build Understanding

▶ How did Gemtasu and Ron Beckett deal with decaying mummies? Fill in the
solution to each problem on the chart below. The first one is done for you.

Problem	Solution
1. Gemtasu discovered that his father's mummy was falling apart.	• Gemtasu and his friend Ulla asked an expert to help.
2. The father's mummy had holes and its skin was falling off.	• Ron Beckett used...
3. Fluids were causing the mummy to decay.	
4. Other Anga mummies were rotting, too.	

QuickWrite

▶ How did Ron Beckett save the mummy? Use the information in Chapter 3 to
help you write your answer.

_____

_____

_____

_____

_____

Resource Links
Library Teaching Resources: p. 123
SAM Keyword: Mummy?

Use with **Library Teaching Resources,** page 122.

System 44 Library 123

Lesson Plan

Killer Plague
by **Trina Robbins**

Moderate 1   **GN220L**

Genre	Pages	Audio CD	Reading
Fiction	**24**	**15 min 19 sec**	**Counts!**

Summary

In 2050, a deadly virus escapes a science lab and causes a worldwide plague. Soon, healthy people have formed gated communities to keep out the sick. When a brother and sister run away from their community, a doctor shelters them in an abandoned medical clinic—and together, the three make a discovery that could lead to a vaccine.

Phonics Focus

- **Long *a* vowel teams in single and multisyllabic words**

See **Master Skills Tracker** in your Teacher's Edition.

Skills Tracker
Preteach   Teach/Practice/Apply   Review/Reinforce   Assess

Smart Words

Words are defined on pages 4–5 of the student book. Page number of first appearance is listed below.

- **contagious*, p. 6**
- **extinct*, p. 6**
- **inoculate*, p. 7**
- **isolate, p. 19**
- **tissue p. 6**
- **virus*, p. 6**

*Spanish Cognates, **page 30**

Option 1: **Decoding**

 Informal Assessment

Ask students to read the Phonics Focus words on the inside back cover of *Killer Plague*. If they struggle with decoding, proceed to targeted instruction.

 Targeted Instruction

For words with long *a* vowel teams: Have the student use the **Word Sort** decoding routine on **page 45** to sort words by *ai* and *ay* spellings. Review that both spellings stand for the long *a* sound.

Option 2: **Academic Vocabulary**

 Informal Assessment

Ask students to read a sentence from *Killer Plague* that contains a Smart Word from the inside back cover. Have students define the Smart Word and identify evidence in the text that helped them determine the meaning. Review definitions on pages 4–5 as needed. Repeat this procedure with other Smart Words. If students demonstrate proficiency, proceed to targeted instruction.

 Targeted Instruction

Use the **Context Clues** vocabulary routine on **page 48** with the Smart Word *tissue* as an example to help the student use context clues to determine meaning.

Option 3: **Fluency**

 Informal Assessment

Ask students to read page 6 of *Killer Plague* aloud. To work on reading with correct phrasing, proceed to targeted instruction.

Targeted Instruction

Use pages 6–7 of *Killer Plague* and the **Phrasing and Punctuation** fluency routine on **page 50** to have the student practice correct phrasing.

Comprehension

Use the questions below and the Graphic Organizer on **page 125** to check comprehension and promote reader response.

After Page 9: *How did the virus spread so quickly from Dan Payton to people around the world?* (The virus is highly contagious and Dan Payton went to the Olympics, an event attended by people from all over the world.)

After Page 14: *Why did Dr. Hassan hide Malik and Layla's plague symptoms?* (Dr. Hassan did not want his children to be kicked out of the gated community, as he later was when he got sick.)

End of Book: *How did antibodies help Layla, Malik, and Dr. Manfred?* (The antibodies identified the disease so that cells in their bodies could fight it.)

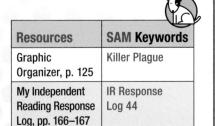

Resources	SAM Keywords
Graphic Organizer, p. 125	Killer Plague
My Independent Reading Response Log, pp. 166–167	IR Response Log 44

Name ______________________________

Killer Plague

Build Understanding

▶ Read the list of events below. Then write the events in the order they happened in the book. The first one is done for you.

Events
Malik and Layla survive the plague.

Dan Payton gets sick with the plague at the Olympics.

Oil workers find an ancient mastodon.

Malik and Layla meet Dr. Manfred.

Dr. Manfred discovers antibodies to the plague.

First *Oil workers find an ancient mastodon.*

Second

Third

Fourth

Last

QuickWrite

▶ At the end of the book, Malik wants to find the outsiders. Why? Write a few sentences to explain. Use details from the book.

____

____

____

____

Resource Links
Library Teaching Resources: p. 125
SAM Keyword: Killer Plague

Use with **Library Teaching Resources,** *page 124.*

Lesson Plan

Left to Die
by **Nancy Honovich**

Moderate 1 350L

Genre	Pages		Audio CD		Reading
Science	**24**		**15 min 31 sec**		**Counts!**

Summary

Joe and Simon challenge themselves to a dangerous mountain climb up the Siula Grande in Peru. They reach the top successfully, but Joe breaks his leg on the climb down. Simon lowers Joe down the mountain with a rope, but then Joe falls into a crevasse. Sure that Joe is dead, Simon leaves him behind to save himself. Joe crawls out of the crevasse back to camp. He shocks Simon, who can't believe Joe is still alive.

Phonics Focus

- **Long *o* vowel teams *oa* and *ow***

See **Master Skills Tracker** in your Teacher's Edition.

Skills Tracker

Preteach   Teach/Practice/Apply   Review/Reinforce   Assess

Smart Words

Words are defined on pp. 4–5 of the student book. Page number of first appearance is listed below.
- **approach, p. 8**
- **gear, p. 8**
- **glacier*, p. 7**
- **struggle, p. 15**
- **summit, p. 8**
- **vertical*, p. 6**

*Spanish Cognates, **page 31**

Option 1: **Decoding**

 Informal Assessment

Ask students to read the Phonics Focus words on the inside back cover of *Left to Die*. If they struggle with decoding, proceed to targeted instruction.

 Targeted Instruction

For words with long *o* vowel teams *oa* and *ow*: Use the **Word Sort** decoding routine on **page 45** to sort words by *oa* and *ow* spellings. Review that both spellings can stand for the long *o* sound.

Option 2: **Academic Vocabulary**

 Informal Assessment

Ask students to read a sentence from the book that contains a Smart Word. Have students define the Smart Word and identify text evidence that helped them determine the meaning. Review definitions on pages 4–5 as needed. Repeat with other Smart Words. If students demonstrate proficiency, proceed to targeted instruction.

 Targeted Instruction

Use the **Context Clues** vocabulary routine on **page 48** with the Smart Word *vertical* as an example to help the student use context clues to determine meaning.

Option 3: **Fluency**

 Informal Assessment

Ask students to read page 14 of *Left to Die* aloud. To practice expressive reading, proceed to targeted instruction.

 Targeted Instruction

Use pages 14–15 of *Left to Die* and the **Read With Expression** fluency routine on **page 53** to have the student practice reading in a varied, expressive tone.

Comprehension

Use the questions below and the Graphic Organizer on **page 127** to check comprehension and promote reader response.

After Chapter 1: *What goal did Joe and Simon have at the beginning of their trip?* (*Joe and Simon wanted to climb the West Face of Siula Grande.*)

After Chapter 4: *After Joe breaks his leg, what does Simon do to help him?* (*He tries to lower Joe down the mountain.*)

End of Book: *How does Joe make it back to camp?* (*He crawls for days.*)

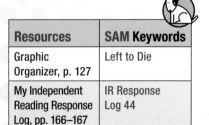

Resources	SAM Keywords
Graphic Organizer, p. 127	Left to Die
My Independent Reading Response Log, pp. 166–167	IR Response Log 44

Name ______________________________

Left to Die

Build Understanding

▶ Joe and Simon face many problems on their climb. Fill in the chart below with the solution to each problem. An example has been done for you.

Problem	Solution
1. Joe breaks his leg. *(Page 14)*	Simon lowers Joe down by ropes.
2. The heavy rope starts to pull Simon down. *(Page 18)*	
3. Joe can't climb up the ice walls of the crevasse. *(Pages 19-20)*	
4. Joe has to get back to camp. *(Page 21)*	

QuickWrite

▶ Why was Joe's solution to problem #3 risky? Use evidence from the text to support your answer.

____

____

____

____

Resource Links
Library Teaching Resources: p. 127
SAM Keyword: Left to Die

Use with **Library Teaching Resources,** *page 126.*

Medical Miracle
by **Allison Langley**

Simple 340L

Genre	Pages	Audio CD	Reading
Science	**16**	**9 min 32 sec**	**Counts!**

Summary

Milagros is born with mermaid syndrome, a condition in which the legs are fused together like a mermaid's tail. Her parents appeal for help, and Dr. Luis Rubio agrees to perform the difficult surgery for free. People across Peru watch the surgery live on TV. Milagros still needs other surgeries, but today she is able to walk.

Phonics Focus

- **Open syllables**
- **Unstressed open syllables**

See **Master Skills Tracker** in your Teacher's Edition.

Skills Tracker

Preteach Teach/Practice/Apply Review/Reinforce Assess

Smart Words

Words are defined on pp. 4–5 of the student book. Page number of first appearance is listed below.

- **artery*, p. 9**
- **fused*, p. 6**
- **prepare*, p. 10**
- **stretch, p. 10**
- **surgery*, p. 9**
- **syndrome*, p. 7**

*Spanish Cognates, **page 31**

Option 1: **Decoding**

 Informal Assessment

Ask students to read the Phonics Focus words on the inside back cover of *Medical Miracle*. If they struggle with decoding, proceed to targeted instruction.

Targeted Instruction

For words with open syllables and unstressed open syllables: Use the **Syllable Strategies** decoding routine on **page 40** to help the student determine the correct vowel sounds in unstressed open syllables.

Option 2: **Academic Vocabulary**

 Informal Assessment

Ask students to read a sentence from the book that contains a Smart Word. Have students define the Smart Word and identify text evidence that helped them determine the meaning. Review definitions on pages 4–5 as needed. Repeat with other Smart Words. If students demonstrate proficiency, proceed to targeted instruction.

Targeted Instruction

Use the **Context Clues** vocabulary routine on **page 48** with the Smart Word *artery* to help the student use context clues to determine meaning.

Option 3: **Fluency**

 Informal Assessment

Ask students to read page 6 of *Medical Miracle* aloud. To work on pacing, proceed to targeted instruction.

Targeted Instruction

Use pages 6–8 of *Medical Miracle* and the **Use Natural, Consistent Pace** fluency routine on **page 51** to have the student practice reading at a natural pace.

Comprehension

Use the questions below and the Graphic Organizer on **page 129** to check comprehension and promote reader response.

After Chapter 1: *What makes Milagros different from other babies? (She is born with her legs fused together.)*

After Chapter 2: *Why does Dr. Rubio put balloons under Milagros's skin? (He does this to stretch her skin so that there will be enough skin to cover both legs after they are separated.)*

End of Book: *What challenges will Milagros face in the future? (She will need to have more surgeries. She will have problems with her kidneys because they don't work well.)*

Resources	SAM Keywords
Graphic Organizer, p. 129	Milagros
My Independent Reading Response Log, pp. 166–167	IR Response Log 44

Name _____

Medical Miracle

Build Understanding

▶ Milagros's parents and doctor face many problems in trying to help her. Fill in the solution to each problem listed below. The first one is done for you.

Problem	Solution
1. Milagros is born with her two legs fused together. *(Chapter 1)*	*Milagros needs an operation to separate her legs.*
2. Sara and Ricardo have no money to help their baby. *(Chapter 1)*	
3. Milagros doesn't have enough skin to cover both legs. *(Chapter 2)*	
4. Milagros has weak kidneys and feet that are not straight. *(Chapter 3)*	

QuickWrite

▶ Why was Milagros's story shown on TV? Explain your answer with evidence from the text.

_____

_____

_____

_____

Lesson Plan

Music Mash-Up
by **Zhang Li**

Moderate 1 | HL330L

Genre	Pages	Audio CD	Reading
Arts	**24**	**18 min 40 sec**	**Counts!**

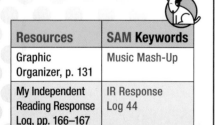

Summary

American musicians and performers have invented and developed many popular types of music over the years. This book explores the origins and defining characteristics of four music genres—jazz, country, rock and roll, and hip hop—and introduces some of the performers who made each genre famous.

Phonics Focus

- Review endings *-ed* and *-ing*
- Review suffixes *-y* and *-ly*
- Prefixes *re-* and *pre-*

See **Master Skills Tracker** in your Teacher's Edition.

Skills Tracker

Preteach Teach/Practice/Apply Review/Reinforce Assess

Smart Words

Words are defined on pages 4–5 of the student book. Page number of first appearance is listed below.

- **emerge***, p. 8
- **entertainer**, p. 7
- **imitate***, p. 12
- **improvise***, p. 8
- **perform**, p. 8
- **reflect***, p. 12

*Spanish Cognates, **page 31**

Option 1: **Decoding**

 Informal Assessment

Ask students to read the Phonics Focus words on the inside back cover of *Music Mash-Up*. If they struggle with decoding, proceed to targeted instruction.

 Targeted Instruction

For words ending in *-ed*, *-ing*, *-y*, and *-ly*, and for words with prefixes *re-* and *pre-*: Use the **Word Parts** decoding routines on **pages 42–43** to identify and use prefixes, suffixes, and inflectional endings.

Option 2: **Academic Vocabulary**

 Informal Assessment

Ask students to read a sentence from the book that contains a Smart Word. Have students define the Smart Word and identify evidence in the text that helped them determine the meaning. Review definitions on pages 4–5 as needed. Repeat with other Smart Words. If students demonstrate proficiency, proceed to targeted instruction.

 Targeted Instruction

The Smart Word *imitate* has many possible synonyms and antonyms. Use the **Extending Meaning** vocabulary routine on **page 47** to extend meaning.

Option 3: **Fluency**

 Informal Assessment

Ask students to read page 6 of *Music Mash-Up* aloud. To work on pacing, proceed to targeted instruction.

 Targeted Instruction

Use pages 6–7 of *Music Mash-Up* and the **Use Natural, Consistent Pace** fluency routine on **page 51** to have the student practice correct pacing.

Comprehension

Use the questions below and the Graphic Organizer on **page 131** to check comprehension and promote reader response.

After Page 8: *How and when did jazz music spread from New Orleans to the northern United States? (In the 1920s, many black Americans moved to the North and took jazz music with them.)*

After Page 16: *How did African Americans help define rock and roll? (They used blues rhythms but played them fast.)*

End of Book: *What are some characteristics of hip hop music? (DJs spin records and mix songs together; they rap; they play "breaks" over and over.)*

Resources	SAM Keywords
Graphic Organizer, p. 131	Music Mash-Up
My Independent Reading Response Log, pp. 166–167	IR Response Log 44

Name _____

Music Mash-Up

Build Understanding

▶ Imagine that you interview some entertainers from *Music Mash-Up*. What might they tell you about themselves and their music? Fill in the speech bubbles. Write a response for each entertainer, using details from the text.

Jimmie Rodgers
(Chapter 2)

Elvis Presley
(Chapter 3)

Kool Herc
(Chapter 4)

QuickWrite

▶ A music "mash-up" is a blend of different styles. Choose one music style in the book. What is "mashed up" about it? Explain, using text evidence.

_____

_____

_____

_____

Lesson Plan

Play Ball!
by **Carmen Mendes**

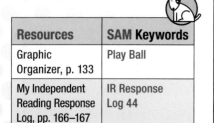

Moderate 1 ◀ **310L**

Genre	Pages	Audio CD	✓ Reading
Social Studies	**16**	**11 min 9 sec**	**Counts!**

Summary

Baseball may be the great American pastime, but the game has roots in medieval English bat-and-ball games, and perhaps even in games invented by the ancient Maya. This book follows the evolution of baseball from its earliest days to its arrival in the United States. The book then presents the development of integrated, modern American baseball and the spread of baseball around the world, to baseball-loving countries such as Cuba and Japan.

Phonics Focus

• **Words with *com-* and *con-***

See **Master Skills Tracker** in your Teacher's Edition.

Skills Tracker

Preteach Teach/Practice/Apply Review/Reinforce Assess

Smart Words

Words are defined on pages 4–5 of the student book. Page number of first appearance is listed below.

• **complex***, p. 7
• **element***, p. 7
• **evolve***, p. 10
• **medieval***, p. 7
• **origin***, p. 7
• **pastime** p. 6

*Spanish Cognates, **page 31**

Option 1: **Decoding**

 Informal Assessment

Ask students to read the Phonics Focus words on the inside back cover of *Play Ball!* If they struggle with decoding, proceed to targeted instruction.

 Targeted Instruction

For words with *com-* and *con-*: Use the **Word Parts** decoding routine on **page 42** to help the student identify and use prefixes.

Option 2: **Academic Vocabulary**

 Informal Assessment

Ask students to read a sentence from *Play Ball!* that contains a Smart Word from the inside back cover. Have students define the Smart Word and identify evidence in the text that helped them determine the meaning. Review definitions on pages 4–5 as needed. Repeat this procedure with other Smart Words. If students demonstrate proficiency, proceed to targeted instruction.

 Targeted Instruction

Use the **Context Clues** vocabulary routine on **page 48** with the Smart Word *evolve* as an example to help the student use context clues to determine meaning.

Option 3: **Fluency**

 Informal Assessment

Ask students to read page 6 of *Play Ball!* aloud. To work on reading with correct phrasing, proceed to targeted instruction.

 Targeted Instruction

Use pages 6–7 of *Play Ball!* and the **Phrasing and Punctuation** fluency routine on **page 50** to have the student practice correct phrasing.

Comprehension

Use the questions below and the Graphic Organizer on **page 133** to check comprehension and promote reader response.

After Page 10: *How did Alexander Cartwright make town ball safer for runners?* (Under Cartwright's new rules, fielders could no longer throw a runner out by hitting him with the ball.)

After Page 13: *How did Brooklyn Dodgers' president Branch Rickey improve baseball?* (Rickey hired the first African-American and Latino players in modern pro baseball, leading to the integration of the sport.)

End of Book: *How did baseball spread from the United States to other countries?* (An American man taught his students to play it. Cuban students attending school in the United States learned the rules of the game; they brought baseball home with them.)

Resources	SAM Keywords
Graphic Organizer, p. 133	Play Ball
My Independent Reading Response Log, pp. 166–167	IR Response Log 44

Use with
Series 14

Name ______________________________

Play Ball!

Build Understanding

▶ Write a short summary of each chapter of the book. Use key ideas and details from each chapter. Chapter 1 has been done for you.

Chapter 1: "Baseball Beginnings"

Modern baseball evolved from much older bat-and-ball games. The ancient Maya played a game that included elements of baseball. People in medieval England played a baseball-type game called stoolball.

Chapter 2: "Baseball in America"

____

____

Chapter 3: "Baseball Grows Up"

____

____

Chapter 4: "Baseball Around the World"

____

____

QuickWrite

▶ Baseball has changed in many ways over the years. Which change described in this book was the most important? Argue your position in a few sentences. Use evidence from the text to support your argument.

____

____

____

Resource Links
Library Teaching Resources: p. 133
SAM Keyword: Play Ball

Use with **Library Teaching Resources,** *page 132.*

Samurai Fighters

by **Mel Friedman**

Moderate 1 | 300L

| Genre Social Studies | Pages 24 | Audio CD 15 min 46 sec | Reading Counts! |

Summary

The first Japanese samurai are warriors who serve and fight for the rich. Eventually, samurai gain independence. Their leader, the shogun, becomes more powerful than the emperor of Japan. Skilled samurai like the swordswoman Tomoe become legends. The shogun brings peace to Japan, but this creates less need for samurai. Unemployed samurai, called ronin, must find other work. Musashi is the last great samurai.

Phonics Focus

- **Long _e_ vowel teams _ea_, _ee_, and _ie_**

See **Master Skills Tracker** in your Teacher's Edition.

Skills Tracker

Preteach   Teach/Practice/Apply   Review/Reinforce   Assess

Smart Words

Words are defined on pp. 4–5 of the student book. Page number of first appearance is listed below.

- **clan*, p. 7**
- **defeat, p. 9**
- **emperor*, p. 8**
- **enemy*, p. 9**
- **legend*, p. 8**
- **samurai*, p. 7**

*Spanish Cognates, **page 32**

Option 1: **Decoding**

 Informal Assessment

Ask students to read the Phonics Focus words on the inside back cover of _Samurai Fighters_. If they struggle with decoding, proceed to targeted instruction.

 Targeted Instruction

For words with vowel teams _ea_, _ee_, and _ie_: Have the student use the **Word Sort** decoding routine on **page 45** to sort words by _ee_, _ea_, and _ie_ spellings. Review that all three spellings can stand for the long _e_ sound.

Option 2: **Academic Vocabulary**

 Informal Assessment

Ask students to read a sentence from the book that contains a Smart Word. Have students define the Smart Word and identify text evidence that helped them determine the meaning. Review definitions on pages 4–5 as needed. Repeat with other Smart Words. If students demonstrate proficiency, proceed to targeted instruction.

 Targeted Instruction

Use the **Context Clues** vocabulary routine on **page 48** with the Smart Word _legend_ as an example to help the student use context clues to determine meaning.

Option 3: **Fluency**

 Informal Assessment

Ask students to read page 7 of _Samurai Fighters_ aloud. To work on pacing, proceed to targeted instruction.

 Targeted Instruction

Use pages 7–9 of _Samurai Fighters_ and the **Use Natural, Consistent Pace** fluency routine on **page 51** to have the student practice correct pacing.

Comprehension

Use the questions below and the Graphic Organizer on **page 135** to check comprehension and promote reader response.

After Chapter 1: _Why do Yoshiie's fighters respect him more than the emperor?_ (The emperor refuses to pay them, but Yoshiie rewards them.)

After Chapter 3: _Who are the ronin, and what do they do to make money?_ (Ronin are former samurai who try to make money in other ways.)

End of Book: _Why does Musashi become a legend?_ (He is never defeated in battle. His book about sword fighting is still read today.)

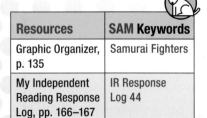

Resources	SAM Keywords
Graphic Organizer, p. 135	Samurai Fighters
My Independent Reading Response Log, pp. 166–167	IR Response Log 44

Name _____

Samurai Fighters

Build Understanding

▶ Fill in the circles with details about the samurai. You may describe their skills, behavior, clothing, and jobs. An example has been done for you.

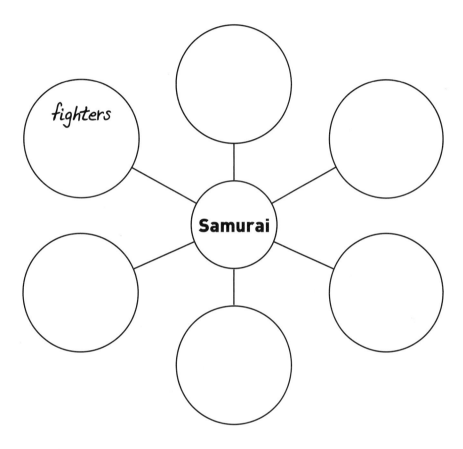

QuickWrite

▶ It's time to hire a new samurai. Write a job ad that describes the skills needed. Use at least two details from the book in your description.

_____

_____

_____

Lesson Plan

The Story of Shi Jin

by **Jennifer Tench**

Moderate 1 | 220L

Genre	Pages	Audio CD	Reading
World Literature	16	9 min 48 sec	Counts!

Summary

In this retelling of an ancient Chinese story, a teen named Shi Jin learns martial arts from a master fighter who is on the run from a powerful and corrupt leader named Gao. Shi Jin becomes leader of his village after his father dies. He defends the village against outlaws. But once he learns the outlaws are battling the villain Gao, he not only helps the outlaws—he leaves the village and joins the outlaws in their fight against Gao.

Phonics Focus

- **Long e vowel teams ea, ee, and ie**

See **Master Skills Tracker** in your Teacher's Edition.

Skills Tracker

Preteach Teach/Practice/Apply Review/Reinforce Assess

Smart Words

Words are defined on pages 4–5 of the student book. Page number of first appearance is listed below.

- defend*, p. 15
- novel*, p. 6
- offer*, p. 11
- outlaw, p. 6
- revenge, p. 11
- villain*, p. 6

*Spanish Cognates, **page 32**

Option 1: **Decoding**

Informal Assessment

Ask students to read the Phonics Focus words on the inside back cover of *The Story of Shi Jin*. If they struggle with decoding, proceed to targeted instruction.

Targeted Instruction

For words with long e vowel teams: Have the student use the **Word Sort** decoding routine on **page 45** to sort words by *ea*, *ee*, and *ie* spellings. Review that all three spellings stand for the long e sound.

Option 2: **Academic Vocabulary**

Informal Assessment

Ask students to read a sentence from the book that contains a Smart Word. Have students define the Smart Word and identify text evidence that helped them determine the meaning. Review definitions on pages 4–5 as needed. Repeat with other Smart Words. If students demonstrate proficiency, proceed to targeted instruction.

Targeted Instruction

The Smart Word *defend* is the base of the words *defended, defender, defense, defensive, defenseless,* and *undefended*. Use the **Extending Meaning** vocabulary routine on **page 46** to build student familiarity with morphological word families.

Option 3: **Fluency**

Informal Assessment

Ask students to read page 6 of *The Story of Shi Jin* aloud. To work on reading with correct phrasing, proceed to targeted instruction.

Targeted Instruction

Use pages 6–7 of *The Story of Shi Jin* and the **Phrasing and Punctuation** fluency routine on **page 50** to have the student practice correct phrasing.

Comprehension

Use the questions below and the Graphic Organizer on **page 137** to check comprehension and promote reader response.

After Page 11: *Why does Wang Jin come to Shi Jin's village? (Wang Jin is fleeing the army leader Gao, who wants to kill Wang Jin.)*

After Page 18: *How does Shi Jin's plan to defend the village work out? (The plan succeeds. Shi Jin and the villagers defeat the thieves and capture Chen Da.)*

End of Book: *Why does Shi Jin sneak away without telling the police or the villagers what he is doing? (Shi Jin thinks the people of the village will not understand why he wants to help the thieves who tried to rob them.)*

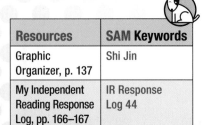

Resources	SAM Keywords
Graphic Organizer, p. 137	Shi Jin
My Independent Reading Response Log, pp. 166–167	IR Response Log 44

Use with Series 17

Name ____________________

The Story of Shi Jin

Build Understanding

▶ Read the list of events below. Write the events in the order in which they happen in the book. The first one is done for you.

Events

Shi Jin becomes the leader of his village.

Wang Jin teaches Shi Jin to be an expert fighter.

Shi Jin becomes an outlaw fighting Gao.

Shi Jin's father dies.

Shi Jin defends his village from thieves.

First Wang Jin teaches Shi Jin to be an expert fighter.

Second

Third

Fourth

Last

QuickWrite

▶ Why does Shi Jin release Chen Da? Cite text evidence in your response.

____

____

____

Resource Links

Library Teaching Resources: p. 137

SAM Keyword: Shi Jin

Use with **Library Teaching Resources,** *page 136.*

The Sweater Thief

by Ayana Carter

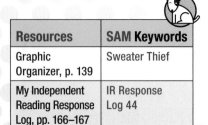

Moderate 1 | 250L

Genre	Pages	Audio CD	✓ Reading
Fiction	24	12 min 36 sec	Counts!

Summary

Tracey's job at an expensive clothing store goes well until Kayla, a popular girl from school, pressures Tracey into letting her steal a sweater. Kayla invites Tracey to a party. Tracey goes, but is plagued by guilt. When Kayla returns to the store and steals again, Tracey tells her boss and learns a lesson about who her real friends are.

Phonics Focus

- **Long *a* vowel teams**

See **Master Skills Tracker** in your Teacher's Edition.

Skills Tracker

Preteach Teach/Practice/Apply Review/Reinforce Assess

Smart Words

Words are defined on pp. 4–5 of the student book. Page number of first appearance is listed below.

- **confused***, p. 12
- **employee***, p. 8
- **expensive**, p. 6
- **ignore***, p. 13
- **include***, p. 13
- **praise**, p. 8

*Spanish Cognates, **page 32**

Option 1: **Decoding**

 Informal Assessment

Ask students to read the Phonics Focus words on the inside back cover of *The Sweater Thief*. If they struggle with decoding, proceed to targeted instruction.

 Targeted Instruction

For words with long *a* vowel teams: Have the student use the **Word Sort** decoding routine on **page 45** to sort words by *ai* and *ay* spellings. Review that both spellings stand for the long *a* sound.

Option 2: **Academic Vocabulary**

 Informal Assessment

Ask students to read a sentence from the book that contains a Smart Word. Have students define the Smart Word and identify text evidence that helped them determine the meaning. Review definitions on pages 4–5 as needed. Repeat with other Smart Words. If students demonstrate proficiency, proceed to targeted instruction.

 Targeted Instruction

Employ is the base of the Smart Word *employee* and the words *employed*, *employees*, *employer*, *employers*, *employing*, *employment*, and *employs*. Use the **Extending Meaning** vocabulary routine on **page 46** to build student familiarity with morphological word families.

Option 3: **Fluency**

 Informal Assessment

Ask students to read page 9 of *The Sweater Thief* aloud. To work on pacing, proceed to targeted instruction.

 Targeted Instruction

Use pages 9–12 of *The Sweater Thief* and the **Use Natural, Consistent Pace** fluency routine on **page 51** to have the student practice reading at a natural pace.

Comprehension

Use the questions below and the Graphic Organizer on **page 139** to check comprehension and promote reader response.

After Chapter 1: *What does Tracey like about her job?* (She likes her boss, and she likes being praised.)

After Chapter 3: *What happens the second time that Kayla comes into the store?* (The alarm goes off. Inez asks Tracey to check out the situation. Tracey sees that Kayla is trying to steal a sweater and lets Kayla steal it.)

End of Book: *What does Tracey realize about Kayla?* (She realizes that Kayla is using her and isn't a person worth being friends with.)

Resources	SAM Keywords
Graphic Organizer, p. 139	Sweater Thief
My Independent Reading Response Log, pp. 166–167	IR Response Log 44

Name _____

The Sweater Thief

Build Understanding

▶ Imagine that Tracey and Kayla have a chance to speak to each other now. What would they say? Fill in the speech bubbles. Use details from the story.

Tracey might say...

Kayla might say...

QuickWrite

▶ In the beginning of the story, Tracey wonders if Kayla is being "fake." Is she correct? Explain your answer with evidence from the story.

_____

_____

_____

_____

Witch Hunt
by Carol Domblewski

Moderate 1 | 300L

Genre	Pages		Audio CD		Reading Counts!
Social Studies	24		15 min 27 sec		

Summary

In 1692 in Salem, Massachusetts, two girls claim that witches have put a spell on them. The girls accuse three women of being witches. The women are arrested. More girls accuse people of witchcraft. The fear of being accused spreads. Innocent people are arrested and hung. Finally, people speak out against the arrests and stop the madness.

Phonics Focus

- **Multiple affixes**
- **Ending -ed with base change**
- **Suffixes -ly and -y**

See **Master Skills Tracker** in your Teacher's Edition.

Skills Tracker

Preteach | Teach/Practice/Apply | Review/Reinforce | Assess

Smart Words

Words are defined on pp. 4–5 of the student book. Page number of first appearance is listed below.

- accuse*, p. 6
- admit*, p. 10
- hearing, p. 13
- release, p. 22
- rumor*, p. 9
- trial, p. 19

*Spanish Cognates, **page 32**

Option 1: Decoding

 Informal Assessment

Ask students to read the Phonics Focus words on the inside back cover of *Witch Hunt*. If they struggle with decoding, proceed to targeted instruction.

 Targeted Instruction

For words with multiple affixes, -ed with base change, and suffixes -ly and -y: Use the **Word Parts** decoding routine on **pages 42–43** to help the student identify and use prefixes, suffixes, and inflectional endings.

Option 2: Academic Vocabulary

Informal Assessment

Ask students to read a sentence from the book that contains a Smart Word. Have students define the Smart Word and identify text evidence that helped them determine the meaning. Review definitions on pages 4–5 as needed. Repeat with other Smart Words. If students demonstrate proficiency, proceed to targeted instruction.

 Targeted Instruction

The Smart Word *hearing* can mean "perceiving sound" or "a court trial." Use the **Multiple-Meaning Words** vocabulary routine on **page 47** with *hearing* as an example to help the student use context to determine the correct meaning.

Option 3: Fluency

 Informal Assessment

Ask students to read page 13 of *Witch Hunt* aloud. To work on reading with correct phrasing, proceed to targeted instruction.

 Targeted Instruction

Use pages 13–15 of *Witch Hunt* and the **Phrasing and Punctuation** fluency routine on **page 50** to have the student practice correct phrasing.

Comprehension

Use the questions below and the Graphic Organizer on **page 141** to check comprehension and promote reader response.

After Chapter 1: *What does the doctor say is the reason the girls are having strange fits?* (He says that the girls are under a spell.)

After Chapter 3: *What happens to the people who are accused of being witches?* (They are taken before a judge who tries to get them to admit that they are witches.)

End of Book: *What do some people do to help end the Salem witch trials?* (Increase Mather says it is wrong to hang innocent people. Thomas Brattle says there is no real proof that people are witches. The governor shuts down the trials.)

Resources	SAM Keywords
Graphic Organizer, p. 141	Witch Hunt
My Independent Reading Response Log, pp. 166–167	IR Response Log 44

Use with
Series 18

Name ____________________

Witch Hunt

Build Understanding

▶ Write a short summary of each chapter of the book. One has been done for you.

Chapter 1: "Scary Rumors"

____

____

Chapter 2: "Arrested!"

____

____

Chapter 3: "Fear Takes Over"

Three accused women are brought before a judge. Two of them say they are innocent. The third woman changes her story. Fear of witches grows.

Chapter 4: "Dangerous Times"

____

____

Chapter 5: "Hang Them!"

____

____

QuickWrite

▶ What happened when people accused the girls of lying? Explain your answer using details from the book.

____

____

____

Resource Links
Library Teaching Resources: p. 141
SAM Keyword: Witch Hunt

Use with **Library Teaching Resources,** *page 140.*

Arabian Nights

A Graphic Classic Based on Traditional Stories by **Terry West**

Moderate 1 | 340L

Genre	Pages	Audio CD	Reading
Graphic Classic	32	23 min 1 sec	Counts!

Summary

In this graphic classic retelling, a sultan's wife and brother plot against him. The Sultan kills his wife by mistake and banishes his brother. Afraid of being betrayed again, the Sultan vows to kill his new wife on their wedding day. Scheherazade, his new wife, soothes the Sultan and keeps herself alive by telling him a new story every night.

Phonics Focus

- *a*, *au*, and *aw*
- Suffixes *-sion* and *-tion*
- Root *graph*

See **Master Skills Tracker** in your Teacher's Edition.

Skills Tracker

Preteach Teach/Practice/Apply Review/Reinforce Assess

Smart Words

Words are defined on pp. 4–5 of the student book. Page number of first appearance is listed below.

- advisor, p. 10
- betray, p. 7
- greedy, p. 7
- majesty*, p. 10
- nightmare, p. 9
- supply, p. 7
- treasure, p. 14

*Spanish Cognates, **page 33**

Option 1: **Decoding**

 Informal Assessment

Ask students to read the Phonics Focus words on the inside back cover of *Arabian Nights*. If they struggle with decoding, proceed to targeted instruction.

 Targeted Instruction

For words with *a*, *au*, and *aw* : Use the **Word Sort** decoding routine on **page 45** to sort words by *a*, *au*, and *aw* spellings.

For words with suffixes *–sion* and *–tion*, and root *graph*: Use the **Word Parts** routine on **page 43** to help the student identify and use suffixes and roots.

Option 2: **Academic Vocabulary**

 Informal Assessment

Ask students to read a sentence from the book that contains a Smart Word. Have students define the Smart Word and identify text evidence that helped them determine the meaning. Review definitions on pages 4–5 as needed. Repeat with other Smart Words. If students demonstrate proficiency, proceed to targeted instruction.

 Targeted Instruction

Advice is the base of the Smart Word *advisor* and the words *advised*, *advises*, *advisors*, *advising*, *advisory*, *advisable*, and *unadvisable*. Use the **Extending Meaning** vocabulary routine on **page 46** to build student familiarity with morphological word families.

Option 3: **Fluency**

 **Informal Assessment**

Ask students to read page 10 of *Arabian Nights* aloud. To work on expressive reading, proceed to targeted instruction.

Targeted Instruction

Use pages 10–12 of *Arabian Nights* and the **Read With Expression** fluency routine on **page 53** to have the student practice expressive reading.

Comprehension

Use the questions below and the Graphic Organizer on **page 143** to check comprehension and promote reader response.

After Page 9: *Why must the Sultan take another wife? (The law says he must remarry, or the kingdom will go to his brother.)*

After Page 19: *In the story of Ali Baba, what happens to Kasim? (Kasim forgets the password and is trapped in the cave. When the thieves return, they kill him.)*

End of Book: *How do Scheherazade's tales help the Sultan? (They ease his mind so that he can fall asleep. The tale of Aladdin gives him hope that he and his wife can be happy.)*

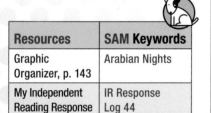

Resources	SAM Keywords
Graphic Organizer, p. 143	Arabian Nights
My Independent Reading Response Log, pp. 166–167	IR Response Log 44

Use with
Series 23 & 24

Name ____________________

Arabian Nights

Build Understanding

▶ Details are bits of information. Fill in the chart below with at least two details about each of the characters. Use information from the text. One has been done for you.

Character	Details
The Sultan	• Was betrayed by his wife and brother • Is scared that any new wife will also betray him
Scheherazade	
Ali Baba	
Kasim	
Morgiana	
Aladdin	

QuickWrite

▶ Why does the Sultan want to kill Scheherazade? Use details from the text to explain your answer.

____

____

____

Resource Links
Library Teaching Resources: p. 143
SAM Keyword: Arabian Nights

Use with **Library Teaching Resources,** *page 142.*

Beauty and the Geek
by **Ayana Carter**

Simple ▲ 380L

Genre	Pages		Audio CD		Reading
Fiction	24		17 min 30 sec		Counts!

Summary

Mia has a crush on Jorge, but Diego, Jorge's geeky brother, has a crush on her. Mia tries to meet Jorge by practicing for band at Diego's house, but is surprised by how much she likes spending time with Diego. Mia sees that Diego is talented and not so geeky after all. Choosing between the brothers is confusing, but eventually Diego wins her heart.

Phonics Focus

- **r- controlled vowels** -air, -are, and -ear
- **Suffixes** -er and -est

See **Master Skills Tracker** in your Teacher's Edition.

Skills Tracker

Preteach | Teach/Practice/Apply | Review/Reinforce | Assess

Smart Words

Words are defined on pp. 4–5 of the student book. Page number of first appearance is listed below.

- **compare***, p. 13
- **impress***, p. 9
- **interest***, p. 6
- **introduce***, p. 8
- **jealous**, p. 13
- **obvious***, p. 9
- **plan***, p. 8

*Spanish Cognates, **page 33**

Option 1: Decoding

 Informal Assessment

Ask students to read the Phonics Focus words on the inside back cover of *Beauty and the Geek*. If they struggle with decoding, proceed to targeted instruction.

 Targeted Instruction

For words with *r*-controlled vowels -air, -are, and -ear: Have the student use the **Word Sort** routine on **page 45** to sort words by -are, -air, and -ear spellings.

For words with suffixes -er and -est: Use the **Word Parts** decoding routine on **page 43** to help identify and use suffixes.

Option 2: Academic Vocabulary

 Informal Assessment

Ask students to read a sentence from the book that contains a Smart Word. Have students define the Smart Word and identify text evidence that helped them determine the meaning. Review definitions on pages 4–5 as needed. Repeat with other Smart Words. If students demonstrate proficiency, proceed to targeted instruction.

 Targeted Instruction

The idiom *got the hang of it* used in the third paragraph of page 17 means "learned how to do something." Build understanding of idioms using the **Idioms** vocabulary routine on **page 49** with this expression as an example.

Option 3: Fluency

 Informal Assessment

Ask students to read page 12 of *Beauty and the Geek* aloud. To work on expressive reading, proceed to targeted instruction.

 Targeted Instruction

Use pages 12–13 of *Beauty and the Geek* and the **Read With Expression** fluency routine on **page 53** to have the student practice expressive reading.

Comprehension

Use the questions below and the Graphic Organizer on **page 145** to check comprehension and promote reader response.

After Chapter 1: *Who does Mia have a crush on?* (a guy named Jorge, a popular older guy in school)

After Chapter 3: *How does Mia plan to meet Jorge?* (Mia arranges to practice for band with Jorge's brother, Diego.)

End of Book: *What things make Mia realize that she has a crush on Diego?* (She can't stop thinking about Diego while she is out with Jorge. She begins to think Diego is cute. She is thrilled when he asks her to go to the movies.)

Resources	SAM Keywords
Graphic Organizer, p. 145	Beauty and Geek
My Independent Reading Response Log, pp. 166–167	IR Response Log 44

Name _____

Beauty and the Geek

Build Understanding

▶ What is Mia thinking? Fill in the thought bubbles below. Write a thought she might have about each topic using details from the text. The first one is done for you.

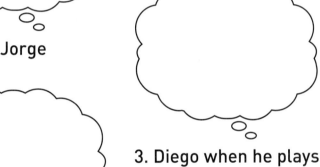

Jorge is the cutest guy at school. I really want to meet him.

1. Jorge

2. Her plan to go to Diego's house

3. Diego when he plays the trumpet

4. The party that Jorge takes her to

5. Diego at the end of the story

QuickWrite

▶ How is Diego different from his brother Jorge? Support your answer with evidence from the text.

_____

_____

_____

Lesson Plan

Everyday Heroes
by Patricia Kean

Moderate 1   440L

Genre	Pages	Audio CD	Reading Counts!
Social Studies	32	24 min 48 sec	✓

Summary

Read about ordinary people who have risked their lives to help others. Four boys save a girl from an attack. Jose LeGrand stops a runaway car with a little girl inside it. Kelli Groves saves a choking baby. Jeremy Hernandez helps evacuate a school bus stuck on a collapsing bridge. And Wesley Autrey keeps a man from being run over by a train.

Phonics Focus

- *oo* and *u*
- Prefixes *dis-* and *mis-*
- Roots *rupt*, *struct*, and *scrib/script*

See **Master Skills Tracker** in your Teacher's Edition.

Skills Tracker

Preteach   Teach/Practice/Apply   Review/Reinforce   Assess

Smart Words

Words are defined on pp. 4–5 of the student book. Page number of first appearance is listed below.

- discovery, p. 10
- distract*, p. 10
- distress, p. 10
- hesitate, p. 12
- instruct*, p. 19
- maneuver*, p. 19
- station*, p. 29

*Spanish Cognates, **page 33**

Option 1: Decoding

 Informal Assessment

Ask students to read the Phonics Focus words on the inside back cover of *Everyday Heroes*. If they struggle with decoding, proceed to targeted instruction.

 Targeted Instruction

For words *oo* and *u*: Use the **Word Sort** routine on **page 45** to sort words by *oo* and *u* spellings. Review that both spellings can stand for the same sound.

For words with prefixes *dis-* and *mis-*, and roots *rupt*, *struct*, and *scrib/script*: Use the **Word Parts** routines on **pages 42 and 44** to use prefixes and roots.

Option 2: Academic Vocabulary

 Informal Assessment

Ask students to read a sentence from the book that contains a Smart Word. Have students define the Smart Word and identify text evidence that helped them determine the meaning. Review definitions on pages 4–5 as needed. Repeat with other Smart Words. If students demonstrate proficiency, proceed to targeted instruction.

 Targeted Instruction

Discover is the base of the Smart Word *discovery* and the words *discovered*, *discoveries*, *discovering*, and *discovers*. Use the **Extending Meaning** vocabulary routine on **page 46** to build familiarity with morphological word families.

Option 3: Fluency

 Informal Assessment

Ask students to read page 13 of *Everyday Heroes* aloud. To work on pacing, proceed to targeted instruction.

 Targeted Instruction

Use pages 13–15 of *Everyday Heroes* and the **Use Natural, Consistent Pace** fluency routine on **page 51** to have the student practice correct pacing.

Comprehension

Use the questions below and the Graphic Organizer on **page 147** to check comprehension and promote reader response.

After Chapter 1: *What happens to Samantha while she is riding her bike? (A car hits her, knocking her onto the grass. When she tries to get up, the driver pulls her back down.)*

After Chapter 3: *How do Jose and Maria help save Reiko? (They let Reiko's car smash into theirs, so that her car will come to a stop.)*

End of Book: *What does Wesley do to save Cameron? (Wesley lies on top of Cameron on the train tracks to protect Cameron from being run over.)*

Resources	SAM Keywords
Graphic Organizer, p. 147	Everyday Heroes
My Independent Reading Response Log, pp. 166–167	IR Response Log 44

Name _____

Everyday Heroes

Build Understanding

▶ Identify the most important things that happen in the chapters listed below. Then summarize each chapter in your own words. One has been done for you.

Chapter 1: "The Fantastic Four"

_____

_____

_____

Chapter 3: "A Baby's Life"

_____

_____

_____

Chapter 5: "Subway Superhero"

A man has a seizure and falls onto the train tracks. Wesley jumps off the
platform to save him. A train passes over them but they are unharmed.
Wesley is honored for being a hero.

QuickWrite

▶ Choose one story from the book. What dangers did the hero or heroes face in order to help someone?

_____

_____

_____

Use With Series 21 & 22 | **Lesson Plan**

Fire! The Triangle Shirtwaist Factory Tragedy by Tracey West

Moderate 1 | **440L**

Genre	Pages	Audio CD	Reading
Social Studies	24	18 min 18 sec	Counts!

Summary

In 1911, a fire breaks out in the Triangle Shirtwaist Factory, killing 146 workers. The factory owners are tried for manslaughter but not convicted. A woman named Frances Perkins protests to prevent future tragedies. Thanks to her, laws are passed to make factories safer places to work.

Phonics Focus

- Diphthongs *oi*, *oy*, *ou*, and *ow*
- Suffixes *-ful* and *-less*

See **Master Skills Tracker** in your Teacher's Edition.

Skills Tracker

Preteach Teach/Practice/Apply Review/Reinforce Assess

Smart Words

Words are defined on pp. 4–5 of the student book. Page number of first appearance is listed below.

- factory*, p. 6
- improve, p. 14
- labor*, p. 14
- prevent*, p. 13
- protest*, p. 14
- strike, p. 14
- tragic*, p. 10

*Spanish Cognates, **page 33**

Option 1: Decoding

 Informal Assessment

Ask students to read the Phonics Focus words on the inside back cover of *Fire!* If they struggle with decoding, proceed to targeted instruction.

 Targeted Instruction

For words with diphthongs *oi*, *oy*, *ou*, and *ow*: Have the student use the **Word Sort** decoding routine on **page 45** to sort words by *oi*, *oy*, *ou*, and *ow* spellings.

For words with suffixes *-ful* and *-less*: Use the **Word Parts** decoding routine on **page 43** to help the student use suffixes.

Option 2: Academic Vocabulary

 Informal Assessment

Ask students to read a sentence from the book that contains a Smart Word. Have students define the Smart Word and identify text evidence that helped them determine the meaning. Review definitions on pages 4–5 as needed. Repeat with other Smart Words. If students demonstrate proficiency, proceed to targeted instruction.

 Targeted Instruction

Use the **Context Clues** vocabulary routine on **page 48** with the Smart Word *strike* as an example to help the student use context clues to determine meaning.

Option 3: Fluency

 Informal Assessment

Ask students to read page 9 of *Fire!* aloud. To work on correct phrasing, proceed to targeted instruction.

 Targeted Instruction

Use pages 9–10 of *Fire!* and the **Phrasing and Punctuation** fluency routine on **page 50** to have the student practice correct phrasing.

Comprehension

Use the questions below and the Graphic Organizer on **page 149** to check comprehension and promote reader response.

After Chapter 1: *Where does the factory fire begin? (in a scrap bin filled with cloth and papers)*

After Chapter 4: *Why does the jury find Blanck and Harris not guilty? (because there is no proof that they knew that the door on the ninth floor was locked)*

End of Book: *How did Frances Perkins react when she saw the fire? (She was angry. She wanted to prevent more tragic fires.)*

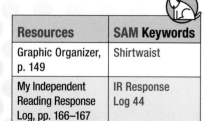

Resources	SAM Keywords
Graphic Organizer, p. 149	Shirtwaist
My Independent Reading Response Log, pp. 166–167	IR Response Log 44

Name _____

Fire! The Triangle Shirtwaist Factory Tragedy

Build Understanding

▶ Why is the Triangle Shirtwaist Factory an unsafe place to work?
Fill in the circles below with reasons from the text. An example has
been done for you.

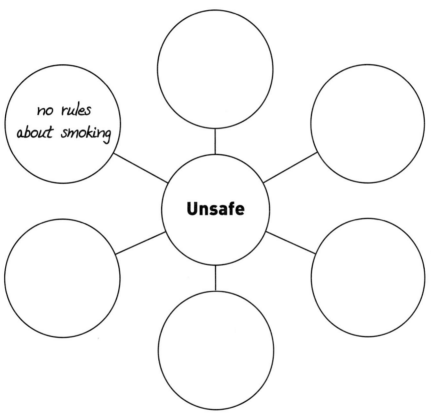

no rules about smoking

Unsafe

QuickWrite

▶ How did the lawyer for the factory workers influence the jury's decision?
Explain your answer with evidence from the text.

_____

_____

_____

Four Rotten Rulers

by **John DiConsiglio**

 Simple — HL380L

Genre	Pages		Audio CD		Reading
Social Studies	**24**		**21 min 10 sec**		**Counts!**

Summary

This book profiles the lives of four rulers who were famous for their ruthless actions. Julius Caesar forced ancient Romans to make him "dictator for life." Spanish conquistador Francisco Pizarro destroyed the Inca in South America. Catherine the Great of Russia stole power from her own husband. And Empress Cixi of China encouraged killing and riots to boost her power.

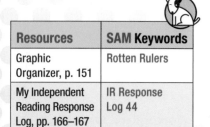

Phonics Focus

- /sh/ spelled *ci* and *ti*

See **Master Skills Tracker** in your Teacher's Edition.

Skills Tracker			
Preteach	Teach/Practice/Apply	Review/Reinforce	Assess

Smart Words

Words are defined on pages 4–5 of the student book. Page number of first appearance is listed below.

- civilization*, p. 6
- conquer*, p. 6
- decline, p. 10
- explore*, p. 12
- foreign, p. 9
- fortune*, p. 6
- tyrant*, p. 10

*Spanish Cognates, **page 33**

Resources	SAM Keywords
Graphic Organizer, p. 151	Rotten Rulers
My Independent Reading Response Log, pp. 166–167	IR Response Log 44

Option 1: Decoding

 Informal Assessment

Ask students to read the Phonics Focus words on the inside back cover of *Four Rotten Rulers*. If they struggle with decoding, proceed to targeted instruction.

 Targeted Instruction

For words with /sh/ spelled *ci* and *ti*: Have the student use the **Word Sort** decoding routine on **page 45** to sort words by *ci* and *ti* spellings. Review that both spellings stand for the /sh/ sound.

Option 2: Academic Vocabulary

 Informal Assessment

Ask students to read a sentence from the book that contains a Smart Word. Have students define the Smart Word and identify evidence in the text that helped them determine the meaning. Review definitions on pages 4–5 as needed. Repeat with other Smart Words. If students demonstrate proficiency, proceed to targeted instruction.

 Targeted Instruction

The Smart Word *explore* is the base of the words *explored*, *exploring*, *explorer*, and *exploration*. Use the **Extending Meaning** vocabulary routine on **page 46** to build student familiarity with morphological word families.

Option 3: Fluency

 Informal Assessment

Ask students to read page 16 of *Four Rotten Rulers* aloud. To work on pacing, proceed to targeted instruction.

 Targeted Instruction

Use pages 16–17 of *Four Rotten Rulers* and the **Use Natural, Consistent Pace** fluency routine on **page 51** to have the student practice correct pacing.

Comprehension

Use the questions below and the Graphic Organizer on **page 151** to check comprehension and promote reader response.

After Page 11: *Why did Roman senators kill Caesar?* (They were unhappy that Caesar had absolute power, and they hoped to make Rome a republic again.)

After Page 15: *How did Pizarro's 200 soldiers defeat Atahualpa's "thousands of warriors"?* (Pizarro's men had rifles and cannons; Atahualpa's warriors had only arrows and spears.)

End of Book: *How did Catherine the Great and Cixi treat poor people in their empires?* (Both rulers allowed poor people to starve while spending money on wars or on luxuries for themselves.)

Name _____

Four Rotten Rulers

Build Understanding

▶ Imagine that you could ask the rulers in the book about their goals as rulers. Write what each ruler would say. Use text evidence.

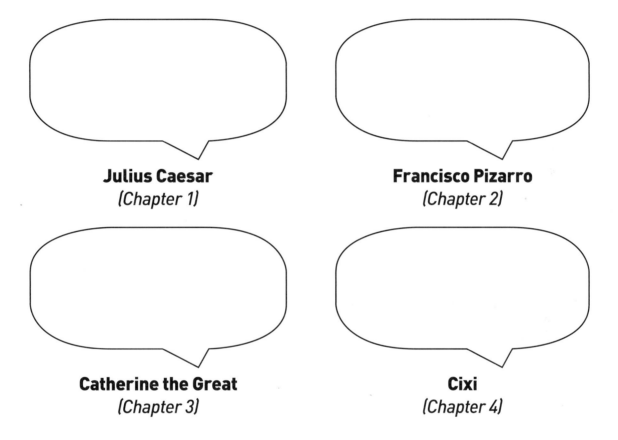

Julius Caesar
(Chapter 1)

Francisco Pizarro
(Chapter 2)

Catherine the Great
(Chapter 3)

Cixi
(Chapter 4)

QuickWrite

▶ Both Julius Caesar and Francisco Pizarro were murdered. Did they deserve to be killed? Write a few sentences to explain your opinion. Support your opinion with text evidence.

_____

_____

_____

_____

Hot Jobs
by Richard Camden

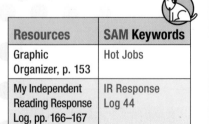

Moderate 1 — 450L

Genre	Pages	Audio CD	Reading
Jobs	32	24 min 42 sec	Counts!

Summary

This book features five people whose jobs involve working under hot conditions. Scientist Cheryl Gansecki studies volcanoes. Firefighter Keisha Wilson saves lives. Chef Yeny Grusenmeyer works in a hot kitchen. Lifeguard Jon Vipond spends his days in the blazing sun. David Garcia blows molten glass in a superhot furnace.

Phonics Focus

- *oo* and *ew*
- Prefixes *mid-* and *sub-*
- Roots *dict* and *port*

See **Master Skills Tracker** in your Teacher's Edition.

Skills Tracker

Preteach   Teach/Practice/Apply   Review/Reinforce   Assess

Smart Words

Words are defined on pp. 4–5 of the student book. Page number of first appearance is listed below.

- career*, p. 16
- equipment*, p. 16
- extreme*, p. 13
- handle, p. 13
- major*, p. 15
- result*, p. 15
- train, p. 6

*Spanish Cognates, **page 34**

Option 1: Decoding

 Informal Assessment

Ask students to read the Phonics Focus words on the inside back cover of *Hot Jobs*. If they struggle with decoding, proceed to targeted instruction.

 Targeted Instruction

For words with *oo* and *ew*: Have the student use the **Word Sort** routine on **page 45** to sort by *oo* and *ew* spellings. Note that both stand for the long *o* sound.

For words with prefixes *mid-* and *sub*, and roots *dict* and *port*: Use the **Word Parts** routine on **pages 42–44** to help students identify and use suffixes and roots.

Option 2: Academic Vocabulary

 Informal Assessment

Ask students to read a sentence from the book that contains a Smart Word. Have students define the Smart Word and identify text evidence that helped them determine the meaning. Review definitions on pages 4–5 as needed. Repeat with other Smart Words. If students demonstrate proficiency, proceed to targeted instruction.

 Targeted Instruction

The Smart Word *handle* can mean "to deal with or take control" or "the part of an object used to move it." Use the **Multiple-Meaning Words** vocabulary routine on **page 47** with *handle* as an example to help the student determine correct meaning.

Option 3: Fluency

 Informal Assessment

Ask students to read page 8 of *Hot Jobs* aloud. To work on expressive reading, proceed to targeted instruction.

 Targeted Instruction

Use pages 8–9 of *Hot Jobs* and the **Read With Expression** fluency routine on **page 53** to have the student practice expressive reading.

Comprehension

Use the questions below and the Graphic Organizer on **page 153** to check comprehension and promote reader response.

After Chapter 1: *Cheryl has a close call while camping at Kilauea. What happens? (The wind changes direction, and burning rocks fly toward her.)*

After Chapter 4: *What ingredients are in mole? (chocolate, chiles, garlic, onions, nuts)*

End of Book: *What skills does a lifeguard need? (Lifeguards need to know first aid and be great swimmers.)*

Resources	SAM Keywords
Graphic Organizer, p. 153	Hot Jobs
My Independent Reading Response Log, pp. 166–167	IR Response Log 44

Name _____

Hot Jobs

Build Understanding

▶ Answer the questions below with details from the book. The first one is done for you.

Chapter 1 Where does Cheryl Gansecki film lava flows? *She films them at the top of a volcano.*	**Chapter 2** How many months of training do firefighters like Keisha Wilson need?	**Chapter 3** Who introduced Yeny Grusenmeyer to cooking?
Chapter 3 What is a sous-chef?	**Chapter 4** What scary rescue does Jon Vipond do at the beach one day?	**Chapter 5** Why does a person need to be strong to blow glass?

QuickWrite

▶ Pick one job described in this book. What makes this job "hot"? Use details from the book to support your answer.

_____

_____

_____

Killer Croc
by **Elizabeth Carney**

Moderate 1 | 430L

Genre	Pages	Audio CD	Reading
Science	24	18 min 5 sec	Counts!

Summary

In Burundi, Africa, a giant killer crocodile prowls the shores of the Rusizi River and terrorizes villagers. A man named Patrice Faye names the croc Gustave and spends years trying to capture it. At one point, it seems that Gustave has died. Then in 2006, a giant croc kills ten people near Lake Tanganyika, and the hunt for Gustave resumes.

Phonics Focus

- *r*-controlled vowels *ar, er, ir,* and *ur*
- Suffixes *–er* and *–or*

See **Master Skills Tracker** in your Teacher's Edition.

Skills Tracker

Preteach | Teach/Practice/Apply | Review/Reinforce | Assess

Smart Words

Words are defined on pp. 4–5 of the student book. Page number of first appearance is listed below.

- **capture*, p. 15**
- **dangerous, p. 8**
- **expose*, p. 15**
- **fail, p. 16**
- **reptile*, p. 6**
- **risk, p. 12**
- **terror*, p. 12**

*Spanish Cognates, **page 34**

Option 1: Decoding

 Informal Assessment

Ask students to read the Phonics Focus words on the inside back cover of *Killer Croc*. If they struggle with decoding, proceed to targeted instruction.

 Targeted Instruction

For words with *r*-controlled vowels *ar, er, ir,* and *ur*: Have the student use the **Word Sort** decoding routine on **page 45** to sort words by *ar, er, ir,* and *ur* spellings.

For words with suffixes *-er* and *-or*: Use the **Word Parts** routine on **page 43** to help the student identify and use suffixes.

Option 2: Academic Vocabulary

 Informal Assessment

Ask students to read a sentence from the book that contains a Smart Word. Have students define the Smart Word and identify text evidence that helped them determine the meaning. Review definitions on pages 4–5 as needed. Repeat with other Smart Words. If students demonstrate proficiency, proceed to targeted instruction.

 Targeted Instruction

The Smart Word *dangerous* has many possible synonyms and antonyms. Use the **Extending Meaning** vocabulary routine on **page 47** to extend meaning.

Option 3: Fluency

 Informal Assessment

Ask students to read page 8 of *Killer Croc* aloud. To work on pacing, proceed to targeted instruction.

 Targeted Instruction

Use page 8 of *Killer Croc* and the **Read With Expression** fluency routine on **page 53** to have the student practice expressive reading.

Comprehension

Use the questions below and the Graphic Organizer on **page 155** to check comprehension and promote reader response.

After Chapter 1: *Why is Gustave so dangerous?* (He's huge and kills large animals and people.)

After Chapter 3: *Why doesn't Faye kill Gustave when he finds him?* (He knows that such large crocs are rare. Capturing the croc alive will allow experts to study it.)

End of Book: *What makes Faye think that Gustave might be dead?* (Gustave disappears for a long time.)

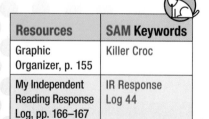

Resources	SAM Keywords
Graphic Organizer, p. 155	Killer Croc
My Independent Reading Response Log, pp. 166–167	IR Response Log 44

Name _____

Killer Croc

Build Understanding

▶ Fill in the circles with words that tell about Gustave, the killer crocodile.
Use information from the text. An example is done for you.

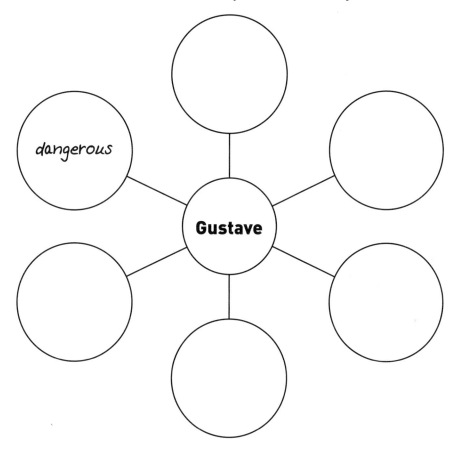

QuickWrite

▶ In 2003, Faye thought Gustave may have been killed. But "surely it wasn't
another crocodile" that killed him. What evidence does the author give to
support this claim?

_____

_____

_____

Lost! Mysteries of the Bermuda Triangle by Emily Costello

Moderate 1 · 440L

Genre	Pages	Audio CD	Reading Counts!
Science	32	24 min 27 sec	✓

Summary

Many ships, planes, and people have vanished without a trace in the Bermuda Triangle. Some people think the area is cursed, but others propose more reasonable explanations. Pirates, the dangerous Sargasso Sea, giant squid, blue holes, sandbars, malfunctioning compasses, and inexperienced pilots are all plausible explanations.

Phonics Focus

- Prefix *tri-*
- Suffixes *-able* and *-ible*
- Roots *phon*, *scope*, *tele*, and *vis/vid*

See **Master Skills Tracker** in your Teacher's Edition.

Skills Tracker

Preteach | Teach/Practice/Apply | Review/Reinforce | Assess

Smart Words

Words are defined on pp. 4–5 of the student book. Page number of first appearance is listed below.

- current*, p. 17
- disappear*, p. 6
- panic*, p. 14
- surrounded, p. 10
- unpredictable*, p. 8
- violent*, p. 16
- visible*, p. 6

*Spanish Cognates, **page 34**

Option 1: Decoding

 Informal Assessment

Ask students to read the Phonics Focus words on the inside back cover of *Lost!* If they struggle with decoding, proceed to targeted instruction.

 Targeted Instruction

For words with prefix *tri-*, suffixes *-able* and *-ible*, and roots *phon*, *scope*, *tele*, and *vis/vid*: Use the **Word Parts** decoding routine on **pages 42–44** to help the student identify and use prefixes, suffixes, and roots.

Option 2: Academic Vocabulary

Informal Assessment

Ask students to read a sentence from the book that contains a Smart Word. Have students define the Smart Word and identify text evidence that helped them determine the meaning. Review definitions on pages 4–5 as needed. Repeat with other Smart Words. If students demonstrate proficiency, proceed to targeted instruction.

Targeted Instruction

Use the **Context Clues** vocabulary routine on **page 48** with the Smart Word *current* as an example to help the student use context clues to determine meaning.

Option 3: Fluency

 Informal Assessment

Ask students to read page 19 of *Lost!* aloud. To practice expressive reading, proceed to targeted instruction.

 Targeted Instruction

Use pages 19–20 of *Lost!* and the **Read With Expression** fluency routine on **page 53** to have the student practice reading in a varied, expressive tone.

Comprehension

Use the questions below and the Graphic Organizer on **page 157** to check comprehension and promote reader response.

After Chapter 2: *Why is the Sargasso Sea dangerous? (It's calm, windless, and filled with seaweed, so ships can get stuck.)*

After Chapter 4: *What could explain why planes get lost in the Bermuda Triangle? (Sometimes compasses don't work in the Triangle. Planes can also get caught in a storm.)*

End of Book: *What are rogue waves and why are they so scary? (Rogue waves are monster waves. They are unpredictable and can form anytime, even in good weather.)*

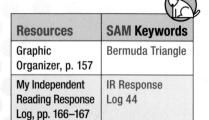

Resources	SAM Keywords
Graphic Organizer, p. 157	Bermuda Triangle
My Independent Reading Response Log, pp. 166–167	IR Response Log 44

Name _____

Lost! Mysteries of the Bermuda Triangle

Build Understanding

▶ There are many explanations for the disappearances in the Bermuda Triangle. Fill in each circle below with an explanation from the text. An example is done for you.

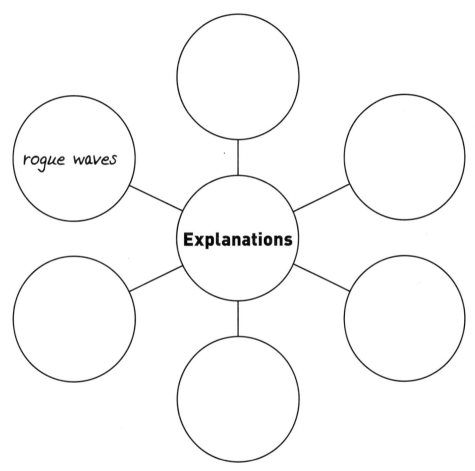

rogue waves

Explanations

QuickWrite

▶ How was the man aboard the "Wild Goose" able to survive the Bermuda Triangle? Use evidence from the text to support your answer.

_____

_____

_____

Use With Series 20

 Lesson Plan

Never Give Up
by Andrew Phan

Simple ▲ **HL410L**

Genre Jobs	**Pages** 24	**Audio CD** 20 min 22 sec	**Reading Counts!**

Summary

The five people profiled in this book are among the most successful in the world in their fields: basketball player Jeremy Lin, TV personality Oprah Winfrey, author J. K. Rowling, Apple founder Steve Jobs, and dog trainer and reality TV star Cesar Millan. All five people persisted despite obstacles and failures to become wealthy, famous, and successful.

Phonics Focus

- **Multisyllable words with /air/**

See **Master Skills Tracker** in your Teacher's Edition.

Skills Tracker

Preteach | Teach/Practice/Apply | Review/Reinforce | Assess

Smart Words

Words are defined on pages 4–5 of the student book. Page number of first appearance is listed below.

- define*, p. 9
- dismiss, p. 9
- failure, p. 6
- obstacle*, p. 6
- persist*, p. 9
- sensation*, p. 9
- underestimate*, p. 7

*Spanish Cognates, **page 34**

Option 1: **Decoding**

 Informal Assessment

Ask students to read the Phonics Focus words on the inside back cover of *Never Give Up*. If they struggle with decoding, proceed to targeted instruction.

 Targeted Instruction

For words with r-controlled vowels -air, -are, and -ear: Have the student use the **Word Sort** decoding routine on **page 45** to sort words according to spelling.

Option 2: **Academic Vocabulary**

 Informal Assessment

Ask students to read a sentence from the book that contains a Smart Word. Have students define the Smart Word and identify text evidence that helped them determine the meaning. Review definitions on pages 4–5 as needed. Repeat with other Smart Words. If students demonstrate proficiency, proceed to targeted instruction.

 Targeted Instruction

The Smart Word *sensation* can mean "someone or something that interests and excites people" or "a physical feeling." Use the **Multiple-Meaning Words** vocabulary routine on **page 47** with *sensation* as an example to help the student use context to determine the correct meaning.

Option 3: **Fluency**

 Informal Assessment

Ask students to read page 6 of *Never Give Up* aloud. To work on expressive reading, proceed to targeted instruction.

 Targeted Instruction

Use pages 6–7 of *Never Give Up* and the **Read With Expression** fluency routine on **page 53** to have the student practice reading with expression.

Comprehension

Use the questions below and the Graphic Organizer on **page 159** to check comprehension and promote reader response.

After Page 9: *Why did the Knicks' coach decide to let Jeremy Lin play? (The Knicks were playing so badly that the coach decided to try something new.)*

After Page 16: *What obstacles did J. K. Rowling face as she tried to finish her first Harry Potter book? (After her divorce, Rowling was jobless and had a baby to support.)*

End of Book: *What qualities do the people in this book share? (Answers will vary but might include persistence, determination, intelligence, talent, ambition, creativity, and originality.)*

Resources	SAM Keywords
Graphic Organizer, p. 159	Never Give Up
My Independent Reading Response Log, pp. 166–167	IR Response Log 44

Name _____

Never Give Up

Build Understanding

▶ The people in this book overcame many challenges. In the chart below, fill in the missing problems and solutions. The first one is done for you.

Problem	Solution
1. Coaches underestimated Jeremy Lin and rarely gave him a chance to play. *(Chapter 1)*	When he finally got a chance, Lin scored 25 points. Then he got to play more.
2. Oprah Winfrey was a troubled teen who ran away many times. *(Chapter 2)*	
3. *(Chapter 3)*	Finally, a publisher bought J. K. Rowling's first Harry Potter book.
4. Steve Jobs wanted to save Apple from its money problems. *(Chapter 4)*	
5. *(Chapter 5)*	Cesar Millan found work grooming and walking dogs.

QuickWrite

▶ Cesar Millan struggled to overcome obstacles. Now that he is a successful dog trainer, how does he help other people who struggle with challenges in their lives? Cite text evidence in your response.

_____

_____

_____

The Promise
by Tracey West

Moderate 1 | 440L

Genre	Pages	Audio CD	Reading
Social Studies	24	18 min 7 sec	Counts!

Summary

Dr. Julian Atim dedicates her life to helping the people of Uganda. She works where she is needed most to help those with HIV and AIDS. She is also a human rights activist, working to get the people of her country proper health care and to end the country's political conflict with enemy rebels. Dr. Atim inspires others by fighting for what is right.

Phonics Focus

- *r*-controlled vowels *or* and *ore*
- /sh/ spellings *ci* and *ti*

See **Master Skills Tracker** in your Teacher's Edition.

Skills Tracker

Preteach Teach/Practice/Apply Review/Reinforce Assess

Smart Words

Words are defined on pp. 4–5 of the student book. Page number of first appearance is listed below.

- accomplish, p. 18
- activist*, p. 17
- conflict*, p. 11
- continue*, p. 10
- dedicate*, p. 7
- mission*, p. 7
- reform*, p. 16

*Spanish Cognates, **page 35**

Option 1: **Decoding**

 Informal Assessment

Ask students to read the Phonics Focus words on the inside back cover of *The Promise*. If they struggle with decoding, proceed to targeted instruction.

 Targeted Instruction

For words with *r*–controlled vowels *or* and *ore*: Have the student use the **Word Sort** decoding routine on **page 45** to sort words according to their vowel spellings.

For words with /sh/ spellings *ci* and *ti*: Have the student use the **Word Sort** routine to sort words by *ci* and *ti* spellings. Note that both stand for the /sh/ sound.

Option 2: **Academic Vocabulary**

 Informal Assessment

Ask students to read a sentence from the book that contains a Smart Word. Have students define the Smart Word and identify text evidence that helped them determine the meaning. Review definitions on pages 4–5 as needed. Repeat with other Smart Words. If students demonstrate proficiency, proceed to targeted instruction.

 Targeted Instruction

Act is the base of the Smart Word *activist* and the words *action*, *active*, *activate*, *activity*, *actor*, and *actress*. Use the **Extending Meaning** vocabulary routine on **page 46** to build student familiarity with morphological word families.

Option 3: **Fluency**

 Informal Assessment

Ask students to read page 9 of *The Promise* aloud. To work on correct phrasing, proceed to targeted instruction.

 Targeted Instruction

Use pages 9–11 of *The Promise* and the **Phrasing and Punctuation** fluency routine on **page 50** to have the student practice correct phrasing.

Comprehension

Use the questions below and the Graphic Organizer on **page 161** to check comprehension and promote reader response.

After Chapter 1: *Where does Dr. Atim work?* (in a hospital in Kitgum, Uganda)

After Chapter 4: *What are two ways that Dr. Atim helps people?* (She works as a doctor. She is also an activist.)

End of Book: *What are some things that Dr. Atim dedicates herself to?* (She is dedicated to fighting for health and human rights, helping orphans and refugees, and helping women earn more money.)

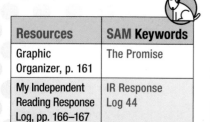

Resources	SAM Keywords
Graphic Organizer, p. 161	The Promise
My Independent Reading Response Log, pp. 166–167	IR Response Log 44

Name ____________________

The Promise

Build Understanding

▶ As you read, think about the most important ideas or events that happen in each chapter. Then summarize each chapter below in the space provided. An example has been done for you.

Chapter 2: "A Country at War"

Uganda has been fighting a war against the deadly disease of AIDS. It has affected millions of people. Uganda is also fighting the LRA, rebels who want to overthrow the president of Uganda.

Chapter 3: "The Making of a Doctor"

____

____

____

Chapter 4: "An Activist Is Born"

____

____

____

QuickWrite

▶ Dr. Atim says her mother "died because of poverty." What does she mean by this? Use evidence from the text to support your answer.

____

____

____

Resource Links
Library Teaching Resources: p. 161
SAM Keyword: The Promise

Use with **Library Teaching Resources,** *page 160.*

The Raven
by Edgar Allan Poe

Complex 1 — NP

Genre	Pages	Audio CD	Reading
Poetry	32	17 min 15 sec	Counts!

Summary

Poe's classic poem takes place one spooky night in the study of the poem's sad and lonely narrator. He is reading to distract himself from thoughts of his lost love, Lenore. He hears tapping at his window, and a raven appears. The bird enters the study—and speaks to him! It says "nevermore" again and again. At first, the narrator likes the bird. But when it says he will "nevermore" see Lenore, the narrator nearly goes crazy!

Phonics Focus

- *or, ore* in single and multisyllabic words
- Diphthongs *oi, oy, ou, ow* in single and multisyllabic words
- Suffixes *-less* and *-ful*

See **Master Skills Tracker** in your Teacher's Edition.

Skills Tracker

Preteach Teach/Practice/Apply Review/Reinforce Assess

Smart Words

Words are defined on pages 6–7 of the student book. Page number of first appearance is listed below.

- **beguile**, p. 18
- **countenance**, p. 18
- **discourse***, p. 19
- **distinctly**, p. 11
- **implore**, p. 13
- **radiant***, p. 11
- **sorrow**, p. 11

*Spanish Cognates, **page 35**

Resources	SAM Keywords
Graphic Organizer, p. 163	The Raven
My Independent Reading Response Log, pp. 166–167	IR Response Log 44

Option 1: Decoding

 Informal Assessment

Ask students to read the Phonics Focus words on the inside back cover of *The Raven*. If they struggle with decoding, proceed to targeted instruction.

 Targeted Instruction

For words with *or* and *ore*, words with *oi* and *oy*, and words with *ou* and *ow*: Have the student use the **Word Sort** decoding routine on **page 45** to sort words by *or, ore, oi, oy, ou* and *ow* spellings.

Option 2: Academic Vocabulary

 Informal Assessment

Ask students to read a sentence from the poem that contains a Smart Word. Have students define the Smart Word and identify text evidence that helped them determine the meaning. Review definitions on pages 6–7 as needed. Repeat with other Smart Words. If students demonstrate proficiency, proceed to targeted instruction.

 Targeted Instruction

The Smart Word *sorrow* has many possible synonyms and antonyms. Use the **Extending Meaning** vocabulary routine on **page 47** to extend meaning.

Option 3: Fluency

 Informal Assessment

Ask students to read page 10 of *The Raven* aloud. To work on reading with correct phrasing, proceed to targeted instruction.

 Targeted Instruction

Use pages 10 and 11 of *The Raven* and the **Phrasing and Punctuation** fluency routine on **page 50** to have the student practice correct phrasing.

Comprehension

Use the questions below and the Graphic Organizer on **page 163** to check comprehension and promote reader response.

After Page 12: *Why does the tapping fill the narrator with "fantastic terrors" and make his heart beat fast? (He thinks Lenore might be there, and he is both hopeful and terrified.)*

After Page 21: *Why does the narrator think the raven's reply is "aptly spoken"? (Something is "apt" when it makes sense in the situation. When the raven says "nevermore," it seems to be answering the narrator's question, not just saying the word at random.)*

End of Book: *How do the narrator's feelings about the raven change during the poem? (At first, the narrator finds the raven amusing. As the bird pesters him, he starts to think it is evil and that it wants to torment him.)*

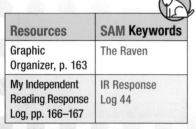

Name _____

The Raven

Build Understanding

▶ Fill in the circles with details from the poem about the raven. Include details about how the bird looks, how it acts, and how it affects the narrator.

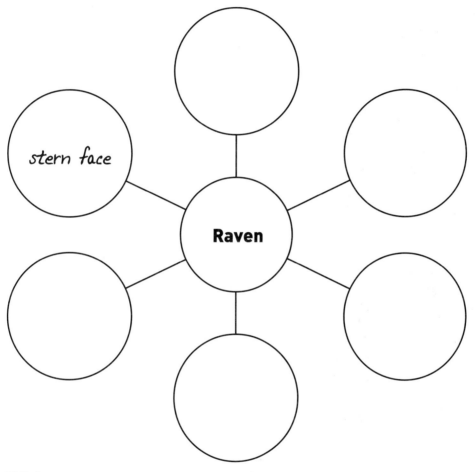

QuickWrite

▶ Edgar Allan Poe wrote "The Raven" more than 150 years ago. Many of the words he used are unfamiliar to readers today. Use your own words to summarize the events that take place in the poem.

_____

_____

_____

Tragedy at Sea
by David Stack

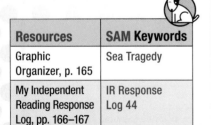

Moderate 1   HL430L

Genre	Pages	Audio CD	Reading
Social Studies	32	25 min 23 sec	Counts!

Summary

In July of 1945, a Japanese sub torpedoed the American warship *Indianapolis*. About 900 men out of 1,200 escaped the sinking ship, only to be attacked by sharks! For four days, the men suffered from shark attacks, injuries, and dehydration before being rescued. Just 317 men survived. Today, these men are honored as heroes. Before the attack, they completed an important job. They delivered an atomic bomb that helped end the war.

Phonics Focus

- **Multisyllable words with *a*, *au*, and *aw***

See **Master Skills Tracker** in your Teacher's Edition

Skills Tracker

Preteach   Teach/Practice/Apply   Review/Reinforce   Assess

Smart Words

Words are defined on pages 4–5 of the student book. Page number of first appearance is listed below.

- **accommodate*, p. 8**
- **crisis*, p. 11**
- **injured, p. 16**
- **mission*, p. 26**
- **perilous, p. 13**
- **surrender, p. 6**
- **warship, p. 6**

*Spanish Cognates, **page 35**

Option 1: Decoding

 Informal Assessment

Ask students to read the Phonics Focus words on the inside back cover of *Tragedy at Sea*. If they struggle with decoding, proceed to targeted instruction.

 Targeted Instruction

For words with *a*, *au*, and *aw*: Have the student use the **Word Sort** decoding routine on **page 45** to sort words by *a*, *au*, and *aw* spellings.

Option 2: Academic Vocabulary

 Informal Assessment

Ask students to read a sentence from the book that contains a Smart Word. Have students define the Smart Word and identify text evidence that helped them determine the meaning. Review definitions on pages 6–7 as needed. Repeat with other Smart Words. If students demonstrate proficiency, proceed to targeted instruction.

 Targeted Instruction

The Smart Word *perilous* has many possible synonyms and antonyms. Use the **Extending Meaning** vocabulary routine on **page 47** to extend meaning.

Option 3: Fluency

Informal Assessment

Ask students to read page 18 of *Tragedy at Sea* aloud. To work on expressive reading, proceed to targeted instruction.

Targeted Instruction

Use pages 18–19 of *Tragedy at Sea* and the **Read With Expression** fluency routine on **page 53** to have the student practice reading with expression.

Comprehension

Use the questions below and the Graphic Organizer on **page 165** to check comprehension and promote reader response.

After Page 14: *Why didn't anyone rescue the sailors immediately after the explosion?* (The captain's SOS call did not go through, so nobody knew the ship had sunk.)

After Page 22: *Why did the American pilot who spotted the survivors almost bomb them?* (At first, the pilot mistook the shipwreck for an enemy submarine. He only realized they were Americans when he got closer.)

End of Book: *Why didn't the government recognize the bravery of the Indianapolis crew right away?* (The government was embarrassed and didn't want to be blamed for the men being left at sea for so long.)

Resources	SAM Keywords
Graphic Organizer, p. 165	Sea Tragedy
My Independent Reading Response Log, pp. 166–167	IR Response Log 44

Graphic Organizer

Use with Series 23

Name ______________________________

Tragedy at Sea

Build Understanding

▶ Read the list of events below. Then write the events in the order they happened. The first one is done for you.

Events
Sharks attack the sailors.
The *Indianapolis* delivers an atomic bomb to an island near Japan.
A Japanese submarine torpedoes the *Indianapolis*.
A U.S. pilot sees the survivors in the ocean.
The U.S. government opens a memorial honoring the men of the *Indianapolis*.

First The Indianapolis delivers an atomic bomb to an island near Japan.

↓

Second

↓

Third

↓

Fourth

↓

Last

QuickWrite

▶ The author writes that the men of the USS *Indianapolis* were "heroic." How were these men heroes? Cite text evidence in your response.

____

____

____

____

Resource Links
Library Teaching Resources: p. 165
SAM Keyword: Tragedy at Sea

Use with **Library Teaching Resources,** *page 164.*

Name _____

My Independent Reading Response Log

Book Title _____

Phonics Focus _____

S.M.A.R.T. Words   Date Completed _____

▶ Write each S.M.A.R.T. Word and rate it. Then, write a sentence that uses each word.

Word	Sentence
1. 1 2 3 4	
2. 1 2 3 4	
3. 1 2 3 4	
4. 1 2 3 4	
5. 1 2 3 4	

During Reading   Date Completed _____

▶ Answer each question on the line below:

1. (page #____) _____

_____

_____

2. (page #____) _____

_____

_____

3. (page #____) _____

_____

_____

After Reading

Date Completed _____

▶ Use the sentence starters to write your answer to the questions.

1. _____

_____

_____

2. _____

_____

_____

Date Completed _____

▶ Answer the reread question here:

_____

_____

_____

Wrap-Up

Date Completed _____

▶ Rate this book by coloring in the number of stars:

☆ ☆ ☆ ☆ ☆

My Reading Counts Quiz Score: _____

Teacher Feedback
Date Completed _____

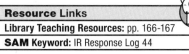

Self-Monitoring Chart

Use this chart to monitor your progress in *System 44* and set goals. Fill in the circle when you complete a Topic and mark a check after you complete the related practice activity or Library book.

Name: _____

	Software Topic	○	44Practice Pages	✔	Decodable Digest	✔	Paperback/Audiobook/eBook	✔	Check-In
SERIES 1	**1.1** Consonants *m, s*	○	p. 8		pp. 9–10		Big! Bugs That Kill Did You Know? Messy Jobs Poster Power They Did What? Wacky Attractions		
	1.2 Consonants *t, n*	○	p. 9		pp. 11–12				
	1.3 Short *a*	○	p. 10		p. 13				
	1.4 Consonants *p, c*	○	p. 11		pp. 14–15				
	1.5 Consonants *b, r*	○	p. 12		pp. 16–17				
	1.6 Sight Words	○	p. 13						
	1.7 Ending *–s*	○	p. 14		p. 18				
	1.8 Success	○	p. 15						
SERIES 2	**2.1** Short *i*	○	p. 16		p. 19		Big! Bugs That Kill Did You Know? Messy Jobs Poster Power They Did What? Wacky Attractions		
	2.2 Consonants *d, f*	○	p. 17		pp. 20–21				
	2.3 Consonants *h, k*	○	p. 18		pp. 22–23				
	2.4 Short *o*	○	p. 19		p. 24				
	2.5 Consonants *l, x*	○	p. 20		pp. 25–26				
	2.6 *–ck*	○	p. 21		p. 27				
	2.7 Sight Words	○	p. 22						
	2.8 Success	○	p. 23						
SERIES 3	**3.1** *s-* Blends	○	p. 24		p. 28		Big! Bugs That Kill Messy Jobs They Did What? Yes!		
	3.2 Short *e*	○	p. 25		p. 29				
	3.3 Consonants *j, w*	○	p. 26		pp. 30–31				
	3.4 Short *u*	○	p. 27		p. 32				
	3.5 Consonants *g, y*	○	p. 28		pp. 33–34				
	3.6 Consonants *v, z, q*	○	p. 29		pp. 35–37				
	3.7 Sight Words	○	p. 30						
	3.8 Success	○	p. 31						
SERIES 4	**4.1** More *s-* Blends	○	p. 32		p. 38		Fast! Plugged In These Are Not Poems Shamila's Goal What's New? Wonders of the World Yes!		
	4.2 Double Consonants	○	p. 33		p. 39				
	4.3 Final Blends	○	p. 34		p. 40				
	4.4 Identifying Syllables	○	p. 35		p. 41				
	4.5 Sight Words	○	p. 36						
	4.6 Success	○	p. 37						
SERIES 5	**5.1** *l-* Blends	○	p. 38		p. 42		Fast! Plugged In These Are Not Poems Wonders of the World		
	5.2 *r-* Blends	○	p. 39		p. 43				
	5.3 More *l-* and *r-* Blends	○	p. 40		p. 44				
	5.4 Two- and Three-Letter Blends	○	p. 41		p. 45				
	5.5 Sight Words	○	p. 42						
	5.6 Success	○	p. 43						

Resource Links
Library Teaching Resources: pp. 168–171
SAM Keyword: 44 Student Chart

Name: _____

	Software Topic	⬤	44Practice Pages	✔	Decodable Digest	✔	Paperback/Audiobook/eBook	✔	Check-In
SERIES 6	**6.1** More Final Blends	◯	p. 44		p. 46		Fast! Plugged In Shamila's Goal These Are Not Poems What's New? Wonders of the World		
	6.2 -ng and -nk	◯	p. 45		p. 47				
	6.3 Closed Syllables	◯	p. 46		p. 48				
	6.4 -nt and -nd	◯	p. 47		p. 46				
	6.5 Sight Words	◯	p. 48						
	6.6 Success	◯	p. 49						
SERIES 7	**7.1** Digraph sh	◯	p. 50		p. 50		Is This Art? Messy Jobs Survival Guide Weird Sports Records Yo, Yolanda!		
	7.2 Digraph ch	◯	p. 51		p. 51				
	7.3 ch, -tch	◯	p. 52		p. 52				
	7.4 sh, ch, -tch	◯	p. 53		p. 53				
	7.5 Ending -es	◯	p. 54		p. 54				
	7.6 Sight Words	◯	p. 55						
	7.7 Success	◯	p. 56						
SERIES 8	**8.1** Digraph th	◯	p. 57		p. 55		Big Steals Crash! DJ Mystery Fashion Flashback Is This Art? Survival Guide When Lisa Met Billy Yo, Yolanda!		
	8.2 Digraph Review	◯	p. 58		p. 56				
	8.3 Ending -ing	◯	p. 59		p. 57				
	8.4 Ending -ed	◯	p. 60		p. 58				
	8.5 More on Ending -ed	◯	p. 61		p. 59				
	8.6 Endings -ing, -ed	◯	p. 62		p. 60				
	8.7 Sight Words	◯	p. 63						
	8.8 Success	◯	p. 64						
SERIES 9	**9.1** Unstressed Closed Syllables (a, e)	◯	p. 65		pp. 61–62		African Journey Big Steals Button Your Lip		
	9.2 Unstressed Closed Syllables (i, o, u)	◯	p. 66		pp. 63–65				
	9.3 Consonant + -le	◯	p. 67		p. 66				
	9.4 Consonant + -el, -al	◯	p. 68		p. 67				
	9.5 Sight Words	◯	p. 69						
	9.6 Success	◯	p. 70						
SERIES 10	**10.1** Long a (a, e)	◯	p. 71		pp. 68–69		Cool Jobs in Basketball The Princess Brat Ripped From the Headlines Unstoppable		
	10.2 Long i (i_e)	◯	p. 72		pp. 70–71				
	10.3 Long a, i (VCe)	◯	p. 73		pp. 72–73				
	10.4 Soft c	◯	p. 74		pp. 74–75				
	10.5 Soft g	◯	p. 75		pp. 76–77				
	10.6 Suffixes -ment, -ness	◯	p. 76		pp. 78–79				
	10.7 Sight Words	◯	p. 77						
	10.8 Success	◯	p. 78						
SERIES 11	**11.1** Long o (o_e)	◯	p. 79		pp. 80–81		Cool Jobs in Basketball Home From War		
	11.2 Long u (u_e)	◯	p. 80		pp. 82–83				
	11.3 VCe Syllables	◯	p. 81		pp. 84–85				
	11.4 More VCe Syllables	◯	p. 82		pp. 86–87				
	11.5 Prefixes un-, non-, de-	◯	p. 83		pp. 88–89				
	11.6 Sight Words	◯	p. 84						
	11.7 Success	◯	p. 85						

Name: _____

	Software Topic	○	44Practice Pages	✔	Decodable Digest	✔	Paperback/Audiobook/eBook	✔	Check-In
SERIES 12	**12.1** Ending –*ing* (drop e)	○	p. 86		pp. 90–91		Crash! El Tiburón When Lisa Met Billy Witch Hunt		
	12.2 Ending –*ing* (with doubling)	○	p. 87		pp. 92–93				
	12.3 Ending –*ed* (drop e)	○	p. 88		pp. 94–95				
	12.4 Ending –*ed* (with doubling)	○	p. 89		pp. 96–97				
	12.5 Sight Words	○	p. 90						
	12.6 Success	○	p. 91						
SERIES 13	**13.1** *y* as a vowel	○	p. 92		pp. 98–103		Back From the Grave Crash! El Tiburón Have You Seen My Mummy? Witch Hunt		
	13.2 Suffixes –*y*, –*ly*	○	p. 93		pp. 104–105				
	13.3 Changing –*y* to *i*	○	p. 94		pp. 106–107				
	13.4 Digraphs *wh*, *ph*	○	p. 95		pp. 108–111				
	13.5 Sight Words	○	p. 96						
	13.6 Success	○	p. 97						
SERIES 14	**14.1** Silent Consonants	○	p. 98		pp. 112–113		Disaster! El Tiburón Have You Seen My Mummy? Medical Miracle Play Ball!		
	14.2 Open Syllables	○	p. 99		pp. 114–115				
	14.3 More Open Syllables	○	p. 100		pp. 116–117				
	14.4 Unstressed Open Syllables	○	p. 101		pp. 118–119				
	14.5 Prefixes *con*–, *com*–	○	p. 102		pp. 120–121				
	14.6 Sight Words	○	p. 103						
	14.7 Success	○	p. 104						
SERIES 15	**15.1** Long *a* (*ai*)	○	p. 105		pp. 122–123		The Sweater Thief Killer Plague		
	15.2 Long *a* (*ay*)	○	p. 106		pp. 124–125				
	15.3 Long *a* Vowel Team Syllables	○	p. 107		pp. 126–127				
	15.4 Sight Words	○	p. 108						
	15.5 Success	○	p. 109						
SERIES 16	**16.1** Long *o* (*oa*)	○	p. 110		pp. 128–129		Left to Die		
	16.2 Long *o* (*ow*)	○	p. 111		pp. 130–131				
	16.3 Long *o* Vowel Team Syllables	○	p. 112		pp. 132–133				
	16.4 Sight Words	○	p. 113						
	16.5 Success	○	p. 114						
SERIES 17	**17.1** Prefixes *re*–, *pre*–	○	p. 115		pp. 134–135		Ant Attack! Hot Jobs Samurai Fighters The Story of Shi Jin		
	17.2 Long *e* (*ea*)	○	p. 116		pp. 136–137				
	17.3 Long *e* (*ee*)	○	p. 117		pp. 138–139				
	17.4 Long *e* (*ie*)	○	p. 118		pp. 140–141				
	17.5 Long *e* Vowel Team Syllables	○	p. 119		pp. 142–143				
	17.6 Sight Words	○	p. 120						
	17.7 Success	○	p. 121						
SERIES 18	**18.1** Long *i* (-*igh*)	○	p. 122		pp. 144–145		Ant Attack! Music Mash-Up Witch Hunt		
	18.2 Other Long Vowel Spellings	○	p. 123		pp. 146–147				
	18.3 Analyzing Word Structure	○	p. 124		pp. 148–149				
	18.4 Sight Words	○	p. 125						
	18.5 Success	○	p. 126						

Name: _____

	Software Topic	○	44Practice Pages	✔	Decodable Digest	✔	Paperback/Audiobook/eBook	✔	Check-In
SERIES 19	**19.1** *ar*	○	p. 127		pp. 150–151		Four Rotten Rulers Killer Croc The Promise		
	19.2 Syllables With *ar*	○	p. 128		pp. 152–153				
	19.3 *er, ir, ur*	○	p. 129		pp. 154–159				
	19.4 Syllables With *er, ir, ur*	○	p. 130		pp. 160–161				
	19.5 Other /sh/ Spellings	○	p. 131		pp. 162–165				
	19.6 Sight Words	○	p. 132						
	19.7 Success	○	p. 133						
SERIES 20	**20.1** *or, ore*	○	p. 134		pp. 166–169		Beauty and the Geek Killer Croc Never Give Up The Promise The Raven		
	20.2 Syllables With *or, ore*	○	p. 135		pp. 170–171				
	20.3 Suffixes *–er, –or*	○	p. 136		pp. 172–173				
	20.4 Suffixes *–er, –est*	○	p. 137		pp. 174–175				
	20.5 *are (scare), air (hair), ear (bear)*	○	p. 138		pp. 176–181				
	20.6 Syllables With /air/	○	p. 139		pp. 182–183				
	20.7 Success	○	p. 140						
SERIES 21	**21.1** *oi, oy*	○	p. 141		pp. 184–187		Fire! The Raven		
	21.2 Syllables With *oi, oy*	○	p. 142		pp. 188–189				
	21.3 *ou (cloud), ow (owl)*	○	p. 143		pp. 190–193				
	21.4 Syllables With *ou, ow*	○	p. 144		pp. 194–195				
	21.5 Sight Words	○	p. 145						
	21.6 Success	○	p. 146						
SERIES 22	**22.1** Suffixes *–less, –ful*	○	p. 147		pp. 196–197		Fire! Hot Jobs The Raven		
	22.2 *oo (boot), ew (news), u_e (tube)*	○	p. 148		pp. 198–203				
	22.3 Syllables With *oo, ew, u_e*	○	p. 149		pp. 204–205				
	22.4 Sight Words	○	p. 150						
	22.5 Success	○	p. 151						
SERIES 23	**23.1** *oo (book), u (put)*	○	p. 152		pp. 206–209		Arabian Nights Everyday Heroes Tragedy at Sea		
	23.2 Syllables With *oo, u*	○	p. 153		pp. 210–211				
	23.3 *aw (paw), au (cause), a (ball)*	○	p. 154		pp. 212–217				
	23.4 Syllables With *aw, au, a*	○	p. 155		pp. 218–219				
	23.5 Success	○	p. 156						
SERIES 24	**24.1** Prefixes *mid–, sub–*	○	p. 157		pp. 220–221		Arabian Nights Everyday Heroes Hot Jobs Lost!		
	24.2 Prefixes *dis–, mis–*	○	p. 158		pp. 222–223				
	24.3 Suffixes *–tion, –sion*	○	p. 159		pp. 224–225				
	24.4 Suffixes *–able, –ible*	○	p. 160		pp. 226–227				
	24.5 Prefixes *uni–, bi–, tri–*	○	p. 161		pp. 228–229				
	24.6 Success	○	p. 162						
SERIES 25	**25.1** Roots *bio, graph, auto*	○	p. 163		pp. 230–231		Arabian Nights Everyday Heroes Hot Jobs Lost!		
	25.2 Roots *port, dict*	○	p. 164		pp. 232–233				
	25.3 Roots *rupt, struct, scrib/script*	○	p. 165		pp. 234–235				
	25.4 Roots *scope, tele, phon, vis/vid*	○	p. 166		pp. 236–237				
	25.5 Success	○	p. 167						

Index

Authors

Aman, Nesar, **72–73**
Bakke, Leslie, **82–83**
Basher, Syed, **84–85**
Bresnick Kendler, Peggy, **56–57**
Caggiano, Juliette, **60–61**
Camden, Richard, **94–95, 152–153**
Carney, Elizabeth, **154–155**
Carter, Ayana, **138–139, 144–145**
Chen, Kevin, **54–55**
Cho, Ellen, **74–75**
Costello, Emily, **156–157**
Daley, Patrick, **120–121**
Davis, Joshua, **78–79**
DiConsiglio, John, **150–151**
Domblewski, Carol, **140–141**
Downes, Polly, **86–87**
Feltes, Kim, **112–113**
Friedman, Mel, **134–135**
Gutiérrez, Peter, **76–77, 88–89, 102–103**
Hakimi, Neda, **106–107**
Hiles, Jaleesa, **68–69**
Honovich, Nancy, **126–127**
Johnson, Jennifer, **100–101**
Jones, Lamar, **66–67**
Kean, Patrick, **146–147**
Kensler, Chris, **104–105**
Langley, Allison, **128–129**
Lebrecque, Ellen, **80–81**
Leviton, Michael, **92–93, 114–115, 116–117**
Li, Zhang, **130–131**
Mendes, Carmen, **132–133**
Nguyen, Grace, **98–99**
O'Connor, Susan, **82–83**
Phan, Andrew, **158–159**
Poe, Edgar Allan, **162–163**
Posner, Tina, **70–71**
Price, Sean, **118–119**
Prieto, Inez, **58–59**
Ramaldo, Jorge, **110–111**
Reyes, Ellen, **112–113**
Robbins, Trina, **124–125**
Sanchez, Daniel, **108–109**
Singh, Sara, **122–123**
Smith, Steph, **90–91**
Stack, David, **164–165**
Takamura, Alan, **62–63**
Taylor, Kimberly Feltes, **96–97**
Tench, Jennifer, **136–137**
West, Tracey, **142–143, 148–149, 160–161**
Williams, Jared, **64–65**

Comprehension Strategies

Idea Web
Fashion Flashback, **95**
Fast!, **61**
Fire! The Triangle Shirtwaist Factory Tragedy, **149**
Is This Art?, **99**
Killer Croc, **155**
Lost! Mysteries of the Bermuda Triangle, **57**
Princess Brat, The, **101**
Raven, The, **163**
Samurai Fighters, **135**

Idioms, Understanding
Button Your Lip and Other Idioms, **87**

Making Inferences
Beauty and the Geek, **145**
Cool Jobs in Basketball, **89**
Disaster!, **119**
Four Rotten Rulers, **151**
Messy Jobs, **63**
Music Mash-Up, **131**
Plugged In, **65**
Sweater Thief, The, **139**
These Are Not Poems, **71**
They Did What?, **73**

Problem and Solution
Have You Seen My Mummy?, **123**
Left to Die, **127**
Medical Miracle, **129**
Never Give Up, **159**
Poster Power, **67**
Survival Guide: How to Keep Your Job, **105**
Unstoppable, **107**
When Lisa Met Billy, **110**
Yo, Yolanda! Advice About Friends, **113**

Read for Detail
African Journey, **83**
Arabian Nights, **143**
Back From the Grave!, **117**
Big!, **55**
Bugs That Kill, **57**
Did You Know?, **59**
Hot Jobs, **153**
Wacky Attractions, **75**
Weird Sports Records, **109**
Yes!, **81**

Sequence of Events
Ant Attack!, **115**
DJ Mystery, **93**
Home From War, **97**
Killer Plague, **125**
Shamila's Goal, **69**
Story of Shi Jin, The, **137**

Tiburón, El, **121**
Tragedy at Sea, **165**
What's New? A History of Invention, **77**

Summarize
Big Steals, **85**
Crash!, **91**
Everyday Heroes, **147**
Play Ball!, **133**
Promise, The, **161**
Ripped From the Headlines, **103**
Witch Hunt, **141**
Wonders of the World, **79**

Curriculum Connections

Arts
Fashion Flashback, **94–95**
Is This Art?, **98–99**
Music Mash-Up, **130–131**
Poster Power, **66–67**

Literature/Language Arts
Ant Attack!, **114–115**
Arabian Nights, **142–143**
Back From the Grave!, **116–117**
Beauty and the Geek, **144–145**
Button Your Lip and Other Idioms, **86–87**
DJ Mystery, **92–93**
Killer Plague, **124–125**
Princess Brat, The, **100–101**
Story of Shi Jin, The, **136–137**
Sweater Thief, The, **138–139**
These Are Not Poems, **70–71**
When Lisa Met Billy, **110–111**

Math
Big!, **54–55**
They Did What?, **72–73**

Physical Education
Cool Jobs in Basketball, **88–89**
Tiburón, El, **120–121**
Weird Sports Records, **108–109**
Yes!, **80–81**

Poetry
Raven, The, **162–163**
These Are Not Poems, **70–71**
When Lisa Met Billy, **110–111**

Science and Technology
African Journey, **82–83**
Bugs That Kill, **56–57**
Crash!, **90–91**
Did You Know?, **58–59**
Disaster!, **118–119**
Fast!, **60–61**
Have You Seen My Mummy?, **122–123**
Killer Croc, **154–155**

Left to Die, **126–127**
Lost! Mysteries of the Bermuda Triangle, **56–57**
Medical Miracle, **128–129**
Plugged In, **64–65**
What's New? A History of Invention, **76–77**

Social Studies/History

Big Steals, **84–85**
Everyday Heroes, **146–147**
Fashion Flashback, **94–95**
Fire! The Triangle Shirtwaist Factory Tragedy, **148–149**
Four Rotten Rulers, **150–151**
Is This Art?, **98–99**
Never Give Up, **158–159**
Play Ball!, **132–133**
Plugged In, **64–65**
Promise, The, **160–161**
Ripped From the Headlines, **102–103**
Samurai Fighters, **134–135**
Shamila's Goal, **68–69**
Tiburón, El, **120–121**
Tragedy at Sea, **164–165**
Unstoppable, **106–107**
Wacky Attractions, **74–75**
Weird Sports Records, **108–109**
What's New? A History of Invention, **76–77**
Witch Hunt, **140–141**
Wonders of the World, **78–79**
Yes!, **80–81**

Decoding Strategies

Blends and Digraphs

Big Steals, **84**
DJ Mystery, **92**
Fast!, **60**
Is This Art?, **98**
Plugged In, **64**
Shamila's Goal, **68**
Survival Guide: How to Keep Your Job, **104**
These Are Not Poems, **70**
Tiburón, El, **120**
Wonders of the World, **78**
Yes!, **80**
Yo, Yolanda! Advice About Friends, **112**

Syllable Strategies

African Journey, **82**
Big Steals, **84**
Button Your Lip and Other Idioms, **86**
Have You Seen My Mummy?, **122**
Medical Miracle, **128**
Plugged In, **64**
Shamila's Goal, **68**
What's New? A History of Invention, **76**

Word Parts

Ant Attack!, **114**
Arabian Nights, **142**
Back From the Grave!, **116**
Beauty and the Geek, **144**
Big Steals, **84**
Cool Jobs in Basketball, **88**
Crash!, **90**
Disaster!, **118**
Everyday Heroes, **146**
Fashion Flashback, **94**
Fire! The Triangle Shirtwaist Factory Tragedy, **148**
Have You Seen My Mummy?, **126**
Home From War, **96**
Hot Jobs, **152**
Killer Croc, **154**
Lost! Mysteries of the Bermuda Triangle, **56**
Messy Jobs, **62**
Music Mash-Up, **130**
Play Ball!, **132**
Princess Brat, The, **100**
Raven, The, **162**
Survival Guide: How to Keep Your Job, **104**
Tiburón, El, **120**
Unstoppable, **106**
When Lisa Met Billy, **110**
Witch Hunt, **140**

Word Sort

Ant Attack!, **114**
Arabian Nights, **142**
Beauty and the Geek, **144**
Big!, **54**
Bugs That Kill, **56**
Cool Jobs in Basketball, **88**
Crash!, **90**
Did You Know?, **58**
Everyday Heroes, **146**
Fire! The Triangle Shirtwaist Factory Tragedy, **148**
Four Rotten Rulers, **150**
Hot Jobs, **152**
Killer Croc, **154**
Killer Plague, **124**
Left to Die, **126**
Messy Jobs, **62**
Never Give Up, **158**
Poster Power, **66**
Princess Brat, The, **100**
Promise, The, **160**
Raven, The, **162**
Ripped From the Headlines, **102**
Samurai Fighters, **134**
Story of Shi Jin, The, **136**
Sweater Thief, The, **138**
These Are Not Poems, **70**

They Did What?, **72**
Tragedy at Sea, **164**
Unstoppable, **106**
Wacky Attractions, **74**
Weird Sports Records, **108**
Yes!, **80**

Fluency-Building Strategies

Phrasing and Punctuation

African Journey, **82**
Big!, **54**
Bugs That Kill, **56**
Cool Jobs in Basketball, **88**
Fashion Flashback, **94**
Fire! The Triangle Shirtwaist Factory Tragedy, **148**
Is This Art?, **98**
Killer Plague, **124**
Messy Jobs, **62**
Play Ball!, **132**
Plugged In, **64**
Poster Power, **66**
Promise, The, **160**
Raven, The, **162**
Story of Shi Jin, The, **136**
These Are Not Poems, **70**
Tiburón, El, **120**
Wacky Attractions, **74**
Weird Sports Records, **108**
Witch Hunt, **140**

Read With Expression

Ant Attack!, **114**
Arabian Nights, **142**
Back From the Grave!, **116**
Beauty and the Geek, **144**
Button Your Lip and Other Idioms, **86**
Crash!, **90**
DJ Mystery, **92**
Home From War, **96**
Hot Jobs, **152**
Killer Croc, **154**
Left to Die, **126**
Lost! Mysteries of the Bermuda Triangle, **56**
Never Give Up, **158**
Princess Brat, The, **100**
Shamila's Goal, **68**
They Did What?, **72**
Tragedy at Sea, **164**
When Lisa Met Billy, **110**
Yes!, **80**
Yo, Yolanda! Advice About Friends, **112**

Use Natural, Consistent Pace

Big Steals, **84**
Did You Know?, **58**

Disaster!, **118**
Everyday Heroes, **146**
Fast!, **60**
Four Rotten Rulers, **150**
Have You Seen My Mummy?, **122**
Medical Miracle, **128**
Music Mash-Up, **130**
Ripped From the Headlines, **102**
Samurai Fighters, **134**
Survival Guide: How to Keep Your Job, **104**
Sweater Thief, The, **138**
Unstoppable, **106**
What's New? A History of Invention, **76**
Wonders of the World, **78**

Genres

Arts
Fashion Flashback, **94–95**
Is This Art?, **98–99**
Music Mash-Up, **130–131**
Poster Power, **66–67**

Classic Retelling
Ant Attack!, **114–115**
Arabian Nights, **142–143**
Back From the Grave!, **116–117**

Fiction
Beauty and the Geek, **144–145**
DJ Mystery, **92–93**
Princess Brat, The, **100–101**
Sweater Thief, The, **138–139**
When Lisa Met Billy, **110–111**

Graphic Novels
Arabian Nights, **142–143**
When Lisa Met Billy, **110–111**

Jobs
Cool Jobs in Basketball, **88–89**
Hot Jobs, **152–153**
Messy Jobs, **62–63**
Never Give Up, **158–159**
Plugged In, **64–65**
Survival Guide: How to Keep Your Job, **104–105**

Life Issues
Yo, Yolanda! Advice About Friends, **112–113**

Literature/Language Arts
Ant Attack!, **114–115**
Arabian Nights, **142–143**
Back From the Grave!, **116–117**
Beauty and the Geek, **144–145**
Button Your Lip and Other Idioms, **86–87**
DJ Mystery, **92–93**
Killer Plague, **124–125**
Princess Brat, The, **100–101**
Story of Shi Jin, The, **136–137**

Sweater Thief, The, **138–139**
These Are Not Poems, **70–71**
When Lisa Met Billy, **110–111**

Math
Big!, **54–55**
They Did What?, **72–73**

Physical Education
Cool Jobs in Basketball, **88–89**
Play Ball!, **132–133**
Tiburón, El, **120–121**
Weird Sports Records, **108–109**
Yes!, **80–81**

Poetry
Raven, The, **162–163**
These Are Not Poems, **70–71**

Science
African Journey, **82–83**
Bugs That Kill, **56–57**
Crash!, **90–91**
Did You Know?, **58–59**
Disaster!, **118–119**
Fast!, **60–61**
Have You Seen My Mummy?, **122–123**
Killer Croc, **154–155**
Left to Die, **126–127**
Lost! Mysteries of the Bermuda Triangle, **56–57**
Medical Miracle, **128–129**
Messy Jobs, **62**
What's New? A History of Invention, **76–77**

Social Studies/History
Big Steals, **84–85**
Everyday Heroes, **146–147**
Fashion Flashback, **94–95**
Fire! The Triangle Shirtwaist Factory Tragedy, **148–149**
Four Rotten Rulers, **150–151**
Is This Art?, **98–99**
Play Ball!, **132–133**
Promise, The, **160–161**
Ripped From the Headlines, **102–103**
Samurai Fighters, **134–135**
Shamila's Goal, **68–69**
Tiburón, El, **120–121**
Tragedy at Sea, **164–165**
Unstoppable, **106–107**
Wacky Attractions, **74–75**
Weird Sports Records, **108–109**
What's New? A History of Invention, **76–77**
Witch Hunt, **140–141**
Wonders of the World, **78–79**
Yes!, **80–81**

Graphic Organizers

African Journey, **83**
Ant Attack!, **115**
Arabian Nights, **143**
Back From the Grave!, **117**
Beauty and the Geek, **145**
Big!, **55**
Big Steals, **85**
Bugs That Kill, **57**
Button Your Lip and Other Idioms, **87**
Cool Jobs in Basketball, **89**
Crash!, **91**
Did You Know?, **59**
Disaster!, **119**
DJ Mystery, **93**
Everyday Heroes, **147**
Fashion Flashback, **95**
Fast!, **61**
Fire! The Triangle Shirtwaist Factory Tragedy, **149**
Four Rotten Rulers, **151**
Have You Seen My Mummy?, **123**
Home From War, **97**
Hot Jobs, **153**
Is This Art?, **99**
Killer Croc, **155**
Killer Plague, **125**
Left to Die, **127**
Lost! Mysteries of the Bermuda Triangle, **57**
Medical Miracle, **129**
Messy Jobs, **63**
Music Mash-Up, **131**
Never Give Up, **159**
Play Ball!, **133**
Plugged In, **65**
Poster Power, **67**
Princess Brat, The, **101**
Promise, The, **161**
Raven, The, **163**
Ripped From the Headlines, **103**
Samurai Fighters, **135**
Shamila's Goal, **69**
Story of Shi Jin, The, **137**
Survival Guide: How to Keep Your Job, **105**
Sweater Thief, The, **139**
These Are Not Poems, **71**
They Did What?, **73**
Tiburón, El, **121**
Tragedy at Sea, **165**
Unstoppable, **107**
Wacky Attractions, **75**
Weird Sports Records, **109**
What's New? A History of Invention, **77**
When Lisa Met Billy, **111**
Witch Hunt, **141**